World Disasters Report 2000

Focus on public health

International Federation
of Red Cross and Red Crescent Societies

ISBN 92-9139-066-6

Printed by SADAG Imprimerie, Bellegarde/Valserine, France

Acknowledgements
The *World Disasters Report 2000* was edited by Peter Walker and Jonathan Walter.
Principal contributors:
Chapter 1, Michael Day and Jonathan Walter; Box 1.1, Fred Pearce; Box 1.2, Michael Day; Box 1.3, Michael Day; Box 1.4, Patrick Fuller (International Federation) and Jonathan Walter; Box 1.5, Jari Vainio (International Federation)
Chapter 2, Jane Cassidy; Box 2.2, Claude de Ville (PAHO); Box 2.4, Michael Day
Chapter 3, John Sparrow
Chapter 4, John Owen-Davies
Chapter 5, Leyla Alyanak; Box 5.1, Sergei Neverkevitch (International Federation); Box 5.2, Jean-Pierre Revel (International Federation); Box 5.4, Shaun Burnie (Greenpeace International)
Chapter 6, Edward Girardet; Box 6.1, Jonathan Walter; Box 6.4, Loretta Hieber (Media Action International)
Chapter 7, Andrew Simms; Box 7.1, David O'Brien and Abby Stoddard (New York University)
Chapter 8, Michael Hoffman (American Red Cross)
Chapter 9, Centre for Research on the Epidemiology of Disasters; US Committee for Refugees
Chapter 10, Box 10.2, World Bank/Disaster Management Facility
Thanks to all those who assisted contributors during travel and research, including Guy Bentham, Aradhna Duggal, Isabelle Grondahl and Fernando Soares.

Contact details:
International Federation of Red Cross and Red Crescent Societies
17, chemin des Crêts, P.O Box 372
CH-1211 Geneva 19, Switzerland
Tel.: (41)(22) 730 4222; fax: (41)(22) 733 0395
E-mail: secretariat@ifrc.org; web site: http://www.ifrc.org
To e-mail the *World Disasters Report* editors: wdredito@ifrc.org

Contents

Section Two **Tracking the system**

Investing in people to bridge the gap

In most people's minds, the Red Cross and Red Crescent is best known for its disaster response, whether in local communities or the international arena. But our day-to-day work has more to do with providing basic health care and welfare – bridging the gap between that which communities and families provide for themselves and that which the state provides.

When disaster strikes, however, community care falters as families are torn apart. State systems crack, and the gap between needs and service delivery dramatically widens. Filling this gap in times of disaster, though, often means that as the threat of disaster recedes, emergency responders find themselves faced with a dilemma. To pull out, knowing that neither community nor state systems have re-established themselves. Or to stay and risk being caught in the open-ended commitment of welfare provision.

Worse still, while sudden disasters hijack headlines and money, it is the silent, ongoing disasters – with less obvious root causes – that are more deadly. Many countries' public health systems are in crisis and grossly underfunded. Weak systems underlie many of today's disasters, and are weakened further in the wake of disaster.

In Africa, the disaster of HIV/AIDS cannot be rolled back though expensive drugs. It requires basic health education and a health system that can deliver consistent care. In DPR Korea – which once boasted a health-care system among the best in the developing world – tuberculosis and malaria are taking hold, while hospitals fuel their heaters with soot gathered from nearby chimneys. Around Chernobyl, millions still live with the nightmare of radiation. Cancer rates continue to rise, 14 years after the disaster, but screening, treatment and psychosocial support remain inadequate. In Kosovo, the health-care system has been irrevocably changed. Rebuilding it will require not just capital but completely rethinking the role of the state in providing care.

I am convinced we must highlight some of the underlying causes of suffering and the long-term consequences of the crises to which we react. The days when disaster response meant 'quick in, quick out' are long gone. We cannot just pack up and go home after the disaster. But pumping inadequate resources into dysfunctional systems is equally flawed.

Today we have to be smarter. Humanitarian organizations must engage in much more focused advocacy and action – through partnerships with local communities, governments, private sector companies, health research bodies and journalists. Public health education and provision within local communities will render them stronger and better able to cope. We need to invest in people, not just in commodities. Encouraging behavioural change is as important as building hospitals. Support for disaster-affected states in providing appropriate public health systems will help prevent future disasters. Advocacy at the international level must address some of the systemic threats to public health – lack of investment in solutions to developing world diseases, shifts from aid towards capital flows which may not serve the needs of the most vulnerable, changes in climate and land use, poverty and poor education.

The International Federation was created in 1919 to respond to the post-war threat of epidemics in Europe. Today, eight decades on, we remain committed to preparing for and responding to not only crises, but chronic threats to people's lives and dignity.

Didier J Cherpitel
Secretary General

chapter 1

Section One

Focus on public health

chapter 1

Public health – has it fallen off the map?

While public health has improved dramatically over the last century in much of the developing world, it is under increasing threat as governments retreat from national health provision and look to the private sector and non-governmental organizations (NGOs) to fill the gap. Diseases such as HIV/AIDS and malaria have become ongoing disasters – less headline-friendly than sudden natural catastrophes or refugee crises, but far more deadly. In 1999, between 70,000 and 100,000 people were killed by natural disasters, but around 13 million died of infectious diseases.

Responding to such chronic public health crises is beyond the capacity of humanitarian organizations alone. International partnerships with governments, the private sector and financial institutions offer one way forward. But often overlooked are local partnerships with the communities facing first-hand the threats of disease and endangered health. Preventive strategies and health education at the front line – promoted by trained volunteers and community health workers – must complement initiatives at an international level.

Chronic health crises dwarf natural disasters

While dramatic catastrophes make the media headlines, chronic, unreported public health disasters continue to claim the lives of millions. Primary health care in the poorer parts of Asia, Africa and Latin America is deteriorating due to lack of resources – drained by conflicts, debt and economic marginalization – as well as misguided resource allocation and failed development.

What are the dimensions of the public health threat facing millions of vulnerable people, aid agencies and governments at the brink of the millennium? First a few facts:

- Public expenditure on health in low-income countries averages 1 per cent of gross domestic product (GDP), compared to 6 per cent of GDP in high-income countries.
- Every day, over 15,000 people are infected with HIV/AIDS – half of them under 25 years old.
- Over 40 per cent of the world lives in malaria-prone areas.
- Five hundred million people alive today will eventually be killed by tobacco.
- One mother dies from pregnancy-related causes for every hundred live births in parts of sub-Saharan Africa.
- An estimated 150 million people have died from AIDS, tuberculosis (TB) and malaria since 1945, compared to 23 million from war between 1945 and 1993.
- Global military spending in 1995 topped US$ 864 billion, compared to an estimated US$ 15 billion spent on prevention and control of AIDS, TB and malaria.
- One B-2 'stealth' bomber costs US$ 997 million compared to the US$ 160 million Africa receives in official aid each year to fight HIV/AIDS.
- Most of the 13 million annual deaths from infectious diseases could be prevented for US$ 5 per person.
- Only 2 per cent of all global public and private biomedical research is devoted to the major killer diseases in the developing world.

Photo opposite page: Raquel Gutierrez tested positive for malaria in a Belize Red Cross clinic for shanty dwellers. Three-quarters of the 1 to 2.6 million who die annually of malaria are children. Since 1970, malaria mortality rates in sub-Saharan Africa have soared 54 per cent.

Photo: Christopher Black, Belize 1995.

Box 1.1 La Niña storms savage Venezuela

For the second year running, Latin America was dealt a massive death toll from flooding and mudslides, after unprecedented rainstorms blew in off the Caribbean Sea. The year before it was Honduras and Nicaragua, mauled by Hurricane Mitch (see 'World Disasters Report 1999'). In December 1999, it was the turn of Venezuela's coastal region, one of the most densely populated areas of the continent.

This time there was no hurricane, and hence no warning from the hurricane watchers in Florida. But two weeks of record rains turned soil to mud and hillsides into tropical avalanches, sweeping hundreds of bodies and entire buildings out to sea. Fifteen-metre waves inundated the coastal state of Vargas, destroying entire communities.

Unofficial estimates put the death toll at around 30,000 – making it Latin America's worst natural disaster of the 20th century. With 23,200 houses destroyed, over 110,000 people were forced to take refuge in schools and stadiums in the capital Caracas, or erect temporary shelters near their vanished villages – despite government efforts to move them to safer ground.

The ingredients of the disaster were eerily similar to those that had killed some 10,000 people in Honduras a year earlier. First, one of the century's most intense episodes of the tropical climate aberration known as La Niña was still bringing fierce storms, hurricanes and heavy rainfall throughout the Caribbean region. Meteorologists had warned at the start of 1999 that "another Mitch" was likely, and so it proved.

Second, the flight of unemployed rural Venezuelans to urban areas in the past two decades had turned the steep coastal hillsides around Caracas, where the rainfall was most intense, into an endless succession of precariously built shanty towns. Some 85 per cent of Venezuela's population of 22 million live in urban areas. Many homes are built on ledges hacked illegally into the hillsides. Few drains have been constructed to channel away flood waters.

And finally, high above these shanty towns on the hilltops, logging had stripped out the trees, the last protection against mudslides. It was a disaster waiting to happen, says Luis Oswaldo Baez of the UN disasters office in Caracas, "yet the population is allowed to grow in these areas." Baez argues that the Venezuelan Environment Ministry should have done more to keep migrants away. Others say people were well aware of the risks. Those with money settled in safer areas. But the poorest, with least choice, ended up "living in areas that should not be inhabited and in houses not designed to resist any unstable movement," says Cesar Centano, forestry professor at Venezuela's Universidad de los Andes.

Dead bodies mixed up in mudslides did not present a significant public health risk, according to the International Federation's Hakan Sandbladh. Concerns focused instead on an increase in diarrhoeal and respiratory diseases, plus surveillance and health education to combat cholera, dengue, malaria and leptospirosis. And to prevent an outbreak of equinine myoencephalitis, 50,000 doses of vaccine were provided. Overcrowding in temporary shelters, collapse of basic services, and above all unsafe drinking water posed the greatest risks to health. Vargas state will have to pump raw sewage into the sea and drink water supplied by road tankers for the next two years, while water and sanitation pipelines running along the coast are repaired.

To meet longer-term public health challenges, the Inter-American Development Bank has approved the reprogramming of US$ 200 million in loans for drinking water distribution, epidemiological surveillance and health education. But with nearly a quarter of a million jobs lost in Vargas state alone, and 29 per cent of the nation's health infrastructure damaged or destroyed, cash to repay loans may be in short supply.

HIV/AIDS – from disease to disaster

Since AIDS was first identified, 50 million people around the world have become infected with HIV, the virus that causes AIDS. Nearly a third of those have died – and each hour, another 300 people die worldwide from the AIDS pandemic (see Chapter 3).

In January 2000, the United Nations (UN) Security Council raised the subject of health for the first time at one of its meetings as it debated the AIDS issue. United States Vice President Al Gore said: "When a single disease threatens everything from economic strength to peacekeeping, we clearly face a security threat of the greatest magnitude," and went on to claim that "the number of people who will die of AIDS in the first decade of the 21st century will rival the number that died in all the wars in all the decades of the 20th century."

Yet while AIDS activists welcomed the US focusing political attention on the pandemic, the extra US$ 110 million pledged by the US was seen as just a start. The president of the World Bank, James Wolfensohn, told the Security Council: "We estimate that the total sum needed for prevention in Africa annually is in the order of US$ 1 billion to US$ 2.3 billion and yet, at present, Africa is receiving only US$ 160 million a year in official assistance for HIV/AIDS." He added that the war chest for the fight against AIDS is "woefully empty". In April 2000, however, HIV/AIDS prevention among the young people of Botswana, Ghana, Tanzania and Uganda was boosted by a pledge of US$ 57 million from the Bill & Melinda Gates Foundation.

AIDS amply demonstrates how a disastrous new disease may disproportionately affect the world's poor. While effective but pricey drug combinations (US$ 12,000 per person, per year) have slashed the number of AIDS deaths and emptied hospital wards in industrialized nations, the death toll in the developing world continues to soar. Sub-Saharan Africa, home to 70 per cent of the world's HIV-positive people but to just a tenth of the earth's population, bore the brunt of the 2.6 million AIDS deaths last year.

Life expectancy figures demonstrate the catastrophic effect the virus is having on public health – and will continue to have on the region's economies. Life expectancy at birth in southern Africa, which climbed from 44 in the early 1950s to 59 in the early 1990s is expected to plunge back to 45 in the next decade. The AIDS pandemic is not just a humanitarian disaster for sub-Saharan Africa and parts of Asia and the Caribbean – it is an economic disaster as well, since the disease targets the most economically active members of society. Half of the 5.6 million people to be infected last year with HIV were under 25 years old.

"With an epidemic of this scale, every new infection adds to the ripple effect, impacting families, communities, households and increasingly businesses and economies. AIDS has emerged as the single greatest threat to development in many countries of the world," said UNAIDS Executive Director Peter Piot recently.

The AIDS issue in Africa raises the crucial question of how best to allocate limited public health resources. The risk of mother-to-child transmission (MTCT) of the virus can be radically cut by treatment with relatively expensive antiretroviral drugs such as nevirapine. But without the necessary public health infrastructure to identify those in need and administer complicated drug regimes, scant health care resources for sub-Saharan Africa may be spent better elsewhere. Essential drugs are needed to combat opportunistic infections such as pneumonia or TB which prematurely claim the lives of so many suffering from HIV. And with 5.6 million new infections last year, resources must be channelled to revitalize community-based prevention and home care.

Political consensus and urgency are desperately needed in Africa. One in four adult Zimbabweans is infected with HIV/AIDS, yet last year the political will to announce a national disaster and allocate resources to the crisis seeemed lacking. Use of condoms is one of the most effective means of preventing transmission of the virus. Yet while thousands of Kenyans continued to die each week of AIDS, President Daniel arap Moi, in a speech in November 1999, criticized the promotion of condoms as "improper".

India and China – the world's two population giants – face their own unfolding disasters. Latest available World Health Organization (WHO) estimates (for 1998) suggest that at least 400,000 Chinese are HIV-positive. As at March 2000, WHO estimated 3.5 million Indians were infected with HIV/AIDS.

Long-term solutions to AIDS in developing countries rest on a combination of successful vaccine research and prevention strategies. According to Seth Berkley, president of the International AIDS Vaccine Initiative, even "with full guns blazing" an AIDS vaccine could take seven to ten years to develop. Meanwhile, a range of short- and long-term preventive measures must be adopted. Such measures include: aggressive and frank health education (greatly underused by many nations at risk); screening of donated blood for the virus; and, ultimately, improving the status of women in developing countries.

Fight against infectious diseases

Dangers posed by new and re-emerging infectious diseases are underlined in a declassified CIA report, dated January 2000, which "responds to a growing concern by senior US leaders about the implications – in terms of health, economics, and national security – of the growing global infectious disease threat. The dramatic increase in drug-resistant microbes, combined with the lag in development of new antibiotics, the rise of megacities with severe health-care deficiencies, environmental degradation, and the growing ease and frequency of cross-border movements of people and produce have greatly facilitated the spread of infectious diseases." The report predicts "economic decay, social fragmentation, and political destabilization in the hardest hit countries".

Comprehensive strategies of surveillance, immunization, treatment and education are needed to tackle the big infectious diseases. Just over 80 years ago, a spectacularly virulent influenza pandemic ('Spanish flu' as it became known) killed up to 40 million people in 12 months. Another potential influenza pandemic was stopped in Hong Kong two years ago by vigilant infectious disease experts. Left unchecked, that outbreak of a deadly bird flu in several Hong Kong residents could have allowed the strain to develop into one transmissible between humans. Influenza experts think it's only a matter of time before such a strain emerges again. And acute respiratory infections (ARIs) such as pneumonia and influenza still kill more people – 3.5 million in 1998 – than any other infectious disease.

Box 1.2 Nicaragua needs a break

Hurricane Mitch, which devastated Central America in late 1998 and killed around 3,000 Nicaraguans, was only the latest in a succession of natural and man-made disasters. Decades of corrupt dictatorships, trade blockades and civil war, on top of volcanoes and floods, have eroded the country's already precarious ability to provide health care.

Post-Mitch, Charles Cherrett of the Dutch overseas aid department said: "There is no such thing as a natural disaster; there are natural phenomena that interact with human activities." The left-wing Nicaragua Solidarity Campaign asked rhetorically in the 5 December 1999 issue of 'New Times': "So why did Hurricane Mitch become such a human and environmental tragedy of catastrophic proportions? Dozens of hurricanes have struck the United States but none in the last 25 years has claimed more than 100 lives."

Caught in a vicious spiral of debt and disaster, Nicaragua is one of many developing nations whose ability to prepare for and cope with catastrophe gets weaker each time disaster strikes. And the burden to provide stopgap health cover falls increasingly on humanitarian agencies.

A quick look at the state of Nicaragua's finances shows why this is happening. In 1997, according to Oxfam, "over half of government revenue went into servicing the US$6 billion debt. The effects on social sector spending have been disastrous..." Although Nicaragua consistently failed to service its debts in full, the amount it repaid in 1997 on loans (over US$ 600,000 per day) was over twice that spent on health and education combined.

Even before the hurricane, over 40 per cent of Nicaraguans did not have access to safe water and sanitation, according to Christian Aid – a factor that plays into the hands of infectious disease agents. And UN figures claim 84 per cent of Nicaraguan children live in poverty. With an estimated 60 per cent of the nation's infrastructure destroyed, including 102 health centres and 512 schools, a moratorium on debt payments was agreed by creditors after Mitch struck. Oxfam suggests that debt relief should be combined with "national development plans", to encourage judicious use of public funds and enable this desperately poor country to break the vicious cycle of poverty and poor public health.

In late October 1999, hundreds of people in Achuapa, 110 km north-west of Managua, were struck by leptospirosis, a disease spread by rats, following heavy rains and flooding. By mid-November nearly 2,500 had become ill. According to David Brandling-Bennett of the Pan-American Health Organization (PAHO): "Leptospirosis is a persistent, often under-recognized problem to which the international community has paid relatively little attention. In Nicaragua, public health interest was sparked by the concern the epidemic of a new disease would pose to other communities and countries."

If a deadlier disease were to emerge in this part of the world it's unlikely that Nicaragua's diagnostic, treatment and containment facilities would be able to cope. Yet there is evidence that dengue fever and its deadly cousin dengue haemorrhagic fever are re-emerging in the region.

The familiar message of "invest now and save later" has never sounded more pertinent. That's not to say Nicaraguans themselves have no responsibilities or bearing on the fate of their country. Why, post-Mitch, did the government choose to spend money widening a four-lane motorway between Managua and Masava, not a yard of which was damaged by the hurricane?

According to President Aleman, it will take 20 years just to regain the level of development reached before Mitch struck. Countries like Nicaragua need a combination of imaginative debt-relief and long-term humanitarian support in order to rebuild the flawed systems that make its citizens vulnerable to disease and natural disaster.

Failure by some of the world's richer developing nations to adopt recommended treatment guidelines mean hundreds of thousands of people are unnecessarily catching and dying from TB, warned WHO. TB kills around 1.5 million people a year, mainly adults and adolescents. HIV/AIDS sufferers are especially at risk – since HIV weakens the immune system, it can activate latent TB infection and is also believed to multiply the risk of initial infection with TB. Around one-third of all AIDS deaths are from TB.

Launching the *Stop* TB initiative, with the World Bank, the US Centers for Disease Control and Prevention, and non-governmental groups, Gro Harlem Brundtland, director-general of WHO, said: "We have a choice to act now and control TB, or we can continue business as usual and let strains of multi-drug-resistant TB thrive. We have the cure; we need to mobilize the world to use it."

Stop TB aims to place TB research and control higher on the political agenda. Previous complacency that TB was on the way out, thanks to the effective DOTS (Directly Observed Treatment, Short-course) therapy, is gone. WHO has identified inadequate treatment

Box 1.3 Minamata – poisonous reminder of the past

Thirty-four years ago in the small coastal town of Minamata, Japan, a new disease was diagnosed among the local population. The condition, which destroyed brains and minds, was named simply after the town where it first appeared. And as this disease was as man-made as the town itself, that seemed entirely appropriate.

Minamata disease is an extreme form of mercury poisoning. Not naturally occurring mercury, but an easily absorbed organic form called methyl-mercury that accumulates in the food chain when large quantities of the metal are released into the environment. At the time, mercury was being used as a catalyst in the industrial production of formaldehyde. The metal was flushed along with waste water into the town's bay, where it was absorbed by small organisms and passed up the food chain into fish and other seafood, before arriving on the plates of locals.

Some 1,500 people suffered damage to their nervous systems with loss of muscle control, fits and personality change. Many children born to those exposed had terrible deformities.

Just as the disease was fading from the world's memory, it sprang up in Latin America. Fishing villages in remote parts of the Amazon have begun to see the tell-tale trembling fits. Japanese experts from the Kumamoto and Yokohama national universities flew to villages around San Luis do Tapajós in Brazil and discovered dangerous levels of methyl-mercury in the bodies of local people. Other researchers, including Donna Mergler of the University of Quebec in Montreal, believe methyl-mercury contamination of the Amazon is more wide-spread that we realize. Experts agree the latest victims were poisoned by eating fish, though it's unclear whether the mercury results from gold prospecting or deforestation.

Mergler contends that mercury occurs naturally in Amazon soils and is released by the slash-and-burn techniques of loggers. Villagers could possibly benefit from eating vegetarian fish which may be less contaminated. But there appears to be no action to address the likely causes. Even with the political will to act, the scale of the clean-up task would be daunting. Japanese authorities spent millions of dollars cleaning up Minamata Bay. What price to decontaminate vast areas of the Amazon Basin?

programmes in Indonesia, Russia and South Africa that are encouraging the spread of the disease. China on the other hand has built up its TB control programme and has achieved 95 per cent cure rates over half the country with DOTS programmes up and running.

Malaria continues to be a major public health problem in over 90 countries. It kills anything from 1 million to 2.6 million people per year – no one knows exactly how many, but three-quarters of them are children. Again, sub-Saharan Africa is disproportionately affected, accounting for 90 percent of deaths. Gains made over the disease in the past 50 years are being reversed by global warming (making transmission possible at higher altitudes and latitudes); increased migration and emergency population displacements; changes in land use such as urban sprawl spreading into endemic areas; and the appearance of drug-resistant strains. The explosion in international travel means cases are turning up in developed countries. Worryingly, malaria is re-emerging in areas such as Azerbaijan and Tajikistan where it was previously under control. WHO claims that 500,000 deaths a year could be prevented with about US$ 1 billion extra spending on strengthened health systems.

In November 1999, the non-profit Medicines for Malaria Venture (MMV) was announced by governmental and inter-governmental organizations, plus, significantly, the International Federation of Pharmaceutical Manufacturers Associations (IFPMA). MMV's aim is to bring about the registration of one new anti-malarial drug every five years. New drugs will be needed to combat emerging drug resistance – particularly in south-east Asia. *Artemether* and similar drugs derived from a Chinese shrub are currently the last line of defence against the deadly *falciparum* strain of malaria in some border regions of Thailand and Viet Nam. If – or when – quinine-resistant variants spread to sub-Saharan Africa, artemether-type drugs will be all that stands between the region and another public health catastrophe.

Preventive education targeted at young adults, seen here on the streets of Maputo, Mozambique, is a crucial strategy in the fight against HIV/AIDS. Each day, 16,000 more people worldwide are infected with the virus – half of them under 25 years old.

Photo: UNAIDS/Neeleman

AIDS, along with the long-standing scourges of ARIs, diarrhoeal diseases, TB, malaria and measles, stand as a grim reminder that the threat of infectious diseases still looms large. Equally worrying are the 28 or so new or re-emerging pathogens, such as ebola and dengue fever. Diphtheria in the former Soviet Union, for example, has shot up from a few thousand reported cases in the 1970s and 1980s to over 50,000 in 1995. Syphilis infection among Russians has increased 40 times since 1989.

Predictably, the poor are hit hardest – 58 per cent of those who die of infectious diseases are among the poorest 20 per cent of the world's population, but only 7 per cent of victims are among the richest 20 per cent. WHO claims in its report *Removing Obstacles to Healthy Development* that the majority of the 13 million deaths a year due to the six main infectious diseases could be prevented for less than US$ 5 per sick person. WHO's Brundtland has stated that vaccination is "one of the most powerful and cost-effective technologies." And politicians and experts alike have often been heard to mutter that if malaria were as common in Europe or the United States as it is in sub-Saharan Africa, there would probably be an effective vaccine against it by now.

Poor health drives poverty...

In addition to the terrible toll on human life exacted by infectious diseases alone, they also accounted for 365 million lost years of healthy life in 1998 – that means 1 million lost DALYs (Disability Adjusted Life Years) each day, according to the WHO. So concerned is WHO about the economic implications of poor health that in January 2000, WHO's Brundtland launched a two-year commission on macroeconomics and health in order to study how concrete health interventions can lead to economic growth as well as reduce inequity in developing countries. And the World Bank's Wolfensohn said in February that 60,000 of the world's poorest, surveyed by the Bank across 60 countries, themselves revealed that "the single largest contribution to poverty is poor health."

While the world's richest nations (the Organisation for Economic Co-operation and Development (OECD) countries) have consistently cut back on government health spending since 1993, World Bank figures for poorer countries show even more disturbing priorities. India, for example, spends just 0.7 per cent of its GDP on health, but more than three times that amount on its military. Turkey spent 4 per cent of its GDP on the military in 1995, but averaged just 2.7 per cent on public health from 1990 to 1997. In eastern Europe, the former Soviet Union and many developing countries, a greater part of health care is being outsourced to private companies and clinics, as part of the transition from state control to market economy. This leaves those who cannot afford such care relying on reduced government services and humanitarian agencies. But what happens to those who fall through the net?

In India, three-quarters of the nation's health care is in private hands, claims Mira Shiva, head of the public policy division for the Voluntary Health Association of India and Asian coordinator of the International People's Health Council. But for the 400 million Indians living below the poverty line, who spend most of their income on food, private health care is hard to afford and often out of reach. Yet people travel great distances at great expense to visit hospital for often 'trivial' complaints. According to Shiva's research, 65 to 70 per cent of outpatient problems in India are totally preventable. But the Western medical model adopted over the past two decades in India, based on 'drugs, doctors and dispensaries' now dominates, with 60,000 drug formulations on the domestic market. As a result, the cost of medical care is emerging as the second commonest cause of rural indebtedness in India.

Public health is under threat, claims Shiva, from pharmaceutical companies pushing non-essential medicines for profit; from centralized, vertical health-care programmes which deal with diseases separately not collectively; and from international loans for capital-intensive health initiatives which poor nations find hard to sustain. Market forces, argues Shiva, are extinguishing traditional health systems such as *ayurveda*, and undermining preventive public health provision, since "the privatization of medical care by its very logic has to be curative care, because nobody profits from public health."

...but poverty and isolation also drive poor health

One place yet to feel the forces of privatization is the Democratic People's Republic of Korea (DPRK) (see Chapter 4). DPRK's public health system was once the envy of developing nations – a system which counted the elimination of TB among its achievements. Today, the system has, according to first-hand witnesses, been brought to its knees by years of political, economic and professional isolation.

Hospital staff are forced to gather soot from local chimneys to burn as heating fuel, in the absence of coal or oil. Many North Koreans are unable to reach hospital simply through lack of transport. And a scant supply of drugs, medical equipment and food keeps many others away. While DPRK has over 600 general hospitals, winter occupancy averages just 15 to 20 per cent.

Following reports of a devastating famine in 1994-96, a nutritional survey carried out in 1998 found that 60 per cent of under-sevens suffered stunting, caused by chronic malnutrition. Malaria is on the increase and TB cases top an estimated 40,000 a year, according to WHO.

Since 1998, three leading NGOs, Médecins sans Frontières (MSF), Oxfam and Action contre la Faim have left DPRK, following problems with access to parts of the country and difficulties monitoring where all their aid supplies were going. The International Federation has stayed on, distributing drugs down to district-level clinics and running training courses for medical staff. Marcel Fortier, desk officer for the International Federation, believes that the humanitarian needs of North Koreans are better served by remaining inside rather than out. "We are doing things today which were impossible 18 months ago", he says.

Poverty brings with it malnutrition which lowers the body's natural resistance to infectious diseases. WHO claims that malnutrition is an underlying factor in more than half of all deaths among children globally – and one in three of the world's children is malnourished. WHO's Brundtland argued recently that "investing in health means improving the conditions of work and the ability to become productive and get out of poverty."

By last year the numbers of people living in absolute poverty (on incomes of less than a dollar a day) had risen to 1.5 billion, and is likely to rise further. Of these, WHO estimates over a billion lack access to safe drinking water. As violent storms along the coasts of Venezuela and India last year tragically showed, it is the poorest whose health will be hardest hit when disaster strikes (see Boxes 1.1 and 1.4).

Political isolation behind the Iron Curtain, followed by economic crisis and poverty since the curtain came down, have taken a heavy toll on the health of literally millions affected by the Chernobyl catastrophe in the former Soviet Union (see Chapter 5). Meltdown of Chernobyl's nuclear reactor in 1986 expelled 100 times more radiation into the earth's atmosphere than the combined effect of the atomic bombs which fell on Hiroshima and Nagasaki at the end of

World War Two. While attracting media attention at the time, it took four years until the first international humanitarian assessment was made.

Box 1.4 Orissa – from cyclone to suicide

Within days of super-cyclone 5B striking the India state of Orissa, government health officials, NGOs and the media were all warning of a looming public health crisis. The tidal surge and heavy rains that accompanied the cyclone caused massive flooding, contaminating thousands of tube wells, swamping crops and killing hundreds of thousands of cattle.

Human and animal corpses littering the affected areas were thought to pose a major health hazard and it seemed likely that a cholera epidemic could claim more lives than were lost during the cyclone itself. Why the predicted epidemic never materialized is still open to question. After the cyclone, people had no choice but to draw water from contaminated sources. In some coastal areas the cyclone destroyed 99 per cent of the coconut trees – but they provided a good supply of green coconuts which served as a valuable source of clean water and nutrients for many who had little or no access to food.

While access to clean drinking water was an acute problem, many knew to boil water before consumption. Comprehension of public health issues, particularly among Orissa's coastal population, has been boosted by the long-term presence of many aid organizations. Following the disaster, mobile clinics reinforced hygiene awareness.

Within days, supplies of water treatment chemicals such as halogen tablets were being distributed as an integral component of most relief distributions carried out by the government and NGOs. Such a rapid and widespread intervention certainly reduced the incidence of water-borne diseases. Water surveillance, epidemiological monitoring for communicable diseases, and a massive programme to clean wells were undertaken. While a small number of cholera and measles cases were reported, these diseases are considered endemic to the coastal region. The initial increase in hospital admissions occurred mainly in bigger towns such as Paradwip and Cuttack where unsanitary, overcrowded conditions led to increased cases of diarrhoeal diseases.

However, longer-term public health impacts of the cyclone may be less obvious and more serious. Endemic poverty in Orissa means people spend four-fifths of their income on food, leading to 'starvation debts' which have forced mothers to sell their own children in order to survive. And around half all Indian children under five are malnourished. Add to this fragile situation a devastating cyclone, and the principal public health crisis – and challenge – becomes food security.

Vandana Shiva, director of the Research Foundation for Science, Technology and Natural Resource Policy in India, argues that commercial exploitation makes matters worse. Sea water swept 20 to 30 km inland because coastal mangrove swamps, which previously acted as a brake on storm surges, had been slashed to make way for shrimp farms. Floods wiped out seed stocks as well as the immediate standing crop. "The corporations are trying to make the crisis an entry point for hybrid seeds," alleges Shiva. Hybrid seeds deliver one great crop but are useless if replanted, she claims. The capital needed to buy new seed annually, plus the herbicides essential for hybrid varieties to survive, is locking farmers into debt. Unable to afford either hybrid inputs or food produced elsewhere, many farmers are taking their own lives. "The epidemic of suicides in India I see as a public health crisis," maintains Shiva.

Today, although the technical problems of securing the leaking sarcophagus which covers the contaminated reactor receive attention, the humanitarian needs of those living nearby remain poorly met by the international community. Yet rates of thyroid cancer – directly linked to the leaked isotope iodine-131 – will not peak until around 2005 – nearly two decades after the disaster. And according to one Belarusian source, birth defects since 1986 have soared by 87 per cent.

Less expected was the psychological fallout from the Chernobyl catastrophe. The mental health of the contaminated – and those who think they were contaminated – was aggravated by the culture of official secrecy which pervaded the region. Some Belarusians were only told they had been contaminated two and a half years after the event. The International Federation launched a psychosocial support project in 1997 to begin assisting the estimated 4 million people still traumatized by what was the world's worst nuclear accident.

It is difficult to determine the direct effect that radiation from Chernobyl has had on emerging cancers, birth defects and psychological trauma in the region. Declining standards of living following the collapse of the former Soviet Union also play a part. But while scientists argue about cause and effect, humanitarian needs remain urgent, long-term and largely neglected.

Sudden-onset disasters leave traumatic legacy

The shock associated with sudden-onset disasters can have an effect on the mental health of survivors which lasts long after the media and relief agencies have packed their bags. As a public health concern, psychological trauma is especially vulnerable to insensitive short-term interventions, and especially aggravated by longer-term systemic crisis.

Survivors of crises involving human rights abuses have in the past attracted more mental health care than survivors of natural disasters. But following last year's crisis in Kosovo and earthquakes in Turkey, psychological concerns were equally at the fore.

By late summer 1999, Kosovo's capital, Pristina, was flooded with humanitarian organizations, many with well-meaning but inappropriate and short-term projects. Confusion reigned as up to 200 agencies – two or three times more than necessary – competed in the health-care sector alone. The self-respect and self-reliance of many of Kosovo's well-trained cadre of professional doctors and nurses were undermined – in turn hampering the psychological recovery of survivors. Worse still, psychosocial issues became 'flavour of the month', leading some attention-seeking agencies to pursue misguided projects such as interviewing rape victims for re-broadcasting purposes (see Chapter 6).

In the aftermath of Turkey's tragic earthquake in August last year, myths and misinformation, spread by ill-informed officials and the media, misled many. Reporters on prominent networks such as the BBC could be heard every night talking about the "frantic race to bury the dead" in order to avert "feared cholera epidemics". Even Turkey's prime minister, Bulent Ecevit, was quoted as encouraging swift action to dispose of dead bodies to avoid epidemics. But Michel Thieren, from WHO's emergency department, emphasized at the time that dead bodies were less likely to pass on infection than live ones. Although bodies left unburied can contaminate drinking water, many Turks were unnecessarily traumatized as lost loved ones were hastily tossed into mass graves or bulldozed into the sea. Millions of Turks were estimated to be suffering from psychological trauma, as thousands of aftershocks continued to rock the region (see Box 1.5).

Nearly two years on from the terrorist bomb – which was meant for the US embassy but destroyed Nairobi's business district in August 1998, killing over 200 and injuring more than 5,500 – the mental suffering goes on. "The wounds do not heal overnight," said the International Federation's head of regional delegation. "It's a long agonizing process, the more so in Kenya where poverty exacerbates the suffering." Such a disaster is unprecedented in this region and the long-term effects on victims' mental health can only be guessed at. A Red Cross mental health programme is targeting 5,000 families of those injured or killed by the blast – as well as 500 relief workers, some of whom suffered severe mental trauma after labouring for over five days to sift the living and dead from the rubble.

Aid agencies as well as governments still have much to do to ensure that long-term, culturally sensitive psychosocial care in disaster settings is given the priority it deserves. The Red Cross/Red Crescent Movement and UNICEF have initiated psychosocial support programmes in the Balkans, and during 1999 WHO and the International Federation developed the first-ever guidelines for rapid mental health needs assessments in the field. But very few disaster managers are specifically trained in this field and many methods appropriate in traditional mental health services don't apply in the extreme situation of major humanitarian crises and disasters. According to Daniel Pierotti, principal officer for crisis relief at the UN Population Fund: "There's still a lot of quackery going on. Things are getting better, but slowly."

Partnerships and priorities for prevention

What are the implications for humanitarian agencies, as decreased primary health care spending leads to a deterioration in public health? According to Peter Walker, director of disaster policy at the International Federation: "Public health disasters are not one-off, they are systemic. But agencies are being asked to pick up systemic problems as if they were still 'emergencies'." And while organizations operating in countries like Somalia are under increasing pressure to take on roles usually reserved for ministries of health, donors are wary of committing funds to long-term projects in case they get stuck without an exit strategy.

Partnerships are a key way forward. In order to prepare better and respond in a quicker, more effective way to meningitis outbreaks, WHO, the International Committee of the Red Cross (ICRC), the International Federation, MSF and UNICEF formed the Interagency Coordination Group (ICG) in 1996. But the control and prevention of infectious diseases is clearly beyond the scope of aid agencies alone. To control malaria, for example, a combination is needed of improved health-system interventions, more insecticide-treated bed nets, better environmental management and new malaria drugs and vaccines. WHO has formed a coalition with other UN agencies, the World Bank, commercial companies and host governments to combat the disease, called *Roll Back Malaria*.

In November 1999, the Bill & Melinda Gates Foundation donated US$ 750 million over five years to establish a global fund for children's vaccines. The fund will be administered by the

Global Alliance for Vaccines and Immunization (GAVI) – a partnership between pharmaceutical companies, national governments, public health and research institutions, the Rockefeller Foundation, UNICEF, the World Bank and WHO. Their aim is to save the lives of the 3 million children worldwide who die each year of vaccine-preventable illnesses. GAVI will use the fund to purchase underutilized and new vaccines, to provide resources to strengthen immunization infrastructure and to support research for developing new vaccines against diseases such as malaria, AIDS and TB. At the official launch of the initiative in February 2000, President Chissano of Mozambique said: "Immunization of our children is a critical pre-condition to ending poverty and establishing a healthy and productive population."

Changing behaviour saves lives

Mortality and morbidity figures from chronic public health disasters are mind-numbing. But vaccination is only one component of a prevention strategy – many lives could be saved by simple preventive measures and changes in behaviour. Research in the US suggests that investment in public health measures such as improving personal hygiene and lifestyles can reduce mortality by over 60 per cent. Yet such investment amounts to just 5 per cent of US government health spending. Meanwhile investment in health infrastructure (hospitals, drugs, etc.) consumes around 90 per cent of the government's national health budget, but its impact on reducing mortality is a mere 11 per cent (see Figure 1.1).

Figure 1.1 Investment in public health pays off

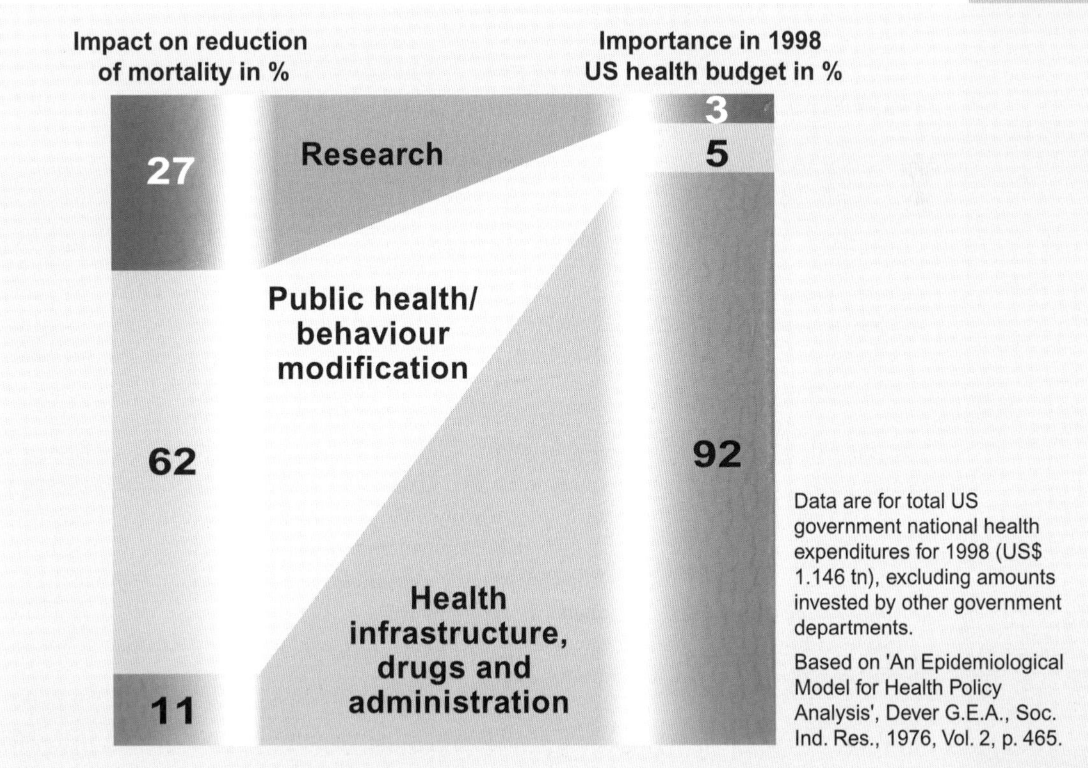

Data are for total US government national health expenditures for 1998 (US$ 1.146 tn), excluding amounts invested by other government departments.

Based on 'An Epidemiological Model for Health Policy Analysis', Dever G.E.A., Soc. Ind. Res., 1976, Vol. 2, p. 465.

"If populations adopted more healthy behaviour patterns," argues Jean Roy, a senior health officer with the International Federation, "we would see a significant decrease in mortality rates among under-fives in Africa." Roy maintains that "physical buildings and hospital facilities are really secondary in terms of addressing the big killers such as HIV/AIDS, ARIs, malaria, diarrhoeas, vaccine-preventable diseases and malnutrition. All of these diseases can be addressed by changing behaviour and seeking appropriate care."

Often it is not the lack of prevention and treatment strategies that bring disease and death, but the failure to use these tools properly. Tens of thousands of lives in the developing world could be saved each year by re-prioritizing existing resources away from tertiary infrastructure towards lifestyle improvements, such as:

- correct handling of drinking water;
- improved sanitation through building and maintaining latrines;
- correct rehydration during bouts of diarrhoea;
- safer sex through condom-use;
- breastfeeding exclusively for the first six months;
- ensuring parents take advantage of existing vaccination opportunities for themselves and their children;
- use of impregnated bed nets in malaria-prone areas;
- more appropriate and nutritious foods; and
- better primary care of acute respiratory infections.

Invest in volunteers

Getting into developing world communities – beyond government hospitals and clinics – is a key priority for the Red Cross/Red Crescent Movement, according to the International Federation's Hakan Sandbladh: "Governments are slipping on their responsibilities for basic, preventive health care. But there is a danger in replacing what the government should normally do," he says, adding: "Pouring money into national health systems is not cost effective, as up to 70 per cent can get siphoned into the big hospitals." Sandbladh advocates training volunteers in the community to enable them to take care of basic health problems. Trained, mobile volunteers can spread prevention strategies against killer diseases like diarrhoea, malaria, measles, HIV/AIDS and ARIs far more effectively than can underresourced hospitals or clinics. And as Sandbladh points out: "Most sick kids die before reaching the peripheral clinics anyway."

ARCHI 2010 (the African Red Cross/Red Crescent Health Initiative) is a collaborative venture engaging the resources of national Red Cross/Red Crescent societies regionwide to focus on high-priority public health interventions, defined through discussion with national health authorities, major health agencies, academics and beneficiaries (see Chapter 10). Priority has been given to activities within the capacities of volunteers and which have a positive impact on health indicators if implemented on a sufficient scale. Red Cross/Red Crescent volunteers are present in virtually every African community and can play a key role in the promotion and delivery of basic health services.

Working with a minimum figure of 1 million existing volunteers across the continent, the International Federation's Roger Bracke argues that, if each volunteer were to target just five families of five members with health education, up to 25 million Africans could be reached. "When someone visits a village for a couple of hours, talks about health, then leaves – that's not prevention," says Bracke. Only by engaging a network of voluntary and paid community health workers in a variety of activities, which consistently pass on the same messages and basic skills, can public health interventions work on the huge scale necessary in, for example, sub-Saharan Africa. But, continues Bracke, the burden of caring for the millions of Africans suffering from AIDS and other diseases is way beyond the capacity of humanitarian organizations alone. ARCHI 2010 can play its part in spreading local-level preventive health education, and can encourage home care for sufferers within that context – but it is the responsibility of governments to establish the continuum of health care from the home to the clinic to the hospital.

Engaging local resources is critical to the success of interventions. Mira Shiva draws a distinction between public health and community health: "Public health can be just a narrow approach, such as throwing chloroquine at malaria – or it can involve the community, for example through vector control." She argues that to achieve a broad, integrated approach, as much money must be spent on training field-based, community health personnel as on distributing and developing vaccines.

In order to encourage the types of behavioural change outlined above, however, it will take more than periodic visits from community health workers. President Chissano told the *World Disasters Report:* "We have eradicated polio in Mozambique because we had the whole population contributing including the business community." He added that, as far as HIV/AIDS was concerned, "the youth in Mozambique did not believe first of all that this disease exists. Today they are engaging themselves in health education campaigns. Before they used to come to us and ask for money for these campaigns. But today they have found their way to sell something in order to have money to continue these campaigns." Peer-to-peer education is key to behavioural change and its role in relation to AIDS is examined in greater detail in Chapter 3, Box 3.3.

Share knowledge locally and internationally

Clearly, many factors other than the level of medical assistance influence the outcome of public health crises. Infant mortality and birth control are directly related to the educational attainment of mothers. David Bryer, director of Oxfam, said in February 2000 that, for every year a young woman spends at school, the chances of her infant dying decrease 5 to 6 per cent, while the risk of dying herself in childbirth plunges by 8 per cent. President Chissano echoed this in saying at GAVI's launch of its child immunization programme: "Education is very important for the success of these activities – especially the education of girls."

Yet despite UN commitments during the 1990s to increase access to basic education to all the world's children, illiteracy is spreading. In sub-Saharan Africa, where AIDS and malaria hit hardest, less children attend school now than ten years ago – 40 million do not even get primary education. In a continent where women are often under pressure to sell sexual favours to survive, thereby exposing themselves to AIDS, education is one of the only ways they can improve their status and income.

Many of the world's poorest nations are not just cash poor – they are knowledge poor as well. Vast inequities in scientific progress between richer and poorer nations will have to be addressed by rich governments – since global capitalism alone is unlikely to do so. As Jeffrey Sachs, professor of international trade at Harvard University, has pointed out, there is no market in malaria. "A hundred IMF missions or World Bank health-sector loans cannot produce a malaria vaccine," he argued in *The Economist* magazine recently. "The root of the problem is a much more complex market failure: private investors and scientists doubt that malaria research will be rewarded financially."

One solution Sachs suggests is that rich nations pledge to buy an effective vaccine for Africa's 25 million babies born each year, if the vaccine is developed. They could guarantee a minimum price of say US$ 10 a dose, with target countries contributing where they can. The pledge would spark vaccine research, which if successful could save millions of lives at a cost around one-quarter of the United States' current debt to the UN. "Such a vaccine would rank among the most effective public-health interventions conceivable," claims Sachs, "and if science did not deliver, rich countries would end up paying nothing at all."

Gordon Perkin, director of the global health programme for the Bill & Melinda Gates Foundation, recently described the foundation's approach to help stimulate the development of new vaccines as a "push, pull, punt". The 'push' is US$ 100 million of grants to help develop candidate vaccines through to early clinical evaluations. The "pull" is the US$ 750 million grant to GAVI to buy existing vaccines and thereby create a market. This should then spur commercial research and development into new vaccines and medicines. Finally, says Perkin: "The 'punt' is a step toward risk reduction, including the provision of loan funds (capital) to facilitate the production to scale of new vaccines."

The past may give us cause for hope. As one WHO official said in 1980: "When the history of the 20th century is written, smallpox eradication will be ranked along with the mastery of flight and the exploration of space as one of the century's greatest achievements." Jean Roy, of the International Federation, points out: "The eradication of smallpox in 1977 was achieved more than 150 years after the discovery of the vaccine – and remarkably, the public health community is about to eradicate polio, this time only 50 years after discovering the vaccine. If there is a will, we can cut the time even shorter between vaccine discovery and control or eradication."

Meanwhile, there is plenty the poorer nations can do while waiting for the rich world to get its act together. When cholera swept through Latin America in 1991, Costa Rica rapidly deployed education and sanitation programmes that kept the disease at bay. Many aspects of Costa Rica's health care compare favourably with first world countries such as the United States – even though its per capita income is ten times less. According to World Bank figures, Costa Rica spends 6 per cent of its GDP on public health measures – ten times more than it does on defence (see Figure 1.2). Costa Ricans live nine years longer than their wealth would predict and infant mortality rates have fallen to levels comparable with industrial nations. Unfortunately, Costa Rica, with its stable democracy and remarkably even wealth distribution is the exception rather than the rule.

Continuity of comprehensive community health care

The range of public health challenges facing governments, humanitarian organizations and the private sector pays no respects to paper distinctions between development and disaster. In order to meet needs stretching from psychosocial trauma in Chernobyl, Kosovo and Turkey to the 10 million AIDS orphans growing up across sub-Saharan Africa, the response must be comprehensive and continuous.

Increasingly, humanitarian agencies who once focused on short-term interventions to alleviate acute suffering find themselves unable to leave after the disaster. There is often no return to normality, no safety net for the most vulnerable, no system for protecting health and preventing disease. No one can walk away from such dilemmas, so agencies have to change the way they work. Advocating for and supporting continuity of basic health education and primary health care become the priorities.

Continuity of health care means investing in people, not just in commodities – whether through supporting peer-to-peer AIDS education in sub-Saharan Africa, or training of midwives and nurses in DPRK. Getting beyond media-driven, reactionary 'band aid' towards committed long-term support is crucial.

Figure 1.2 Public expenditure on health as a percentage of GDP

Source: World Development Report 1999/2000

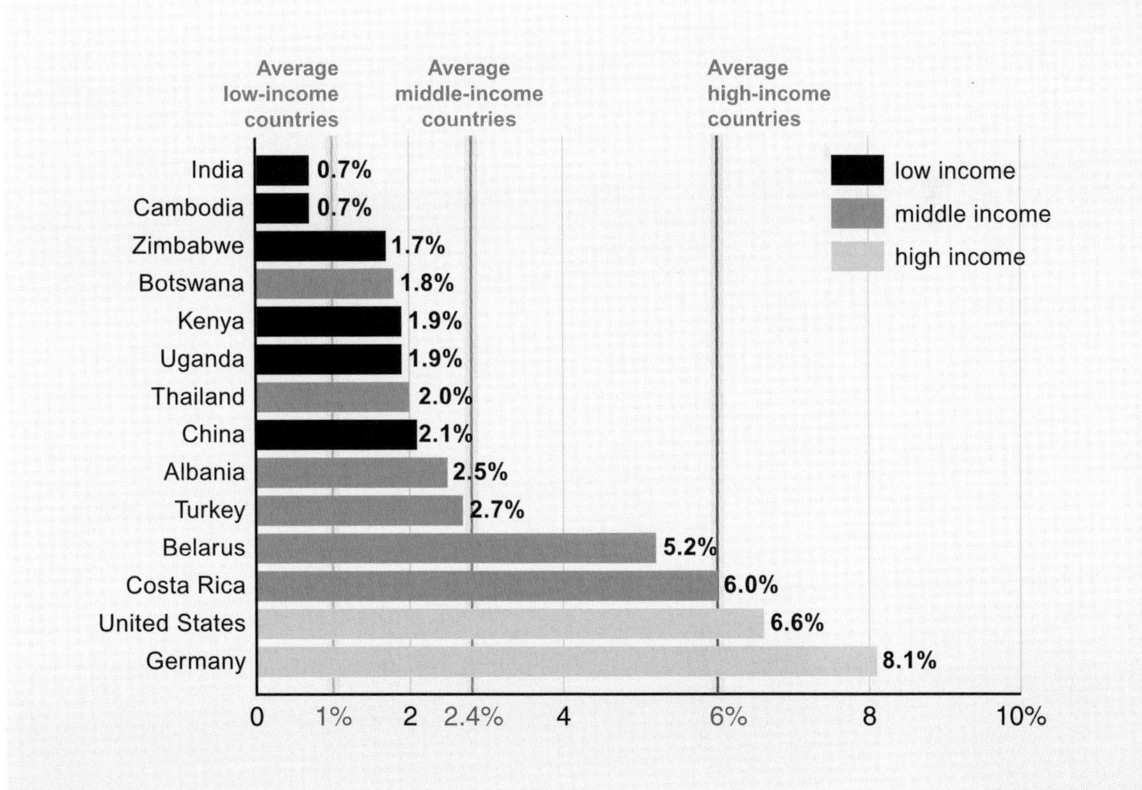

Box 1.5 Turkish earthquakes leave long-term legacy

The ground shook for just 45 seconds, but the damage was devastating: over 17,000 dead, 44,000 injured, millions psychologically affected. The massive earthquake which struck north-western Turkey at 3 a.m. on 17 August 1999 measured between 7.4 and 7.8 on the Richter scale. It damaged or destroyed around 340,000 buildings, hitting Izmit hardest – an industrial city of 1 million inhabitants. The floors of apartment blocks collapsed "like a loaf of sliced bread", according to one observer, crushing thousands in their sleep. As the seabed dropped suddenly along the fault line, a tidal wave as high as six metres swamped the coast.

Over 1,300 aftershocks followed, culminating in a second major quake on 12 November around 100 km east of Izmit. Rated 7.2 on the Richter scale, it killed at least 845 people and injured nearly 5,000 more. A further 40,000 homes and buildings were destroyed.

The sheer scale of the first catastrophe caught everyone off guard, prompting the Turkish government to declare a state of emergency and request international assistance. Initial fears – widely publicized in local and international media – that epidemics of cholera would be spread by dead bodies beneath the rubble proved unfounded. Emergency public health activities focused on surveillance of communicable diseases; providing clean water and sanitation equipment for survivors living in tent cities and prefabricated settlements; and distributing medicines and medical equipment to hospitals, clinics and rehabilitation centres.

While the international media publicized the work of dozens of international search-and-rescue teams lifting injured survivors out of the rubble, these images disguised the reality that most of the rescue work, in the first crucial hours after the disaster, was done by neighbours, often digging with bare hands. And the spontaneous but professional action of Turkish health workers – many of whom had themselves lost homes and family members – undoubtedly saved lives.

Estimates of the survivability of victims buried under collapsed buildings in Turkey indicate that within six hours less than 50 per cent of those buried were still alive. With even the quickest international rescue teams taking 12 hours to reach the disaster zone, clearly it is local people and institutions that need to be strengthened and supported to cope whenever disaster strikes.

An assessment team deployed by the International Federation shortly after the first earthquake was surprised to find few patients in the disaster area. Turkish health personnel had already evacuated seriously injured patients to Istanbul or Ankara, while 'walking wounded' had moved to safer areas.

Nevertheless, temporary clinics and hospitals were needed to meet the demands of non-earthquake-related patients. The pre-quake 5,000-bed capacity of the 25 hospitals in the most seriously affected provinces dropped to just 300 beds after the earthquake – and half of this capacity was in 'buffer hospitals' outside the immediate disaster zone. Tented, 'container' and, later, prefabricated hospitals provided temporary clinical health services in the earthquake area.

But while international aid organizations focused on the epicentre of the earthquake, looking to support hospitals that suffered structural damage, the buffer hospitals received the bulk of patients – and hardly any international assistance. The Kandira State Hospital, to the north of the August epicentre, had a tenfold increase in admissions and operations. "I performed 11 caesarean sections within the first day after the earthquake and the midwife assisted in 35 births," said hospital director Ismail Yilmaz. Hundreds of patients were admitted to his hospital, despite the lack of tele-communications, staff, medication, clean water or electricity. "Today, seven months later, we continue to face serious personnel, financial and structural constraints," explained Yilmaz.

In the aftermath of disasters, international aid could make more difference if it were focused on 'helping the helpers'. That means, within the health context, material support for the buffer hospitals bearing the brunt of treating patients, and physical and psychological support for local hospital and health personnel.

Local and international health professionals considering the long-term public health implications of the two earthquakes agree that,

.../

.../

besides widespread damage to health facilities, at least two other direct consequences of the disasters will be felt for years to come: the need for essential physical rehabilitation of severely disabled quake survivors; and the importance of addressing the psychosocial needs of the affected population.

Since August 1999, the International Federation's health team in Turkey has visited many of the Istanbul hospitals to which most seriously injured patients were transferred. One 17-year-old boy, who lost his home and entire family, is now paralysed from the neck down and still waits for medical rehabilitation seven months later. An estimated 4,000 quake survivors are suffering from spinal-cord injuries, peripheral nerve lesions, multiple bone fractures and extremity amputations. The majority of these victims received emergency treatment immediately after the earthquakes. However, due to the limited capacity of local health institutions, many patients must wait up to a year for crucial, often lifesaving, physiotherapy and rehabilitation.

The earthquakes and aftershocks caused severe psychological disturbances and many still suffer from post-traumatic stress symptoms, including sleep disorders, irritability, hyperarousal, anxiety, depression and psychosomatic disorders. In addition, the constant predictions, widely advertised by the Turkish media, that another strong earthquake could hit Istanbul at any time, have added to survivors' distress. The International Federation has initiated a community-based psychosocial programme – starting in Avcilar, Istanbul – aimed at providing immediate support to quake survivors, medical personnel and relief workers.

Long-term efforts in the health sector will not only focus on psychosocial support, physiotherapy and rehabilitation for severely injured quake survivors, but also on public health issues, first-aid training and upgrading the Turkish Red Crescent Society's nationwide blood programme. Other key areas for the Red Cross/Red Crescent include reconstruction of health, education and social facilities, social welfare and disaster preparedness.

What has been learnt in the aftermath of disaster? A comprehensive disaster preparedness plan encompassing the government, non-governmental and civil society organizations, health institutions and individual families is needed. The following list highlights some of the important public health aspects to be taken into consideration when serious disasters strike:

- Assess the damage and consider the immediate needs of hospitals and clinics in the disaster zone. Main needs often include: clean water and food; staff; medicine and medical items; and electricity.
- Assess the needs of buffer hospitals and clinics surrounding the disaster area, which may receive a high number of victims in addition to their regular caseload and may quickly become overwhelmed.
- Helping the helpers: the basic needs of health personnel must be quickly met to enable them to perform their duties effectively.
- Swiftly organize psychological debriefing for both local and international health and aid personnel.
- Mobilize additional medical staff from outside the disaster area.
- Organize additional field hospitals/temporary clinics in the disaster area within 24 hours – not for lifesaving purposes, but for filling temporary gaps in the health service.
- Health personnel must be trained beforehand in triage and first aid, while the general public needs prior training in basic rescue and first-aid skills.
- Public health surveillance is crucial in a disaster-stricken area. Fast response must follow up any detected needs.
- A disaster preparedness plan must provide for sufficient relief items and medical stocks, availability of transport to evacuate patients quickly, good communication, generators for hospitals, and a database of available human resources.
- Recovery programmes should include the reconstruction of the health structure and facilities as well as the physical and psychological rehabilitation of the affected population.

Comprehensive responses will only be possible through public/private partnerships such as ARCHI 2010 and GAVI, which can act in an integrated rather than vertical fashion. The causes and consequences of public health disasters reach far beyond the medical realm. In January 2000, James Wolfensohn told the UN Security Council: "Many of us used to think of AIDS as a health issue. We were wrong. AIDS can no longer be confined to the health or social sector portfolios. AIDS is a global issue. It forces us to bring all our understanding together – of security, health, economics, social and cultural change. It forces us to bring all actors together – from developed and developing countries, communities and governments, business and NGOs, science, faith and civil society."

The same is true of the less reported public health disasters which maim lives and manacle social and economic development. Such disasters are not one-off – they are symptoms of an often systemic failure of development and public health provision. Countering these negative trends will take courage, vision and commitment at a global level – there is more than simply health at stake.

Sources and further information

British Medical Journal, vol. 319, pp. 412 and 415, August 1999.

Emerging Infectious Diseases, vol. 5, no. 4, July-August 1999.

Hurrelmann, Klaus and Laaser, Ulrich (eds.). *The International Handbook of Public Health.* Greenwood Press, 1996.

International Federation of Red Cross and Red Crescent Societies. *World Disasters Report 1999.* Geneva: International Federation, 1999.

Leaning, Jennifer (ed.). *Humanitarian Crises: The Medical and Public Health Response.* Cambridge, MA: Harvard University Press, 1999.

Noji, Eric K. *The Public Health Consequences of Disasters.* Oxford: Oxford University Press, 1997.

Panos Institute. *Young Lives at Risk, Adolescents and Reproductive Health.* London: Panos Briefing No. 35, July 1999.

Reich, Michael et al. "Pharmaceutical Donations by the USA: an assessment of relevance and time to expiry". *WHO Bulletin*, vol. 77, p. 8, 1999.

US National Intelligence Council. *The Global Infectious Disease Threat and Its Implications for the United States.* National Intelligence Estimate 99-17D, January 2000.

World Bank. *World Development Report 1997 and 1998/1999.* Oxford: Oxford University Press, 1997 and 1998.

World Health Organization (WHO). *The World Health Report 1999 – Making a Difference.* Geneva: WHO, 1999.

WHO. *WHO Report on Infectious Diseases: Removing Obstacles to Healthy Development.* Geneva: WHO, 1999.

Wuyts, et al. *Development Policy and Public Action.* Oxford: Oxford University Press, 1992.

Web sites

BBC News – http://news.bbc.co.uk
Disaster relief – http://www.disasterrelief.org/
European Union – http://europa.eu.int/
Human Rights Watch – http://www.hrw.org/reports/
International Federation of Red Cross and Red Crescent Societies – http.//www.ifrc.org
New York Times – http://www.nytimes.com
Organisation for Economic Co-operation and Development – http://www.oecd.org
US Center for Mental Health Services – http://www.mentalhealth.org
UNICEF – http://www.unicef.org
World Bank – http://www.worldbank.org/
World Food Programme – http://www.wfp.org
World Health Organization – http://www.who.int

Section One

Focus on public health

chapter 2

Assessing and targeting public health priorities

The world in which relief organizations are now operating has changed faster than anyone could have predicted. Post-Cold War fragmentation in the Balkans and continuing floods and refugee crises in sub-Saharan Africa have taken a heavy toll on public health. A series of '100-year' storms whipped up by the El Niño/La Niña event of 1998-99 killed tens of thousands and devastated swathes of infrastructure across Latin America. As a result, many poorer states have to divert precious resources to deal with disasters, leaving little to support medium- to long-term public health provision.

Disasters destroy progress in public health and feed off weak public health infrastructure. This vicious spiral of cause and effect is drawing humanitarian agencies into situations more complex than they ever imagined. A short-term refugee crisis in Kosovo is becoming a medium- to long-term reconstruction of the province's health system. Famine in the Democratic People's Republic of Korea (DPRK) during 1994-96 may have been the widely reported disaster – but the ensuing public health crisis is more serious still. The HIV/AIDS pandemic in sub-Saharan Africa has been termed a 'complex emergency' in its own right, demanding both immediate and longer-term responses.

Such crises suggest the era of the quick fix is over. Decision-makers must come to terms with long-term involvement in areas where emergency interventions were once the rule. But facing up to unlimited public health needs with limited resources demands ever more rigorous assessing and targeting of priorities.

The textbook version of how to plan relief responses is often set out in diagram form (see Figure 2.1), but what looks so clinically easy in theory can become impossibly complex in the field. This chapter explores some of the tools and principles that enable agencies to meet post-disaster public health needs more effectively.

How best to collect and disseminate data? How cost-effective are high-tech assessment tools? How should international agencies engage with local communities? Effective targeting of public health aid demands coordination of standards and delivery in the disaster zone. Should we have lead agencies or lead methodologies – tools or turf? How can the impact of health interventions be multiplied to create maximum effect?

Increasingly, questions are being raised about the legitimacy of humanitarian actors and their often self-proclaimed agenda. So how should organizations improve and monitor the standards of service they offer to beneficiaries? If humanitarians are to wield the power of life and death, they must prove their competence to intervene and be accountable for their actions.

Photo opposite page:
While international partnerships are vital to tackle the world's ever greater public health needs, the tools to deliver preventive and curative care only work in trained hands. Improving public health means investing in local people as well as in technology.

Photo: Jenny Matthews/ International Federation, Sudan 1999.

Forward planning and partnerships key to data collection

The idea that data collection starts in the aftermath of a disaster is flawed. Health professionals working in development settings recognize the value of tracking disease patterns and studying epidemic cycles to forecast and prepare for outbreaks – such as the cycles of meningitis that until recently struck sub-Saharan Africa once a decade (see Box 2.1). The regularity of these cycles has been broken down by population movement and climate change – Médecins sans Frontières (MSF) reports that meningitis outbreaks can now happen anytime, anywhere in Africa – making data collection and analysis even more critical.

Fruitful partnerships have developed with meteorologists who can map severe, changeable weather conditions, helping prepare for floods, hurricanes and drought. The Famine Early Warning System (FEWS), focusing on the Sahel, is one well-established example.

But much more useful information remains to be tapped, especially by disaster response planners. Epidemiologists are now monitoring socio-economic data on issues such as crime rates, political changes and corruption, compiled by political scientists, military planners, economists and intelligence agencies. Such information sources help pinpoint areas of potential conflict, enabling planned responses well ahead of public health crises.

Figure 2.1
The planning cycle

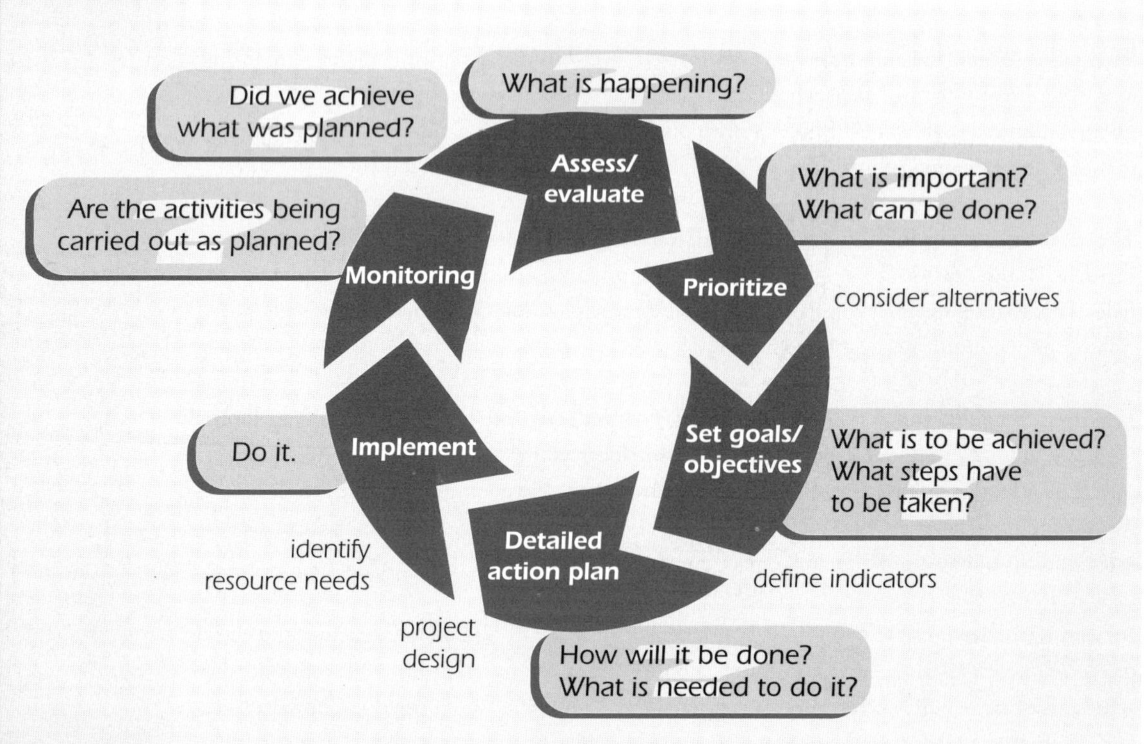

Kosovo, Angola and East Timor were all highlighted as potential hot spots for 1999 – and using this information, Eric Noji, of the World Health Organization's (WHO) emergency and humanitarian action department, visited Kosovo in the run-up to the NATO bombing campaign on a forward-planning mission.

There, Noji built up baseline information on Kosovo and its neighbouring states so that when refugees started pouring across the border, emergency teams had access to a communicable disease profile and information on issues such as vaccination status and existing health problems in the Kosovar population. These included high incidence of tuberculosis (TB) (often multi-drug-resistant strains) and Balkans Renal Syndrome, leading to kidney failure and requiring the transfer of refugees for dialysis. Also recorded were details of the public health infrastructure and information about health professionals in neighbouring Albania and Macedonia, where hundreds of thousands sought refuge.

One attempt to formalize information gathering is HINAP (Health Intelligence Network for Advanced Contingency Planning), launched by WHO in December 1999 – an early warning system designed for use by all organizations involved in public health relief in emergencies involving sudden population displacements. Its main goal is to consolidate, analyse and redistribute background and health information to the right people, at the right time, in the right format, in order to promote better-informed and -targeted interventions. Information aims to be country-by-country, covering communicable diseases, immunization coverage and nutrition, along with overviews of economy, government structures and existing infrastructure – analysed in the context of current events to highlight main issues of concern.

By focusing on countries where latent or low-level tensions have gone unnoticed but could escalate, and by early detection of negative trends in key health and medical indicators, HINAP also aims to spur preventive decision-making and contingency planning – at both governmental and non-governmental organization (NGO) levels. By February 2000, the HINAP web site had information on nine countries: Albania, Angola, Colombia, Yugoslavia/Kosovo, Macedonia, Indonesia, Nigeria, Tajikistan and Uganda.

While HINAP has not yet proven itself, it does hold promise for the future. According to Ronald Waldman, of the Program on Forced Migration and Health at the Mailman School of Public Health of Columbia University in New York City, HINAP should analyse the quality of the data available. "HINAP is a very innovative and potentially useful idea", says Waldman, "and will be all the more useful if it filters, assesses and selects the information it is disseminating, so that the user can rely on that information to be of the highest possible quality." Although HINAP may be helpful as emergencies unfold, its ability to predict where future public health disasters will occur remains to be seen.

High-tech tools map public health priorities...

The Kosovo crisis marked a technological leap forward for agencies in the field. In Albanian camps, 'cyber-points' were set up to enable refugees to e-mail relatives around the world and to trace missing family members via the Internet. Communication breakdowns and incompatibilities which dogged recent relief efforts from Rwanda to Afghanistan are being consigned to history. Now, reports from the field can be transmitted swiftly back to base. The latest generation of international mobile phones, carrying cordless e-mail and Internet capabilities, will make front-line aid workers of the 21st century even more connected.

Box 2.1 Volunteers vital for meningitis vaccination

Sudan has experienced widespread meningitis epidemics in ten-year cycles during the dry seasons in 1979 and 1989. Although outbreaks are now reported at any time of year and outside the so-called 'meningitis belt' of sub-Saharan Africa, epidemiologists tentatively predicted 1999 as the year for another major outbreak. So, close monitoring was already in place when numbers of reported cases and mortality rates began to climb in December.

On 12 December 1998, 25 cases of cerebrospinal meningitis were reported in North Darfour state which escalated to 190 cases within a month. The highest disease rates are found in the young, with older children, teenagers and young adults also affected. The mortality rate was very high and prompted plans for a mass vaccination campaign by Sudan's Ministry of Health (MoH).

A Red Cross/Red Crescent training of trainers workshop during the first week of February 1999 covered vaccination techniques, methods for preventing the spread of the epidemic, and active case-finding. As part of the awareness programme, 10,000 posters and pamphlets were produced and distributed and 250 volunteers took part in the North Darfour vaccination campaign.

Outbreaks were reported in 12 other states in February, transmitted along the main road and rail transport routes. Weekly coordination meetings between the MoH, the Sudanese Red Crescent (SRC) and the Inter-agency Coordinating Group (ICG, comprising the International Federation, WHO, UNICEF and MSF) decided priority regions and presented new figures on reported cases and deaths.

The average number of cases reported per day was 135, but a very sharp increase took place between 21 and 31 March, when 3,454 cases and 146 deaths were reported over the ten-day period. The SRC and ICG launched a vaccination and health education campaign on 1 March which could be implemented quickly thanks to swift donor response to both an initial appeal and an appeal for further funds following the rapid spread of the epidemic.

Within three weeks, drugs and vaccines were delivered to begin targeting people aged from 2 to 30 years, lowering morbidity and mortality rates and controlling the spread of the disease in the initial target area. Peaking at the end of April, having spread to 17 states, meningitis infected more than 33,000 people and killed at least 2,375 of them. Eleven million people nationwide were targeted with vaccines, and, as part of the intervention, a disaster preparedness plan was put in place, which included stocking 30,000 vials of oily chloramphenicol at five strategically-located treatment facilities.

SRC volunteers were described by the annual ICG meeting as crucial in helping organize the vaccination programme and identifying suspected cases early for treatment. Local radio and television, posters and leaflets were used to help spread information.

To try to contain a future meningitis epidemic as quickly and efficiently as possible, response plans are now being set up by the MoH and SRC. A local-level prevention training programme is now planned for the seven states where the SRC has a major presence, to try and ensure treatment campaigns take place as soon as the next cycle of disease sweeps through the region.

Computer software packages to aid decision-making are now becoming commonplace. Geographic Information Systems (GIS) are graphically presented databases allowing the user to click on a map of a chosen country to access multi-layered information.

But some organizations making GIS and image processing software available to agencies believe it is being underused. Global Resources Information Database (GRID) is, according to its director Ron Witt, "an application in search of users." Digital maps, satellite images and aerial survey results are included in GRID's data archive, part of a worldwide network of 15 environmental data centres developed by the United Nations Environment Programme (UNEP) and available free on-line.

WHO and UNICEF have jointly developed HealthMap – a GIS-based application which maps public health resources and diseases in relation to the local environment and infrastructure. By plotting the locations of, for example, villages, schools, health centres and clean water sources onto one map, then overlaying the spread of specific diseases, public health professionals can prioritize needs and target resources far more effectively.

Satellite imaging systems are now becoming so sophisticated they can accurately estimate displaced populations, making the technology extremely helpful in assessing and targeting health needs. During the Somalian floods of 1997, satellite images showed the Juba River inundating towns way off its usual course. This helped the International Committee of the Red Cross (ICRC) pinpoint areas to target before relief teams arrived, saving valuable time and resources on the ground.

When ICRC teams in the field asked villagers how many of them were affected by flooding, answers for one location could vary from 10,000 to 50,000 people. "The figures can be grossly exaggerated," said Riccardo Conti, who heads ICRC's water and habitat unit.

But use of satellite images plus GIS software containing the results of a 1991 census survey and databanks of information positioning wells, boreholes and donated seed distribution, gave Conti and his team a head start in assessing and planning their response.

"Satellite images not only differentiate water from soil, they can reveal vegetation and germination rates. We could see where the donated seed had been planted and whether it had been flooded or not," said Conti.

Risk Map, developed by John Seaman of Save the Children Fund, is a software tool that helps decision-makers in Africa prioritize areas in need of food aid, using complex analysis based on information collected via rigorous fieldwork about how rural households live in normal years. The programme formalizes previously patchy approaches to vulnerability analysis and famine prediction, standardizes methods of data collection and analysis, and has developed databases on the economies of several African countries.

The user can analyse a large geographic area composed of many different food economy zones simultaneously, can predict to some degree how prices of various commodities will be affected by a given problem – such as crop failure, sick livestock, or closure of markets – and can then determine how rural households will be affected by these changing prices.

"Inefficient use of resources kills a lot of people and impoverishes a lot more. Getting it right is actually quite important," says Seaman, who has been working on Risk Map for eight years, and is completing a training manual to help spread its use. It has already been taken up by the governments of several countries in Africa. Seaman can see enormous scope for developing his technology to help model health and social service systems.

Emergency response units (ERUs) taking part in relief health operations for refugees can tap into Health Monitoring System (HMS), a database and analysis software tool developed by Oleg Blinnikov for the International Federation of Red Cross and Red Crescent Societies, to help epidemiological monitoring and health management of refugees and displaced populations. Easy to learn and use, the basic version contains databases of camp population, patients, staff and drug use, plus a diagnosis list of the most common communicable diseases in refugee camps. A more complex version designed for mobile referral hospitals can be used by any in-patient department, and features surgical and maternity databases as well as a diagnosis list covering diseases most frequently encountered by displaced rural African populations. A third pharmacy version lists most types of drug and material used in the field.

At Johns Hopkins University School of Hygiene and Public Health, Jonathan Patz is an environmental health scientist who is combining geography, spatial statistics, high-speed computer simulations and satellite surveillance to investigate the health effects of climate

Figure 2.2 Satellites map Mozambique's floods

Source: Canadian Space Agency

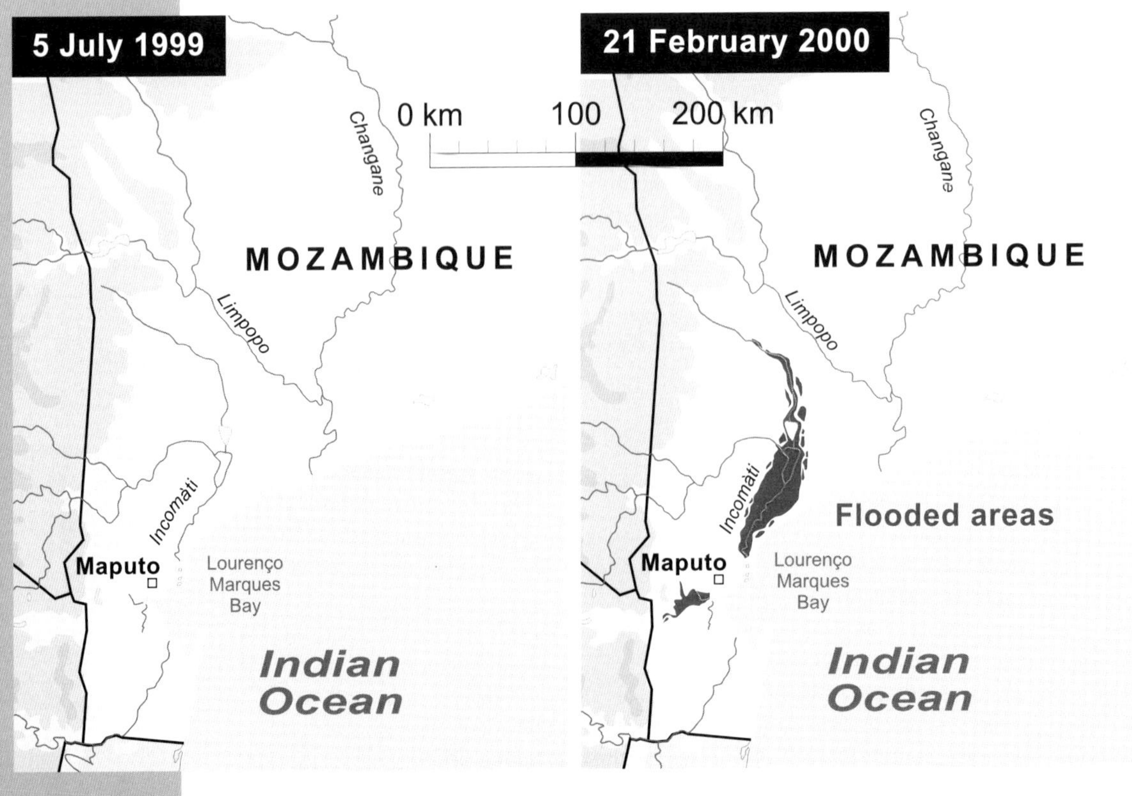

change and global warming. He and colleague Gregory Gurri Glass, an infectious disease ecologist, are using satellite photos to map areas of moisture and vegetation in order to predict regions prone to malaria outbreaks.

However, both accept the limitations of their high-tech approach, reporting that such technology is prohibitively expensive for developing countries, and that orbiting cameras are useless on cloudy days during the rainy season – precisely when malaria-carrying mosquito populations are at their worst. With this in mind, they looked for simpler prediction methods, using the amount of water held in soils in the region. Analysing the biting rates and infectiousness of local mosquitoes in Kenya, and combining the data with information on local temperature, rainfall, humidity, wind speed and solar radiation, they produced a model which could be easily used in the field.

...but field-based tools deliver the detail

Joachim Kreysler, formerly of the US Centers for Disease Control and Prevention, and the International Federation, argues that public health priorities should be dictated by needs on the ground and questions the value of computer modelling. "There is a dangerous convergence between virtuality and reality," he says. "We avoid the horror of disasters through using computer screens."

High-tech tools may deliver the public health planner with a more complex and detailed overview of a crisis – but they can't replace simple field methods. A satellite photograph will never reveal refugees scattered across wide areas or sheltering in the homes of host families. Only 'quick and dirty' field surveys will identify hidden people in need.

But even these existing field-level epidemiological methods can be improved upon. Cluster sampling, for example, is a popular method of needs-assessment, but as a method it has important limitations, argues Columbia University's Waldman. Given the changing nature of emergencies, and changing information needs, the means of collecting and analysing data need to change as well. Developmental methods such as participatory

Humanitarian crises continue to attract inappropriate drug donations – sometimes offloaded by pharmaceutical companies seeking tax breaks. Sorting through them soaks up valuable resources, and shipping out or destroying useless medicines can cost millions.

Photo: Mikkel Oestergaard/ International Federation, Turkey 1999.

rural appraisal should also be adapted to emergency settings, suggests Waldman. "We need to find the optimum combination of quantitative and qualitative methods", he says, "which can generate data to guide the design and implementation of humanitarian interventions."

The WHO-led *Roll Back Malaria* initiative is employing a range of surveillance tools to fight a disease which claims an estimated 1 to 2.6 million lives each year. While depending on GIS mapping technology to plan anti-malaria interventions, WHO is exploring cheaper technologies to diagnose malaria. High-tech microscopy used to be the only means of testing for malaria, and it is still useful for detecting parasites and TB. But microscopy is a hospital-based technology, which requires electricity and well-trained technicians. Since many areas where malaria is endemic often lack the public health infrastructure to support such technology, WHO has developed diagnostic dipsticks that can be distributed at low cost and easily taught to local health workers and volunteers.

In order to reach and test a greater proportion of people living in malarial zones, some unusual volunteers have stepped forwards. Barmen in Brazil and teachers in Bangladesh, for example, have been taught to use dipsticks in their place of work to test anyone suffering from a fever. By placing a pinprick of blood on the dipstick, they can diagnose within 15 minutes whether the patient has malaria. The dipstick method has several advantages – it can be used by volunteers, minimal training or infrastructure are needed, and it cuts down the time between diagnosis and cure.

Useless drug donations dog disaster zones

Attempts to plan ahead of public health crises must be matched by serious efforts to cut wasteful and inefficient practices still dogging relief efforts. Tax breaks benefit US pharmaceutical companies which offload drugs on disaster zones – a bitter pill, if those 'donations' turn out to be useless.

WHO has long promoted good drug-donation practices, and issued interagency guidelines three years ago – updated in September 1999 and based on a consensus among 15 major United Nations (UN) and international agencies. They appealed for donors to ensure contributions are based on consultation with recipients and are of maximum benefit. Yet a WHO survey during the Kosovo crisis reveals unacceptable practices are still taking place.

Of 108 drug-donation lists submitted to the Albanian Ministry of Health during May 1999, only half mentioned trade names and many of these were unknown to local health professionals. Just 56 per cent included information on shelf-life, 41 per cent had a remaining shelf-life of less than a year, and 18 per cent of donations contained small packs of free samples or drugs returned to pharmacies.

Unsolicited and inappropriate donations flooding into Turkey after the massive August 1999 earthquake seriously hampered restocking of regular and emergency medical supplies, according to the International Federation. It seems little has been learned since Bosnia in 1997, when a joint study by Epicentre and Pharmaciens sans Frontières estimated almost two-thirds of drug donations were inappropriate.

The cost of flying in and then disposing of unsolicited donations is bad enough. Often classified as chemical waste, drugs must be disposed of in purpose-built facilities, such as incinerators, to minimize potential environmental contamination. Shipping them out is the costly alternative. The United States will be paying US$ 2 to 4 million to ship 1,000 tonnes of inappropriate pharmaceuticals and medical supplies from Croatia for appropriate disposal.

One tool, developed by the Pan American Health Organization (PAHO), to rationalize drug donations in emergencies is SUMA – a Supplies Management system which inventories and filters incoming medicines (see Box 2.2).

Drug supplies can filter into a population and actually worsen the health situation. In the former Soviet republic of Georgia, drug donations to combat tuberculosis triggered a market for uncontrolled use – this in a region where the only hope of limiting TB is strict control of drug distribution to reduce lethal multi-drug resistant strains.

Such drug donation is a crime, says Ann Aerts-Novara, of ICRC's health services unit. She welcomes legislation introduced by the Georgian government, allowing only licensed doctors to prescribe TB medication, in an effort to stamp out unofficial supplies. Perhaps other

Box 2.2 SUMA in East Timor

Traditionally, disasters attracting prime-time media coverage are also those which stimulate unsolicited donations. Humanitarian workers and disaster managers are all too familiar with mountains of inappropriate supplies – medical or other – competing for space, transportation and time against those items of critical importance.

Alarmed by early indications that huge amounts of all kinds of supplies for Timor were piling up in Darwin, Australia, WHO despatched four experts in Supplies Management (SUMA) – a computerized system for sorting, classification and inventory of humanitarian supplies.

They found that, while large amounts of supplies were stacked in the Darwin warehouses, most had been ordered, requested and expected by humanitarian organizations. Few supplies were unsolicited or donated by the public or industry.

Had the international community suddenly learnt to refrain from sending unsolicited and inappropriate donations, like those dispatched in large quantities to Kosovo and Central America? One explanation was the logistical difficulty and cost of shipping supplies first to Australia then on to East Timor, an island without commercial communications with the outside world. A similar situation prevailed in the enclave of Iraqi Kurdistan when the military was in full control.

SUMA proved to be a coordination success in East Timor. In addition to standardizing information among agencies, over two tons of unclaimed medical supplies in Darwin were listed and referred for decision to the Health Coordinating Committee in Dili. Medical supplies were salvaged from looted warehouses and inventoried for use by the participating agencies. Collaboration over SUMA between sister UN agencies and both international and local NGOs contributed to a transparent exchange of information – proving the feasibility and value of a common inventory and data management approach to supplies management, whether in complex emergencies or natural disasters.

countries should follow Georgia's example. Fines could be levied against those who fall foul of WHO's guidelines.

Coordination or cooperation?

Tools to assess and target effective public health interventions are useless without coordination or at least cooperation between disaster stakeholders. The cornerstone of effective humanitarian action lies in coordination between governments, donors, the UN and NGOs, with clear lines of responsibility, an identified lead agency, sharing of information, timely surveillance data, and agreed strategy and objectives – so wrote Anthony Zwi, head of the health policy unit at the London School of Hygiene and Tropical Medicine (LSHTM), and two colleagues in the *European Journal of Public Health* during the Kosovo crisis last year.

Yet, they noted, the humanitarian disaster following NATO air strikes was met with inadequate support services for the hundreds of thousands of refugees fleeing over the border into Albania, one of Europe's poorest nations.

Kosovo's refugee crisis was an "intensely politicized" event, claims the independent evaluation of the role of the Office of the UN High Commissioner for Refugees (UNHCR) in the emergency, published in February 2000. The political/military agenda of NATO states at times competed with the humanitarian agenda of aid organizations, leading to poor information sharing and lack of coordination. As an illustration of external constraints, the evaluation notes that NATO refused flight clearance for the aircraft supposed to carry UNHCR's first emergency response team into Albania on 31 March 1999.

Coordination between, and even within, agencies continues to be an uphill struggle. "We had two or three months when we knew NATO was going to intervene in the Kosovo crisis. Surveys were done. We had a good perception of the situation on the ground," says ICRC's Riccardo Conti. "But why didn't Geneva-based agencies hold a single common meeting during those months?"

WHO's Eric Noji criticizes the "false dichotomy" institutionalized within relief agencies whereby totally different medical communities respond to natural disasters and complex humanitarian emergencies – and rarely meet. Yet lessons from one side have value for the other, and assessments during all these disasters follow much the same criteria, he argues.

By late summer 1999, around 400 different agencies had converged on the Kosovar capital Pristina, swamping local resources and in some cases undermining local efforts to recover. Over-assessments and duplicated relief efforts wasted energy and resources, and antagonized those supposedly being helped. People in shock from the trauma of losing loved ones, or returning to see their homes turned to rubble, were not well served by being asked the same questions again and again by different visiting delegations.

Some have warned that unless the proliferation of organizations working in international aid get their own houses in order, others will do it for them: "Steps toward greater efficiency, effectiveness and community transparency either will come because we can collectively learn from our mistakes, or they will be forced upon us, at some point, by the people we are attempting to serve," observed Jennifer Leaning, senior research fellow at the Harvard Center for Population and Development Studies.

In the aftermath of the Turkish earthquake, the government quickly designated the International Federation as the lead humanitarian organization, and daily meetings were held to promote interagency communication and coordination. For the first time, Oxfam channelled their water and sanitation relief through the International Federation, taking part in joint assessment missions.

However, this fell well short of 'coordination'. No one, for example, coordinated the deluge of search-and-rescue teams that arrived from dozens of different countries. And relief efforts were continually complicated by conflicting, lengthy or non-existent flows of information between the International Federation, the Turkish Red Crescent and Turkish government officials at local, provincial and national levels.

WHO gets operational

WHO is moving to assume more of a leadership role in crises with a public health dimension. Violence in East Timor in September 1999 forced more than 500,000 people into forest and mountain camps, where water, food and health services were in short supply. A further 170,000 were displaced into West Timor. Having taken part in a health assessment in April 1999, and several interagency missions in August and September, WHO was well placed to identify problems and priorities.

WHO identified key areas of concern: all surveillance and epidemic response activities had ceased for nearly a year; the majority of the population had insufficient food, shelter, clean water or sanitation for extended periods; most had no access to medical or preventive care; and public health programmes such as immunization and vector control had been seriously disrupted. Many health professionals had fled, nearly all the health infrastructure was seriously damaged, and most medical supplies had been looted or destroyed.

Based on this information, WHO appealed for US$ 9 million in September 1999 to revitalize health infrastructure, continue coordinating the control of key infectious diseases such as malaria and TB, and initiate programmes on mental and reproductive health. Although the appeal had raised only US$ 2 million by the end of 1999, WHO was able to implement its *Roll Back Malaria* initiative in East Timor, with MERLIN as the main implementing agency and the International Rescue Committee providing insecticide-impregnated bed nets.

Using the fledgling state's crisis as an entry point, this anti-malaria partnership aims to establish long-term training of local health professionals, health education for East Timor's communities, drug availability and early warning mechanisms.

Some believe WHO's strengths lie in data collection and analysis, dissemination of statistics in emergencies and guidelines for best practice, and that the organization cannot compete operationally with well-established front-line agencies, not least because of its bureaucratic administration. However, argues Maire Connolly, who led WHO's response in East Timor, the organization is taking a more active role in health coordination, and has implemented surveillance systems for the emergency phase in Macedonia, Kosovo and East Timor. "WHO can be operational, in providing not health care, but technical coordination at the field level," maintains Connolly.

Tools not turf

The much-discussed concept of overall lead agency, however, seems unworkable in practice. Some sources privately admit this is because established agencies don't like to be ordered around by 'new kids on the block' like OCHA, the UN's Organization for the Coordination of Humanitarian Affairs. Some claim the relief world is not authoritarian in structure, like the military, and therefore has no culture of obeying orders.

During the devastating floods in Mozambique in March 2000, the head of relief for one leading international aid agency publicly admitted that coordination was impossible, given the range of military and humanitarian assets deployed by both regional and international actors.

The question of coordination can be looked at another way. Instead of arguing about lead agency status, it may be more productive to focus on 'lead methodologies' around which collaboration and cooperation could be built – 'tools not turf'.

While the humanitarian response to Kosovar refugees last year was slow to start, in Macedonia, teams from a number of separate agencies worked together to assess needs. Key to their success was their commitment to hold regular 'coordination' meetings (hosted by WHO and UNHCR) and to use a common disease-surveillance form provided by WHO in April 1999. The teams were given three days to take away the form, study and return it with comments before it was put into use as an agreed template.

The survey results were collated and analysed by WHO on a weekly basis. Published in a weekly report and handed out, this showed that the information was being used to decide priorities. The teams got feedback showing their efforts were appreciated and decisions leading to action flowed from the information they had gathered, spurring them to maintain interest in their work. The bulletins were also made available in electronic form, so agencies could e-mail them back to their headquarters quickly and easily.

A lead methodology developed by WHO for treating TB is DOTS (Directly Observed Treatment, Short-course), which ensures that patients complete the full regime of drugs to avoid multi-drug-resistance. In order to combat TB in Georgia, the ICRC agreed to intervene only if the DOTS method was used – an argument that eventually was won. Now DOTS is accepted nationally as the treatment which gives the best results.

In Cambodia last year, the Red Cross, WHO, the government, local volunteers and the media joined forces to contain an epidemic of dengue haemorrhagic fever (see Box 2.3). Joint needs assessments, common response and prevention strategies were key to the success of this operation. And a health education campaign using local Cambodian radio and TV helped disseminate ways of preventing further outbreaks of dengue fever.

Using journalists and mass media to help target public health interventions, in both disaster and development situations, is a tool often overlooked or underexploited. While some aid agencies may view the media with suspicion, partnerships with radio professionals can greatly magnify public health messages.

Box 2.3 Dengue fever contained by cooperation in Cambodia

Close cooperation between the Cambodian Ministry of Health (MoH), the International Federation and the Cambodian Red Cross (CRC), during a seven-month operation ending in February 1999, helped bring under control a serious epidemic of dengue haemorrhagic fever (DHF). A rare and deadly outcome of dengue fever, DHF is a viral disease spread by the 'aedes aegypti' mosquito which mainly affects children under 14 years.

The seasonal DHF outbreak in Cambodia escalated into an epidemic from June to October 1998. Peaking in August, 4,434 patients were admitted to hospital and at least 185 children died. Recorded cases throughout the year reached over 16,000.

The International Federation's regional health and information delegates arrived on 7 August to assist the CRC. They reviewed health data on population and numbers of new cases, provided by the MoH and WHO, in order to identify high-risk provinces.

Red Cross teams then carried out village-level spot checks with the MoH outreach team, monitoring use of insecticides and the practice of covering water storage jars. The CRC, MoH and WHO carried out a needs assessment during a joint field visit to hospitals in the two worst-affected provinces and the national paediatric hospital in Phnom Penh, where they assessed the situation of hospital wards and drug supplies. What the teams found in the field corresponded closely with centralized data.

The information they collated enabled them to identify urgent medical supply, insecticide and staffing needs and set up a variety of preventive and education campaigns bolstered by CRC youth and volunteer training. There is no known vaccine to help combat DHF, making other preventive measures like reducing the population of mosquitoes and health education the most effective form of control.

Immediate objectives aimed to reduce mortality rates by targeting hospitals, carrying a DHF caseload of more than 150 as of 31 July, with medical supplies and blood transfusion kits. A health education campaign via TV, radio, leaflets and posters urged people to store water in specially cleaned containers, to use lids to cover them and to add larvicide to the water. The education campaign also advised mothers in high-risk areas how to recognize early symptoms so that children could receive prompt medical treatment.

Simultaneously, Red Cross volunteers helped promote early hospitalization and mass environmental clean-ups, while larvicide and insecticide supplies airlifted into the country were distributed via the MoH and WHO.

Monitoring was based on drug consumption and hospital records. Evaluation was carried out after three months using epidemiological data provided by the MoH and WHO, hospital patient records and drug consumption records. Success of preventive measures was determined by monitoring behavioural changes of the population and spot checks helped evaluate participation in clean-up campaigns.

Longer-term, the Red Cross aims to reduce the vulnerability of the urban population to DHF outbreaks with the introduction of a dengue module in their community-based first-aid training, and through regular environmental clean-ups organized by CRC youth groups.

Broadcasting editorially independent 'news you can use' via local radio stations reaches populations otherwise out of reach, especially women and children who may in some, especially Moslem, cultures be required to stay at home. Radio can be used in emergencies to help trace missing family members, to direct people towards aid, or to communicate messages of psychosocial support (see Chapter 6, Boxes 6.3 and 6.4).

Radio has played a key role in targeting vaccines to children in need. According to Carol Bellamy, executive director of UNICEF, "the use of mass media...has been crucial to the success of immunization campaigns so far. No matter how much money or how many vaccines, without some kind of mobilization, it's not going to work." And radio can be used in longer-term interventions to diffuse health education messages, often through the medium of soap opera.

A more comprehensive attempt to focus on tools not turf is the Sphere Project (see *World Disasters Report 1999*), during which hundreds of agencies came together to reach consensus on operational minimum standards in disaster response. These professional standards, which include health services, may even take their place in a future international disaster response law (see Chapter 8, Box 8.3).

While Sphere presents humanitarians with an unparalleled opportunity to cooperate in disaster response, monitoring adherence to the minimum standards remains an elusive goal. "The project has no interest to act as judge and jury," says Sphere's project manager Nan Buzard. She suggests that the task of enforcing accountability and compliance may lead to partnerships between donors and NGOs.

Accreditation and evaluation benchmark best practice

Accountability and transparency of agencies involved in public health interventions could be boosted by a system of accreditation, whereby agencies demonstrate competence in a range of different fields.

In particular, suggests Anthony Zwi, agencies may come under pressure to show that they adhere to accepted guidelines, can monitor and evaluate their own work, and are open to independent review and evaluation. Especially important, argues Zwi, is a demonstrated willingness to document field experience, to highlight strengths and weaknesses, and to propose remedial action to avoid recurrent problems.

Those best demonstrating that they were building appropriate standards into services could be offered incentives by donors and governments who would refer to the accreditation system when deciding what to fund and with whom to work.

"The accreditation mechanism, however, would need to reflect the concerns of a wide range of stakeholders – such as donors, beneficiaries, the UN, service-providers and NGOs – if it is to stand a chance of being successfully implemented. Participants would need to consult actively and work together to agree the standards and guidelines they wished to promote," Zwi suggests. He stresses the importance of making resources available to assist those smaller and poorer agencies with integrity, so they are not frozen out of accreditation schemes because of resource-consuming, but necessary, reporting requirements.

Box 2.4 Consigning polio to the grave

In March 1999, WHO announced poliomyelitis had been eradicated from the western Pacific region. WHO and its partners in the global push to consign the crippling viral infection to the grave say the disease is unlikely ever to return to this region, which includes all of China.

Polio, which can be prevented by simple oral vaccination, most commonly strikes young children, with devastating effects – infants can become paralysed within hours, and in severe cases death by asphyxiation follows.

Thanks to mass immunization campaigns, the number of polio cases worldwide fell from an estimated 350,000 in 1988 to some 6,400 confirmed cases in 1999, according to WHO. Eradication relies on a combination of: routine polio vaccination; vaccination through campaigns, known as National Immunization Days (NIDs); and close surveillance for signs of the acute flaccid paralysis caused by the disease.

WHO and its partners (UNICEF, Rotary International and Western governments) aim to eradicate the virus from the whole world by the end of 2000. In addition to the goal of total eradication, the polio initiative provides broader benefits. The NIDs – or 'Days of Tranquillity' – can contribute towards stopping conflict, at least temporarily, as combatants lay down their arms to permit immunization of children, whatever their origins and affiliations. And NIDs strengthen existing vaccine delivery systems in sub-Saharan Africa and south Asia.

While some argue it would be more cost-effective to control the caseload of polio at a manageable level rather than aim for total eradication, WHO says eradication and the eventual halt of polio immunization worldwide would save US$ 1.5 billion a year. WHO's rationale for eradication is that: polio only affects humans, so there is no animal reservoir; an effective, inexpensive vaccine exists; immunity is lifelong; there are no long-term carriers; and the virus can only survive for a very short time in the environment.

Predictably, polio is proving most persistent in nations where public health systems are fragmented or nearly non-existent. Although only three major areas of transmission remain, they include the highly populated countries of India, Pakistan and Nigeria, together with the war-torn states of Afghanistan and parts of central Africa.

And UNICEF has warned that declining commitment to public health in Iraq is prompting an upsurge of the disease there. According to WHO, the migration of minority populations across Iraq's national boundaries with Iran, Jordan, Kuwait, Saudi Arabia, Syria and Turkey, plus civil unrest and poor case management, have created perfect conditions for the polio virus to spread.

Conflict-torn Angola suffered one of the largest-ever outbreaks in Africa in early 1999, when over 1,000 children were affected and 58 died. But in the Democratic Republic of the Congo, 75,000 health workers managed to vaccinate over 80 per cent of the country's under-fives, during a specially brokered ceasefire between the warring parties in August 1999. WHO's director-general, Gro Harlem Brundtland, welcomed the achievement but warned that "war is one of the greatest hurdles that we now face in our effort to eradicate this disease."

Despite attempts to promote 'credentialing' in the United States, many relief agencies have no established requirements of competence, according to Columbia University's Waldman. And attempts by donors to hold NGOs accountable for their performance are only in preliminary stages. "Essentially, anyone can provide health care to refugees," he claims, adding that "no licensing and no certification are required." Frequently, the credentials of health care personnel are not reviewed by the country in which they will be practising. This issue took on renewed importance during the Kosovo crisis, when national authorities sought to review the credentials of foreign personnel. Not all agencies complied, nor did UNHCR require them to. Yet, points out Waldman, most European and North American countries do not allow foreigners to practise health care delivery without passing stringent examinations.

As for the idea of an ombudsman (an independent individual who can investigate complaints and disagreements), Zwi prefers the idea of a community 'ombuds-group', set up in relation to a particular event or conflict, constituted at a high level, with a mandate to pull together a respectable team, drawing on local expertise and concerns and with some input from regional NGOs, academics and UN agencies.

"The team would look at what's going on in 'real time' rather than provide *post hoc* analysis, and would challenge NGOs to work together and the UN to perform its function. And it would be able to make statements about the role of the military and the relationship between indigenous and international NGO communities," he says.

How can one introduce calm and measured analysis and reflection into a working environment dominated by the need for rapid response to increasing numbers and types of crises? Overwhelming pressure to perform is aggravated by a pervading atmosphere of rivalry, as agencies compete for dwindling donor budgets. Couple this with the rapid turnover of staff working in disaster settings, with very few making emergency health their career, and there is a danger that skills can be lost and best practice is not passed on.

"NGOs see their job as providing services and often do not have the resources to reflect upon and maximize the learning of lessons from their own experience and that of other agencies. Some are much more reflective than others," says Zwi. He believes one way of stimulating research and analysis about front-line practices lies in promoting partnerships between academic institutions and humanitarian organizations to allow staff to discuss and document their work.

As has been done at the Johns Hopkins University and Columbia University Schools of Public Health, among others, LSHTM and MERLIN have set up a joint project to support a senior lectureship in evidence-based humanitarian aid. They hope the model can be replicated with academic/NGO partnerships worldwide, and that donors will be prepared to help fund them.

Waldman adds that "although health concerns tend to dominate our interventions in emergencies, there's been very little done to formally evaluate those factors which contribute to successful outcomes." He points to recent evaluations of the humanitarian response to Kosovo which analyse issues of coordination and relations with the military in some detail but which fail to address health-sector issues in a detailed fashion. Zwi also intends to host writing, reflection and policy (WRAP) workshops allowing aid workers from different settings to share evidence and experiences from the field – with the goal of documenting lessons learned, facilitating policy refinements and stimulating peer debate.

Partnerships multiply impact of interventions

As we have seen, technical partnerships – with meteorologists, economists, social scientists, journalists and academics – can produce new tools to assess and target public health interventions.

Strategic partnerships – between, for example, humanitarian organizations, governments, international banks, pharmaceutical companies and philanthropists – can multiply the impact of existing tools, such as immunization (see Box 2.4). The Global Alliance for Vaccines and Immunization (GAVI), launched in November 1999 with a US$ 750 million donation from the Bill & Melinda Gates Foundation, aims to save 3 million children's lives a year by ensuring they are vaccinated against preventable diseases (see Chapter 1).

But no amount of new tools or international partnerships will make much impression on public health without trained hands on the ground, in disaster-affected communities, ready to turn theory into reality. Jean Roy, senior health officer with the International Federation, argues that building and multiplying local capacities is crucial: "A strong volunteer network in a community can address several problems sequentially," he says, "for example, an effective immunization programme contributes to polio eradication which can then lead to measles control and even the introduction of new vaccines."

Volunteers are sometimes only thought of and brought into use during emergencies, then left to lapse into inactivity in the periods between crisis situations. But the skills of local people and local organizations must be developed to build continuity and make projects sustainable. Nowhere is this more appropriate than in the field of public health, where preventive action is always needed and its effectiveness can be measured.

In addition, community health workers trained in first aid not only promote long-term good health, they are also more than likely to be the first on the scene of a major disaster, saving lives long before international teams arrive.

Training and investment in humanitarian staff – both professional and volunteer, local and international – is woefully lacking, especially when compared to the sums spent on national military training. If donors are serious about meeting humanitarian needs, then redirecting their emphasis to invest in people is long overdue.

The International Federation's African Red Cross/Red Crescent Health Initiative (ARCHI 2010 – see Chapter 10) is working through Red Cross and Red Crescent societies to motivate and support local volunteers in Africa, where the presence of western NGOs can all too often diminish the notion of self-help. Basic incentives are being worked on at branch level to motivate those whose efforts are needed over long periods and to try to decrease the drop-out rate. Priority health areas have been identified by National Societies, as well as an agreement to focus on health prevention and first-aid activities, rather than curative projects.

Local knowledge is useful in making preventive services more accessible to remote or service-shy populations. This was found to be the case during a Romanian mass measles immunization campaign from October 1998 to January 1999, which followed an epidemic of 33,000 cases and 21 deaths. Intensive efforts were made to reach children who were out of school, living in inaccessible gypsy communities, working, or perhaps itinerant. Romanian Red Cross volunteers led social mobilization efforts, bringing visibility and accessibility to the campaign. As a result, the risk of future measles outbreaks among targeted adolescents was greatly reduced.

From knee-jerk to helping hand

Trained volunteers and community health workers bridge the gap between disaster and rehabilitation often left yawning by humanitarian responders. This is especially relevant in the case of post-disaster psychological trauma, which in areas contaminated by the Chernobyl nuclear catastrophe, for example, is still affecting millions of people 14 years after the event.

Developing best practice in psychosocial response is problematic for international teams, which struggle to offer therapy and support to those of a different language and culture. Psychiatric intervention in humanitarian emergencies may prove inappropriate – but there are plenty of common-sense approaches which non-specialist aid workers should adopt (see Chapter 6, Box 6.1). Nevertheless, local capacity building is likely to be the only effective way of delivering the kind of context-sensitive, long-term response needed to heal mental scars.

Investing in local capacities – both human and infrastructural – will mitigate the effects of ongoing public health crises and future disasters. Local people are on the scene of a disaster long before international agencies arrive, and they remain long after the agencies have gone.

Humanitarian organizations can use disasters as a way in to longer-term contributions that build rather than reduce local self-dependence. If, for example, a fraction of the money poured into Tanzanian refugee camps during the Rwandan crisis had gone into health infrastructure, the country would still be reaping the benefits years after the refugees had gone home. Why spend money, for example, putting in a collapsible bladder tank when you could use the resources on a water system that will keep working in the medium to long term?

If agencies need to adjust their perspective to think longer-term, then so do donors. Those in the relief world are crying out for an end to knee-jerk, stop/start funding, most easily gained in an emergency, but harder to come by for preventive and preparedness projects. The sequential nature of current funding mechanisms mean there are often damaging delays between emergency, rehabilitation and reconstruction funding.

The distorting effect of the media spotlight on emergencies such as those that afflicted Kosovo and Turkey leads some agencies to seek higher individual profiles (and therefore funds) at the expense of inter-agency cooperation. Worse still, the glare of TV cameras can distort donor resource allocations geographically, so that some (nearest to home) gain at the expense of others (usually in Africa) who are forgotten. There is, perhaps, a need for more trust funds, independent of donor government-driven priorities which may favour specific geographical areas or certain times of year in which to spend annual budgets.

Warped funding priorities affect the ability of agencies to operate where they feel there is the greatest need. "It's a real balance. Agencies have to work to have a raison d'être and to survive financially. And the pressure to follow 'where the bees are buzzing' to get funding is very powerful," says MERLIN's Bruce Laurence.

"We work mainly in areas of chronic emergency – in areas of conflict where there is grinding poverty – that often receive very little media coverage, like Irian Jaya, which we plugged and plugged." Laurence says that the only way to act reasonably and ethically is to continue working in underreported crises and fight for as much public money as possible.

Cooperation between agencies and donors involves more than just information-sharing. It involves taking on the burden of the less media-friendly humanitarian causes: "We're trying to persuade other agencies to come in and help us in Sierra Leone because we're on the edge of being overwhelmed. But people aren't interested in coming because organizations tend to build up loyalties to their own countries. Sierra Leone's not in the public eye and it's insecure," says Laurence. "We're very overstretched, but then most agencies are. We're all trying to face unlimited needs with limited capacity."

Old enemies and new challenges

The retreat of many governments from public health provision, combined with increasing urbanization, climate change and environmental degradation, is opening the door to new disasters and fresh public health challenges. Old enemies, such as malaria and TB, are reasserting their influence, and new diseases continue to emerge. To deal with the enormity of the task ahead, agencies must redefine their roles.

Margareta Wahlström, under-secretary general for disaster response and operational coordination at the International Federation, warns that humanitarian agencies are often too self-limiting in the way they are operating, and too slow to detect the scale of the public health and social welfare challenges ahead: "The problems have been so big, so vast, nobody felt inclined to get involved, thinking, 'if I put my foot into that I'm going to be swallowed whole'," she says.

"But you can't defend not doing anything, particularly if the humanitarian system is the only system that can mobilize resources. We must change our attitude to the problems we're facing. We have much more global responsibility. Many, many more people are looking to us for help."

Yet, simultaneously, aid agencies are under attack for being unaccountable, undemocratic and uncoordinated. So how can humanitarian actors meet these challenges? Three principles emerge:

- **Tools not turf:** agencies and donors must collectively seek out, develop and embrace common methodologies and benchmarks – rather than exploiting disaster zones to build profile.
- **Strategic and technical partnerships**: cooperation across borders and disciplines will throw up new tools and multiply their effects.
- **Local capacities:** tools only work in trained hands. Improving public health means investing in people as well as technology.

To make these principles a reality, humanitarians must take forward planning, training and disaster preparedness more seriously – which in turn requires funding that is consistent and unwavering in face of media hype. Humanitarians must cooperate rather than compete – a well-worn mantra, but one which has yet to be taken on board. And they must think beyond their own limits – to work in more imaginative, and more local, partnerships. It is a case of adapting not only to survive, but to help others to survive.

Sources and further information

Boudreau, Tanya. *Ethiopia Risk Map Report.* Save the Children Fund, January 1999.

British Medical Journal. Vol. 319, 14 August 1999. Special issue on medicine and international law.

European Journal of Public Health. 1999, 9:81-82.

International Federation of Red Cross and Red Crescent Societies. *World Disasters Report 1997.* Oxford: Oxford University Press, 1997.

International Federation of Red Cross and Red Crescent Societies. *World Disasters Report 1999.* Geneva: International Federation, 1999.

Johns Hopkins Public Health. Johns Hopkins University School of Hygiene and Public Health, Spring 1999.

Leaning, Jennifer (ed.). *Humanitarian Crises: The Medical and Public Health Response.* Cambridge, MA: Harvard University Press, 1999.

Noji, Eric K. *The Public Health Consequences of Disasters.* Oxford: Oxford University Press, 1997.

Vidal, John. "Blacks need, but only Whites receive", *The Guardian,* 12 August 1999.

World Health Organization (WHO). *Rapid health assessment protocols for emergencies.* Geneva: WHO, 1999.

Web sites

Columbia University's Program on Forced Migration and Health – http://cpmcnet.columbia.edu/dept/sph/popfam/rp/forced_health.html
Drug donations guidelines – http://www.drugdonations.org
European Community's Humanitarian Office (ECHO) – http://europa.eu.int/
Global Resources Information Database (GRID) – http://www.grid.unep.ch
Health Monitoring System (HMS) – http://www.geocities.com/~endopediatric/HMS/project.htm
International Federation of Red Cross and Red Crescent Societies – http://www.ifrc.org/
Médecins sans Frontières – http://www.epicentre.msf.org
United Nations Office for the Coordination of Humanitarian Affairs (OCHA) – http://wwwnotes.reliefweb.int/
Organisation for Economic Co-operation and Development – http://www.oecd.org/
Pan American Health Organization (PAHO) – http://www.paho.org
PAHO's Virtual Disaster Library – http://www.vdl-bvd.desastres.net
Sphere Project – http://www.sphereproject.org/
The Lancet – http://www.thelancet.com
World Health Organization HINAP – http://www.who.int/eha/hinap

Section One

Focus on public health

AIDS in Africa: no longer business as usual

Real estate can be cheap in western Kenya these days, and outsiders are acquiring land. It's a buyer's market. Property lies empty in many a rural community as funeral follows funeral and Africa's HIV/AIDS pandemic intensifies.

Those who sell their inheritance, some of them orphans, do so reluctantly, but the burden of poverty the disease has imposed leaves them little option. Those infected and affected by the human immunodeficiency virus (HIV) take life a day at a time, short of food, health care and social support, often barely able to survive.

The poor soil of the villages along the banks of the Kibos River in Nyanza Province does not help. It never brought prosperity. Now where the weak and the sick are left to till the land, there is even less to sustain them. AIDS widows and children go hungry, say Kenya Red Cross workers, and the nutritional needs of the seropositive are as critical as the shortage of basic drugs to treat opportunistic infection.

Gezia is 23, lives alone in a bare earth hut, and is seriously ill with AIDS. The disease which is now the leading cause of death in sub-Saharan Africa has decimated her family. Her husband died of AIDS in 1997, and their second daughter was born with its virus. The children are elsewhere today, cared for by a sister, while a destitute Gezia contends with her persistent ailments, diarrhoea and pneumonia among them. Her body is wasting, her skin tormented by mosquito bites that take forever to heal.

She spent short spells in hospital, but in Kenya more than 50 per cent of hospital beds are occupied by AIDS-related cases and long-term hospital treatment is out of the question. So, like millions of AIDS sufferers across the African continent, she was sent home prematurely, and there she must wait to die. She counts herself fortunate. A Red Cross home-care programme is helping – there is someone to nurse, counsel and encourage her. But there are days when she goes without eating, and her strength is sapping away.

Hardly a home along the Kibos River is unaffected by HIV/AIDS. Neighbours can no longer help neighbours, overwhelmed by their own misfortunes. "It isn't just the virus, or the absence of drugs," said a despondent community worker. "People are dying from hunger and poverty. This isn't some disease. It's a disaster."

Few people would argue with that. Less than 20 years since AIDS was first recognized, the United Nations (UN) describes it as "the worst infectious disease catastrophe since the bubonic plague". Over the next decade, the UN tells us, AIDS will kill more people in sub-Saharan Africa than all the wars of the 20th century.

But somehow urgency is missing from Nyanza. Had the problems of Kenyans worst affected by HIV/AIDS been related to famine, an alert would have sounded, emergency relief would have been sent in. Hunger scares due to drought elsewhere in Kenya last year brought

Photo opposite page:
This Tanzanian mother is HIV-positive. Over 23 million sub-Saharan Africans are estimated to be infected, including 1 million children. Nearly 42 million children worldwide are predicted to lose one or both parents to AIDS by 2010.

Photo: Sean Sprague/ Panos Pictures, Tanzania.

indignation and response. But the acute nutritional needs of AIDS patients aroused no special concern. Is AIDS a disaster or isn't it?

Credibility gap

Care for the infected and affected on a continent with weak health-care systems is one of many issues sparking debate. There are disturbing questions: Are all African governments serious yet ? Why is the virus still spreading when countries claim high public awareness? How do you change patterns of behaviour?

There are perplexing questions: Can African nations access new and expensive Western drugs that control the progress of infection? Should they bother? Or should they divert resources elsewhere, to boost structures of prevention and care?

There are also questions for humanitarians. There is a growing grass-roots perception that donors, 'experts' and governments are out of touch. Billions of dollars pour in but often the impact is negligible. The issue, one African physician says, is that "we don't have a clear understanding of what's going on with respect to the HIV/AIDS situation and responses. Nor is the continent positioned today to understand and lead its own prevention and mitigation efforts. Experts continue to develop their responses based on very limited data, simplistic analyses and assumptions. Most importantly, these responses are developed with very limited communication with the African people." As the new millennium dawns, Africa is threatened as much by disarray and deception as by the disease itself.

Time is on no one's side. Since the pandemic began, 50 million people worldwide have been infected with HIV, of whom over 16 million have died. The 1999 update from the Joint United Nations Programme on HIV/AIDS (UNAIDS) and the World Health Organization (WHO) revealed that AIDS deaths reached a record 2.6 million last year, with new infections soaring to 5.6 million – the majority in sub-Saharan Africa.

Over 23 million Africans south of the Sahara are estimated to be infected with HIV, around 70 per cent of the global total in a region home to just 10 per cent of the world's population. Africans have the poorest access to care, says UNAIDS, and the social and economic safety nets that help families cope are badly frayed, partly due to the epidemic itself.

The severity of the African crisis was reflected in January 2000 when the UN Security Council confronted the issue, the first time ever that health had been placed on its agenda. US Vice President Al Gore told the session that the havoc wreaked by HIV/AIDS imperilled political stability and regional security.

Reflecting on the recent findings, Peter Piot, executive director of UNAIDS, said, "With an epidemic of this scale, every new infection adds to the ripple effect, impacting families, communities, households and increasingly, businesses and economies. AIDS has emerged as the single greatest threat to development in many countries of the world."

Worse still, development gains are being reversed. The UN Development Programme (UNDP) reported in 1999 that some African nations had fallen in the Human Development

Box 3.1 Save the orphans

A teenager hovers self-consciously as a bar fills up in the port of Kisumu on Lake Victoria. Ill at ease, her sheepish glances from a doorway are curious in a place where women don't care for modesty. In their endlessly languid games of pool, they put on display all that they have for sale. The nervous girl in the decent dress does not belong here. When a man beckons her over, the women she passes catch her arm, whispering advice. She's in desperate need of some.

She should be at home with her parents, doing her homework, helping her mother care for her brothers and sisters. Only she has no parents and since her mother died she has found no other way of surviving. Her name is Evelyn. She is one of Africa's 10 million AIDS orphans. Evelyn is perhaps 16 or 17, but pretends, when asked, that she is 20. For less than US$ 7 an hour she risks encountering the virus that killed her parents. She may risk all for twice that and copulate without a condom.

There are many Evelyns in the night-time streets of Kisumu, girls and boys, and some are very much younger. The authorities chase them from public places, but the youngsters find shelter in the slums and along Lake Victoria's beaches. Sex remains a prime source of income. In better times, the extended family would care for an orphan but AIDS has overwhelmed traditional systems. Many families cannot cope and numbers of street children are increasing.

Agencies are responding, the Kenya Red Cross among them. By the end of 1999, it counted 1,352 orphans among the 25,000 people living within a home-based care project area. Resources are few and most are deprived of proper care, but one 28-year-old Red Cross counsellor has shown his community that something can be done. He has started an orphans-for-orphans operation.

The counsellor knows about orphans. His father died of AIDS when he was a student, obliging him as the eldest son to quit college – someone had to provide for six brothers and sisters. A few months later, AIDS claimed his mother, then an uncle and aunt. Before he knew it, he was head of a 15-child family. When the 28-year-old himself contracted HIV, another African tragedy might have had a predictable end, except that he refused to accept it. The care and support his family needed were required by many others. So he initiated income-generation projects, a revolving fund and communal care that allows all but the infants to stay in their homes – considerably changing their prospects. Life is not easy but the children involved do not drop out of school, nor do they go hungry.

Across Africa, local responses to the plight of AIDS orphans provide compelling evidence of how community-based organizations hold the answers to many problems. But response is ad hoc and poorly supported, given the dire straits faced by millions of children today and which many millions more will face in years to come as the full force of AIDS is felt. In Zimbabwe, UNAIDS forecasts, the number of AIDS orphans could rise to almost a million by 2005, from the present 600,000. "Who is going to look after these children?" asks Loveness Mupfeka, orphan coordinator for the AIDS Counselling Trust (ACT). There is no clear answer – but ACT's call for sound and comprehensive policy is echoed elsewhere on the continent.

ACT fears ad hoc responses may be unsustainable and is nurturing community solutions. Occupied with prevention, control of infection and care for victims, ACT has 550 orphans under its wing. Says Mupfeka, "Many children now head households or are in the care of poor grandparents. Many are barely making it." ACT is encouraging community care, forming support groups who alert them to problems and facilitating income generation. "It is important", says Mupfeka, "that children remain in the community and in contact with their relatives." If it can, ACT also pays school fees where a child would otherwise drop out. For without proper parenting or education, the road ahead for Africa's orphans will be a bleak one.

Index, a ranking based on levels of health, wealth and education. Most major changes in rank, it said, could be attributed to declining life expectancy as a result of AIDS, notably in southern Africa. There, life expectancy at birth had climbed from 44 in the early 1950s to 59 in the early 1990s, but it would drop to 45 between 2005 and 2010.

Losing economic gains

Slowly southern African governments have conceded that HIV/AIDS is eroding economic development. Zimbabwe fears a serious slump in gross domestic product (GDP). Osias Hove, director of the National Economic Planning Commission, says, "We used to worry so much about drought, but now with drought management in place and no solution for AIDS in sight, I fear the disease surpasses everything. There is no major policy statement today that does not mention this scourge."

Hove says the most productive age group, from 16 to 49, is perishing, and with projections that a quarter of the adult population is infected, the future is bleak. UNAIDS points out that due to the long incubation period between infection with the virus and onset of disease, many consequences have yet to be fully felt.

The UN's analysis suggests that, because of AIDS, by 2005 the GDP of most southern African countries will have shrunk by at least 14 per cent. Per capita income will drop 10 per cent. Labour costs are rising due to morbidity and absenteeism, and training new workers brings an added burden. So firms will switch to more capital-intensive, automated production methods, as evident in South Africa.

Threat of famine

Hove's greatest fears are for agriculture and rural people, who number 68 per cent of Zimbabwe's 12 million population. The economy is largely agrarian, poverty is acute in the countryside – and HIV/AIDS makes it worse. His fears are shared by the International Federation of Red Cross and Red Crescent Societies. A report produced for its Harare-based regional delegation suggests that HIV/AIDS, combined with the effect of recurrent drought, greatly increases the threat of famine in southern Africa.

Zimbabwe's drought management policy, with its emphasis on water harvesting and greater agricultural productivity, could be jeopardized. According to Jerry Talbot, the International Federation's regional head, "when a country has 1,200 people a week dying of AIDS, to say nothing of those who are ill, it soon has insufficient people tilling the fields. Commercial farms may be in a position to replace their workers but most people depend on communal farming lands. The impact at the household level will be severe." The situation in eastern Africa is no better. A 1999 UNDP/Food and Agriculture Organization study of Kenya's commercial farms spoke of "a severe social and economic crisis" in a sector which accounts for 30 per cent of GDP and 70 per cent of export earnings.

HIV/AIDS in Africa has been perceived as an *urban* problem. The response has been primarily urban because analyses have been based mainly on urban findings. Rural areas have reported lower HIV prevalence, and hence have received less attention. Yet of an estimated 160 to 170 million Africans infected and affected by the virus today, the majority are probably living in rural areas.

The fabric of African society ensures it. In countries like Rwanda, 90 per cent of the population is rural. A UNDP/FAO report illustrates the case in Kenya. In 1994, close to 600,000 rural adults and 300,000 urban ones were living with HIV, while the reported rural prevalence rate of 5 to 6 per cent was less than half the urban rate.

Accuracy of rural prevalence figures is threatened by poor surveillance mechanisms, and a UN study concludes, "Rural HIV remains, to some extent, silent and invisible – in other words, an unknown entity for policy-makers and planners with potentially far-reaching implications for the rural economy."

What is known for sure is that rural HIV-infection rates continue to rise in most African countries. Underlying influences include conflict and refugee movements, migration, trade, an itinerant workforce and increased rural-urban mobility. In Rwanda, the rural infection rate for people between 20 and 44 increased tenfold over a decade, rising from 1.3 per cent in 1986 to 10.8 per cent in 1997. The Ministry of Health says the worsening situation is in part the consequence of social upheaval. Conflict in the 1990s drove hundreds of thousands out of their homes or into refugee camps. Where there is war, prostitution, promiscuity and rape commonly increase – safe sex is rarely a priority.

Rural-urban migration has helped spread HIV in the Zimbabwean countryside. Poverty is driving more and more job-seekers to the towns and mines, where prevalence rates are higher. Contacts with home remain strong, however, and workers return for weekends and holidays bringing the virus with them. One recent study by the Ministry of Health and Child Welfare showed rural infection rates closing on those in urban areas. A random survey in Matabeleland disturbed health officials by revealing that 45 per cent of pregnant women tested in urban Victoria Falls were HIV-positive. But a rural community wasn't far behind, with 42 per cent. "AIDS", the provincial medical director commented, "is no longer a problem of tourist or urban areas alone."

A change of thinking is required for the countryside, say underfunded agencies working there. Rural response is inadequate and often fails to take account of illiteracy, inequality and cultural practices. Compared to towns, there are fewer information, education and communications programmes, there is less HIV testing and counselling, less access to condoms and hence less HIV/AIDS awareness, despite what authorities may claim.

Victims of a vicious circle

A couple of hours from Harare, poverty spreads through eastern Mashonaland and HIV is its travelling companion. Even without HIV, life would be hard in the wide, open country of maize, wheat and tobacco fields where Robert Mugabe was born and still maintains a home. HIV is not the cause of the region's demise but it feeds on its problems and multiplies them. Mugabe's backyard is vulnerable. Good roads provide a trade route through Mashonaland, trucks lumber along it, up to Mozambique, down to South Africa. As they travel, truckers bring business to roadside settlements, and leave more than their money behind them. So do the migrant labourers home from the city for the weekend.

Rising illness and mortality, overwhelmed health services, orphans and child-headed households tell the story. The extended family is cracking under pressure. Bongai Mundeta, secretary general of the Zimbabwe Red Cross, sees social fabric unravelling. Caring for 5,000 AIDS patients countrywide, a Red Cross home-based programme finds more and more coping mechanisms failing.

All his life Pemias has been a hard-working man. He is too proud to confess what ails him to a stranger. The belief promulgated in capital cities that AIDS is losing its stigma hasn't reached his corner of the countryside. People living with AIDS face discrimination, so Pemias keeps his own counsel. He suffers from tuberculosis (TB), a disease HIV encourages. Parts of Africa have seen TB incidence treble since the onset of the pandemic. Pemias has a persistent cough, and gets breathless. He has lost considerable weight and his body itches all over. Catherine Malunga, a Red Cross worker, keeps an eye on him. She calls once a week. Catherine *is* someone he confides in.

But his problems are not only health-related. Pemias is caught in a vicious circle. He and his wife are impoverished. At 13, their eldest daughter has dropped out of school because the cost is way beyond their means. He cannot even afford transport to the district hospital for treatment Catherine has recommended. The last time he went there he was prescribed medication but, penniless, he never bought it. What he has always comes from Catherine.

The old man does have land, but he's too sick to work it, or his neighbour's. Farmers here labour for one another, and those whose fields you plant will be working yours tomorrow. HIV is undermining the system. Pemias has been ill for so long, help is no longer forthcoming. His land lies idle. Soon his neighbour's may follow.

The burden on the countryside isn't always local. Pemias has lived here all his life, but others are coming home to die. Many town dwellers with HIV head back to their villages of origin. It is cheaper here, they say, and care is easier to find. Relatives pay the price, opening up the doors of the African extended family. But the strain of nursing the sick, the cost of food, medicine and funerals has left many families impoverished. The continent's social safety net is ripping apart – the carers cannot cope.

Burden for women

Women in sub-Saharan Africa bear the greatest burden. It is women who provide most of the care, women who are AIDS's greatest victims. In 1999, UNAIDS produced evidence showing clearly for the first time that more women are infected with HIV than men.

Electa, 35, came home to her mother in Mashonaland after her husband abandoned her. It was he who had passed on the virus, but, when he learned from television how to recognize AIDS, he showed her the door and divorced her.

Today she is practically ostracized. Too ill to leave home for long, she cannot access the essential drugs that could control the opportunistic bacterial infections that afflict her. The nearest hospital never seems to have them, and with less than enough to eat she cannot afford to buy them. Her plight reveals the weakness of an inadequate health-care system, but her story is the story of women.

South of the Sahara, 55 per cent of infected adults are female. UNAIDS estimates that 12.2 million African women and 10.1 million African men aged 15 to 49 are living with HIV. Disparity is greater among the young. African girls aged 15 to 19 are six times more likely to be HIV-positive than boys. Girls are more vulnerable, says UNAIDS, because of greater ease of male-to-female sexual transmission, and because girls often have sex with older, infected men. And the risk of contracting the virus during unprotected sex is two to four times higher for women than for men.

More crucial, however, is economic dependence on men. AIDS raises questions of women's authority over their bodies. According to Millicent Obaso, a leading Kenyan authority on reproductive health, "most African women are unable to say 'no' to sex, even when they know they should, because to do so would threaten their security."

Obaso, formerly a reproductive health coordinator for the Red Cross/Red Crescent, points to poor job opportunities, income and status: "It is women in the main who are entrusted with the care of the children. But women have very little access to resources. We need to empower them, so that they can say to a man: 'I no longer trust you, you have multiple partners and I am not going to have sex with you'."

The World Bank has argued that improving female socio-economic status and ensuring tough penalties for sexual abuse are essential to protect vulnerable women from HIV/AIDS. Less clear is the danger from traditional practices.

In Obaso's home province of Nyanza, widow inheritance – found elsewhere in eastern and southern Africa – once brought social security. When a man died, another of his clan was assigned to shelter his family. He inherited more than the woman, and ensured she could care for the dead man's children. Sex, says Obaso, was never the dominant factor, and indeed was often frowned upon.

Somehow, in recent years, tradition changed, and sexual relations with inherited widows have helped western Kenya to the highest HIV rates in the country. Says Obaso, "Women are inherited for one thing, and instead of caring for the dead man's family, inheritors purloin what he left behind."

A UN report speaks of the "sinister dimension" of wife inheritance. A pattern is clear. A man infects his first wife and then the widow he inherits. He dies, his women are passed on to others. Those men die, and the virus continues to spread. Children are born infected or become orphaned, or both. Despite official assertions that 99 per cent of Kenyans are "aware" of HIV and AIDS, men seem little discouraged by the dangers. In Nyanza they speak of "cleansing" the widows with the sexual act, of "driving out the devil". Professional cleansers are operating and "inheritance" is reduced in some cases to a single night-time visit by a man paid to have sex with a widow.

Women have begun to take a stand. When Consulata, a widow from a Kibos village, refused to be inherited for a second time, her case became a *cause célèbre*. Her refusal left her homeless but with Red Cross support, and her church behind her, a roof was put over her head. She is poor, HIV-positive, and undeterred. Today she visits funerals to rally women, and widow alliances are growing steadily, nurtured within Red Cross programmes.

The right to say 'no' could save women from even more virulent practices. If most Kenyans know what spreads HIV, there are many who don't know what doesn't. Rural folk in Nyanza fear *chira* – a sickness which comes from breaking taboo – and *jinni* – a magical spirit used to harm one's enemies. Myths they may be, but people credit them with causing AIDS, just as they credit other myths with preventing the disease.

Many Africans believe a man can rid himself of HIV by having sex with a virgin. One girl known to the Red Cross was 12 when she became a victim in Nyanza. The perpetrator was her elder sister's husband. Her parents had consented – to them it was a cleansing ritual. The girl was raped. The man has since died and she has been left with the virus. So has the child she gave birth to nine months later.

Critical research

How aware is Africa really? It was a question asked in western Mashonaland by the Women and AIDS Support Network (WASN), a ground-breaking Zimbabwean non-governmental organization (NGO), counselling and caring for women and girls. What they found in baseline surveys across the Chikwaka communal lands underlined the need for far greater levels of information, education and communication.

Women are left to work the land, while most of the men seek employment away from home, in Harare, in townships, or on commercial farms. When men return, HIV comes with them. WASN is working to increase community knowledge, to ensure that in their sex lives women are able to make informed choices. Surveys in Chikwaka have found that:

- most women do not practise safe sex and contraception;
- most know the dangers, but feel powerless to change things; and
- most say male unfaithfulness is inevitable.

More than 76 per cent of married women polled said only "loose women" carried condoms, and young women indicated that they preferred sex unprotected. Reproductive rights were never raised, said the women, and less than 22 per cent of those WASN surveyed were aware they had a right to refuse sex.

Chiedze Musengezl, WASN's director, said things were no better among adolescents. Cases of girls having sexual relations with farm workers, bus conductors, truck drivers and other older men were common. Money and presents were prime motivations of many. The 'sugar daddy' phenomenon is widespread in Chikwaka where girls drop out of school due to economic hardship.

Box 3.2 Herbal healers and HIV

Traditional healers in Uganda help HIV patients with ailments hospitals cannot treat. Where biomedicine fails, some herbal remedies score success. So impressed is Uganda's Ministry of Health, it is now helping the healers process and package their products for wider distribution.

While quacks still sully the name of traditional healing in many parts of Africa, peddling phoney potions to the desperate, clinical evidence shows that plant medicines from skilful practitioners do alleviate HIV-related conditions. Chronic skin and diarrhoeal complaints are among those successfully treated.

Donna Kabatesi is a public health specialist with the Ministry of Health's STIs unit. She spends her mornings preoccupied with conventional medicine at Kampala's Old Mulago Hospital but, come afternoon, heads off to direct Traditional and Modern Health Practitioners Together against AIDS (THETA). Besides researching herbal remedies, THETA is nurturing dialogue and cooperation between healers and health workers. Healers are trained to recognize symptoms and determine what they can treat and what should be referred to clinics. Workshops demystify traditional medicine for modern health personnel. These are still early days, concedes Kabatesi, but it is no longer unusual in Uganda for doctors to refer patients to healers if hospital treatments are not working.

In a country where there may be one doctor for 30,000 people, and a chronic shortage of competent health workers, trained healers could bridge many gaps – and not only for HIV/AIDS. Says Kabatesi, "Every village has its healers, and we estimate there is one for every 100 adults across the nation. In a population of 22 million that is an interesting statistic. I just returned from a workshop in a county which has 20 health workers but a minimum of 300 operating healers."

The potential has not gone unnoticed elsewhere. Over half a million healers reportedly practise in South Africa, where there are more than 650 traditional healer organizations. USAID and others have funded training of trainers there, covering HIV prevention, counselling, management of symptoms, care and support.

THETA evolved from the interest of Mulago doctors who discovered some of their own HIV/AIDS patients consulted healers as well. Curious to know if they had answers to some of the hospital's enduring problems, the doctors gained healers' consent to set up a study group. Over a one-year period, 250 patients were observed to see if herbal treatment could remedy what doctors could not. Three useful treatments were discovered, including one for herpes zoster. Says Kabatesi, "We discovered patients came to the healers not only for the effectiveness of their herbs but for the comfort they provided. They had excellent communication and counselling skills which needed only reinforcement with greater knowledge of HIV and AIDS."

Obstacles remain. Healers are suspicious of the establishment, afraid researchers will misappropriate their secrets, mindful too of how they have been harassed, arrested and imprisoned in the past for their practices. Many doctors and health workers remain sceptical there is a place for traditional medicine. But President Yoweri Museveni has come out strongly in favour of inclusion, as has WHO.

WHO's regional office for Africa is developing a strategy for traditional medicine that would integrate it into national health-care systems for the general treatment of disease. Regional director Ebrahim Samba has said traditional medicinal products could eventually be exported for the economic benefit of African countries, and he has called for the protection of healers' intellectual property rights by appropriate patenting.

But no one was talking about these problems. Even among themselves, women did not discuss sexually transmitted infections. WASN has begun to break the silence. On World AIDS Day, behind a small country church, men, women and children gathered in the open-air to discuss HIV/AIDS together for the first time. Among the men were husbands, fathers, a schoolteacher, community elders and local government officials. The awareness of those who have authority over women is being raised as well.

For four hours they talked about poverty, morality, health care, living with HIV, and condoms. A schoolgirl exposed sugar daddies, a nurse introduced the female condom, women condemned *nhaka* (widow inheritance). No one has any illusions. The road will be a long one. When WASN asked parents if they would permit the provision of condoms to sexually active children, there was stern opposition. "You will only encourage them more," said one woman. "It is perhaps better that they die."

Slowly does it

With suffering at appalling levels and the full force of AIDS yet to come, Chiedza Musengezl says prevention and care must be scaled up. "We need management of this epidemic. We need movement from everyone. There must be an all-embracing, comprehensive, holistic approach, and the messages must be consistent." Slowly it is coming, some would say too slowly.

Peter Piot believes African AIDS could be at a turning point. "Everywhere I go," he said, "I hear the top African leaders speaking out about AIDS as the major threat to the continent's development. This gives me grounds for hope that in the coming years we will see stronger, more effective responses in many more sub-Saharan nations."

But political urgency remains missing from much of Africa. With one in four adults infected, 600,000 AIDS orphans and 400,000 cases of full-blown AIDS reported since the epidemic began, Zimbabwe last year seemed in two minds as to whether it had a national catastrophe. It certainly hesitated to announce one at home. A senior source in the Ministry of Health said, "Making HIV/AIDS an official disaster would force the government to allocate resources, and respond to it. This has been advocated for some time now."

An AIDS conference in Lusaka in September 1999 had seen Zimbabwe join Burkina Faso, Lesotho, Malawi, Mozambique, the Republic of Congo, Swaziland, Tanzania and Zambia in declaring HIV/AIDS a national disaster requiring emergency response. The domestic position, however, remained a confused one. If there was a change of status, most AIDS organizations were unaware of it, and some people viewed Lusaka as a stance for international consumption only.

Political will may be growing to some extent. The US ambassador in east Africa who summoned aid agencies to a crisis meeting in the summer of 1997, to ask, "Why is there silence at the top?" would be less frantic today. Africa has progressed but the will is often equivocal. The disaster declaration from Lusaka had raised hopes of more forceful governmental responses. But, asked a Zimbabwean official, "How many African presidents were there? You should look at the status of the people making the speeches. How much influence do they have back home?"

When leaders gather, there are often disappointments. Africa has a powerful lobby in the 54-nation Commonwealth group made up of former British colonies, but its November 1999 summit in South Africa left many AIDS experts astonished. The pandemic was relegated to item 55 in the end-of-summit communiqué.

Some argue that the advent of multiparty politics has made matters worse. The absence of clear policies on HIV/AIDS in Kenya in the 1990s brought frustration and media criticism, but senior officials stayed silent. Commentators speculate that faced by constitutional crises and political opposition on other fronts, the government avoided AIDS because it was contentious. Churchmen were burning condoms in public and evangelicals were speaking of divine retribution. Churches sway votes in Kenya. Even after finally conceding that AIDS was a national disaster last year, President Daniel arap Moi maintained it would be "improper…to encourage the use of condoms".

Politicians have been hesitant because of the stigma, said Philip Moses, acting director of Zimbabwe's National AIDS Co-ordination Programme. "Political life is a career in Africa. Most politicians have nothing else, no other profession like you have in the West. They make sure they tread carefully. But on HIV and AIDS they have to speak out, irrespective of whether it wins them votes."

Support from the top

President Yoweri Museveni of Uganda was the first to show the importance of high-level political involvement, and UNAIDS argues it is a common denominator of effective programmes. Uganda, which in the 1980s had the world's highest infection rate, was the first African country to confront AIDS. Museveni, who came to power in 1986, soon adopted a policy of candour, speaking wherever and whenever he could.

The president pushed for a multi-sectoral approach, because Ugandans saw causes and consequences that went beyond the realm of health, and sought support from religious and traditional leaders. From national debate came consensus. Health education, public campaigns, rallies and radio messages followed, telling Ugandans what AIDS was, how it was spread, and how they could control it – through abstinence, fidelity and safer sex. Condom sales soared. Surveys show that casual sex is decreasing and young people are delaying their first sexual encounters. Today, urban HIV infection rates are falling.

Uganda has come far. Elsewhere in Africa, the model is used for comparison. Said a senior UNDP source in Nairobi, "What you see in Uganda is the result of action taken in the 1980s, the creation of an enabling environment. Kenya is beginning to get to where Uganda was ten years ago. Most certainly we will endure another decade of tragedy."

Uganda's own tragedy, though, is far from over, and while much can be learned from its success stories, there are also lessons in its shortcomings. Nearly 2 million people are said to be infected, 500,000 have died, Uganda has more than a million AIDS orphans, and the average HIV prevalence rate is still around 7 per cent. Charles Wendo, health and environment correspondent with *The New Vision* newspaper, says: "I fear there is too much praise for Uganda. We do deserve credit for the way we provided public awareness, and for reducing the stigma around the disease. But the suffering remains unacceptable. For the average Ugandan living with HIV or AIDS the level of care is pathetic. People should be living much longer. There is a great deal left to do."

HIV/AIDS aggravates existing structural problems. Predominantly rural, 57 per cent of Ugandans do not have access to health care. Few live near a health unit, and those units are often short of medicine and trained personnel. Wendo believes improvements are occurring but calculates there is only one doctor per 30,000 people. Ugandans, he charges, are dying of infections like meningitis because essential drugs are unavailable to them. "There is an urgent need to find out how we can help these people. The government has done hardly anything; they have left it to the NGOs. But the NGOs cannot cover the entire population." The Uganda AIDS Commission (UAC) admits it must widen its programmes to rural areas.

According to Agathe Lawson, country programme adviser for UNAIDS, "If you live in Kampala and you have the money, health care is excellent. Once you are out of town it's finished. People are not receiving the treatment you would expect. Even drugs that are supposed to be free you pay for out there. The situation is worse than in some countries poorer than Uganda."

Given the donor money that has poured in since the 1980s, observers question Uganda's performance. Lawson says that in terms of cost effectiveness, no other country has achieved less. "A lot of effort will be made to improve that. There is provision for every HIV patient to be treated correctly, but there is so much corruption." Lawson claims that less than 30 per cent of the drugs and services foreseen in a US$ 75 million World Bank programme reached the Ugandan population.

Very little funding has gone to strengthen infrastructure. Health care was close to collapse when Museveni took over and AIDS hit the country before it had a chance to recover. The UN reports that almost 70 per cent of Ugandan hospital beds are occupied now by HIV/AIDS-related cases, and the authorities say this crowds out patients with other illnesses. An air of fatalism pervades overcrowded wards and corridors of eastern and southern African clinics and hospitals. But, some suggest, AIDS is not so much disabling health services as exposing their weaknesses.

Uganda, however, has got a great deal *right*. The multi-sectoral approach showed Africa the road ahead. All Ugandans, national policy determined, had individual and collective responsibility to involve themselves in the control of AIDS, from government to grass-roots level. The UAC was established to coordinate, located not in the Ministry of Health, but in the office of the president. John Rwomushana, director general of the UAC, says, "There was a need to be in a neutral position where we would have clout but also the freedom to rally all government, and other, sectors, and eventually have equitable resource allocation." The UAC's first chair was Museveni himself, and a 24-person board included a dozen cabinet ministers, NGO leaders, and churchmen.

In 1999, Kenya and Zimbabwe were moving in similar directions. A five-year strategic plan for Kenya, running to 2003, sees the introduction of a national AIDS council, a high-level multi-sectoral body. In Zimbabwe, a bill before parliament is slated to bring in an independent

National AIDS Council (NAC) to replace the National AIDS Co-ordination Programme (NACP) that was a ministry department.

Resembling a parastatal, Zimbabwe's NAC will bring together government, NGOs, churches and the commercial sector. Said the NACP's acting director Moses, "The move will give us more muscle power, cut bureaucracy, and bring more prominence to HIV and AIDS. As a ministerial department we have been seriously constrained."

Continuum of care

Other Ugandan pioneers have made progress. The AIDS Information Centre (AIC), provider of voluntary counselling and testing (VCT) to more than 450,000 people since it began, and The AIDS Support Organization (TASO), have decentralized to meet rural needs better.

VCT contributes to the prevention of HIV transmission. It also helps people cope with infection and is critical for obtaining proper care. People need to know and accept their HIV status if they are to access timely and correct treatment, and to prepare for the future. But VCT is commonplace in rich, industrialized countries where prevalence rates are low, and rare in high-prevalence developing nations. UNAIDS estimates that over 90 per cent of infected Africans are unaware they have the virus. Uganda's AIC is trying to change this. During the 1990s, it developed a nationwide network of VCT sites, most recently into the conflict-affected north of the country.

"This is my husband's bike", says Jennifer Ayoo, a Ugandan mother of two. "The slogan has to do with AIDS. My husband is good and the slogan helps keep other women away."

Photo: Crispin Hughes/ Panos Pictures, Uganda.

VCT is the entry point to what WHO characterizes as the 'continuum of care' needed through all stages of HIV infection. Access to it must be provided from VCT sites, hospitals, social services, community-based support groups and home-based care. The concept is subscribed to by TASO.

TASO is Africa's largest NGO dealing exclusively with HIV/AIDS, and provides medical services, counselling and social support for the infected and their dependents. Most of its clients are the rural poor, and where it has no permanent presence it trains community-based organizations to deliver services, building district capacities. "Access to care in the countryside is hindered by poverty," says director Sophia Mukasa Monico. "People cannot afford transport to hospital and, at the parish level, health units are poorly equipped to deal with HIV and AIDS."

The biggest hurdle facing TASO is access to drugs. "Our budgets cannot acquire them, and our clients most certainly cannot afford them," said Monico. "TASO has proved you can live positively with HIV for many years, and even meagre resources can improve the quality of life. If we had drugs, of course, things would be so much better."

The drugs she alludes to are common ones which can control opportunistic infections like pneumonia and meningitis. These relatively inexpensive drugs would ensure that the 2 million Ugandans living with HIV do not suffer, and die, from curable diseases. "Don't even think about antiretrovirals," she said.

Wonder drugs or disease genocide?

With enormous resources still required to elevate HIV-prevention to an acceptable level, and to strengthen and widen care, the comment was a practical one. Meanwhile, fevered debate surrounds antiretrovirals (ARVs), the 'wonder' drugs that suppress HIV replication and have revolutionized treatment in the west.

ARVs are not a cure, nor are they a global panacea – a third to a half of the patients who start therapy drop out due to the side effects – but they enable many HIV-positive citizens of industrialized lands to live much longer, freed from the misery of AIDS's symptoms. Mortality rates have fallen. Most of the 33 million HIV-sufferers across the globe, however, have no access to these drugs. They are hugely expensive. To increase effectiveness and to minimize a risk that a single ARV can encourage resistance in the virus, the drugs are taken in triple combination therapies. A year's treatment, WHO estimates, costs an average US$ 12,000 per person, and Charles Wendo, the *New Vision* journalist, calculates 0.5 per cent of infected Ugandans can afford them.

The public debate around Africa primarily concerns equitable access. When HIV/AIDS causes such enormous suffering, some argue, how can Africans be denied ARVs? The arguments are usually reduced to one issue: affordability. Either the pharmaceutical industry or the international community should place them within reach of the African pocket, it is said.

But to administer ARVs successfully requires an effective delivery infrastructure which many sub-Saharan nations lack. And ARVs must be taken with the correct dosage, frequency and duration to be effective, says WHO. For that, the health-care system must be capable of diagnosing and monitoring HIV-related conditions, and must provide trained health-care workers for appropriate treatment and psychosocial support. More disturbing is that uncontrolled use of ARVs and deviations from strict regimes could trigger drug-resistant HIV mutations. The Zambian government is so concerned, it is taking steps to prevent the sale of ARVs on the black market.

Yet the arguments for access to ARVs remain compelling. Peter Mugyenyi heads Uganda's Joint Clinical Research Centre, a pioneering Kampala institute where Africa's first HIV-vaccine trials have taken place. It is treating between 500 and 600 patients with ARVs but, he says, "When patients come to us for these drugs we spend most of the time discussing economics. Mostly you end up telling people not to start the treatment because they are unlikely to be able to continue."

The despair is palpable. "Here are people who know we have the drugs that could save their lives but we turn them away. Because of *cost*. I have had to refuse my own relative," laments Mugyenyi. "It is the most shameful thing in medicine today. We have our contemporaries in the West who have a solution, and it is being kept from the people who need it most. If this situation were to occur in the United States, indeed if any country outside Africa had such a large proportion of its population that was going to die of HIV/AIDS, it would be treated as a disaster. All the red flags would be in the air, every force would be mobilized. But the world

Box 3.3 Generation of hope

Will Africa's youth prove to be a lost generation or a generation of hope?

Of the 33 million people worldwide living with HIV/AIDS today, 11 million are aged between 15 and 24. In sub-Saharan Africa, three in five of the newly infected fall into that age group. More than 16 young people are infected there every five minutes and, in 1999 alone, 1.7 million under-25s acquired the virus. Between 10 and 20 per cent of 15 to 24 year olds are already seropositive in much of the region and while no figures exist for under-15s, the dangers are apparent.

Studies show African youngsters start sex earlier than previous generations, have multiple partners and make little use of condoms. A 1995 Ugandan study of 12 to 19 year olds found that 62 per cent of boys and 38 per cent of girls had had sexual intercourse.

Clearly sex education needs to start early. "There is a window-of-hope age group we should target," says Esther Ogara of Kenya's National AIDS/STIs Control Programme. "These are the 9 to 12 year olds. You really must be talking to these children before they are sexually active." Evaluations of teenage smoking and pregnancy prevention programmes back this up. Success has come where they have reached the youngsters in advance of risky behaviour.

Few countries have compulsory AIDS education in schools, partly because of fears of controversy. Some African authorities have banned sex education and in at least one country materials have been publicly burned. The mood may be changing but, says Ogara, there is a need to emphasize the evidence that sex education does not induce promiscuity. Education delays first encounters and leads to less and safer sexual activity, as Uganda has most recently proven.

Esther Ogara is a prominent participant in a pan-African initiative to improve reproductive health and reduce the spread of HIV/AIDS among the young. Known as 'Africa Alive!' it has begun in eight countries – Ghana, Kenya, Nigeria, South Africa, Tanzania, Uganda, Zambia and Zimbabwe – with an estimated audience of 150 million youngsters. More countries are expected to follow. "Around 60 per cent of Africa's population consists of young people", she says, "and there is an urgent need to provide them with better reproductive health information and services."

The 'Africa Alive!' concept evolved from informal discussions between Africans, Johns Hopkins University and USAID. They believed a synergetic regional partnership would be the most cost-effective way to improve adolescent reproductive health. Since 1998, national 'Africa Alive!' chapters in participating countries have begun to develop their own programmes around common objectives. Young people themselves will play a major role in the network. The initiative aims to stimulate sexual responsibility, reduce discrimination against people with AIDS, develop sustainable information strategies, and generate and distribute funds for prevention.

is watching while disease genocide takes place on this continent. It is the most glaring injustice, and inequality, of our age."

Breaking scientific ice

Amid the acrimony, Africa is also making its own way. The first HIV-vaccine trials, which began in 1999, were as significant for themselves as for their content. Uganda has long debated the ethics of testing in Africa. "There was a lot of suspicion surrounding trials in general," says Mugyenyi. "Some people thought Africa would be used as a guinea pig for testing things other countries would not be comfortable with. But in our case we went looking for something that could be useful to us. These trials have broken the ice. Normally developing countries test finished products. Here we are involved in basic scientific research to develop a product, and because that can be done in Uganda, other countries now know it can be done in theirs. They are already jumping on board, Kenya and South Africa among them."

So far, two interesting drugs have emerged from other African trials, both cheaper alternatives to expensive Western therapies. The first was hydroxyurea, an old drug that has been used for leukaemia and anaemia in the past. Mugyenyi's institute is among those who have found that combined with low doses of the HIV drug ddI it suppresses levels of the virus in the blood. Southern African researchers have presented this as a "more affordable" cocktail than triple therapy.

The other African discovery is a long-acting antiretroviral, nevirapine, which disturbs the enzyme essential to HIV replication. Studies at Kampala's Mulago Hospital suggest it can substantially reduce mother-to-child transmission (MTCT) of the virus at a unit cost of roughly US$ 4. With UNAIDS and WHO estimating that around 450,000 sub-Saharan children were born with the virus, or infected through breastfeeding, in 1999, the drug could have enormous impact.

For all that, nevirapine will not be quickly available in southern Africa, caught up in a controversy raging over another antiretroviral, AZT, commonly given to HIV-positive pregnant women in the West. In November 1999, health ministers from the 14 nations of the Southern African Development Council (SADC) said they were "gravely concerned" about toxic side effects of AZT and nevirapine, and the potential development of resistance to them. Some suggest the verdict was influenced by South Africa, whose health minister had told parliament that the cost of providing AZT would be ten times the country's health budget. NGOs described the SADC decision as a serious setback in the region's fight against AIDS.

Myths and morals

Chilling moral issues abound. Since HIV-positive mothers will die prematurely, won't the prevention of mother-to-child transmission simply produce more AIDS orphans? Won't the astronomical cost of caring for more orphans weigh against other needed interventions? Won't drugs such as nevirapine only encourage HIV-infected women to have children? Shouldn't abortion, illegal in most African countries, now be made available, along with counselling?

Spread of HIV in sub-Saharan Africa

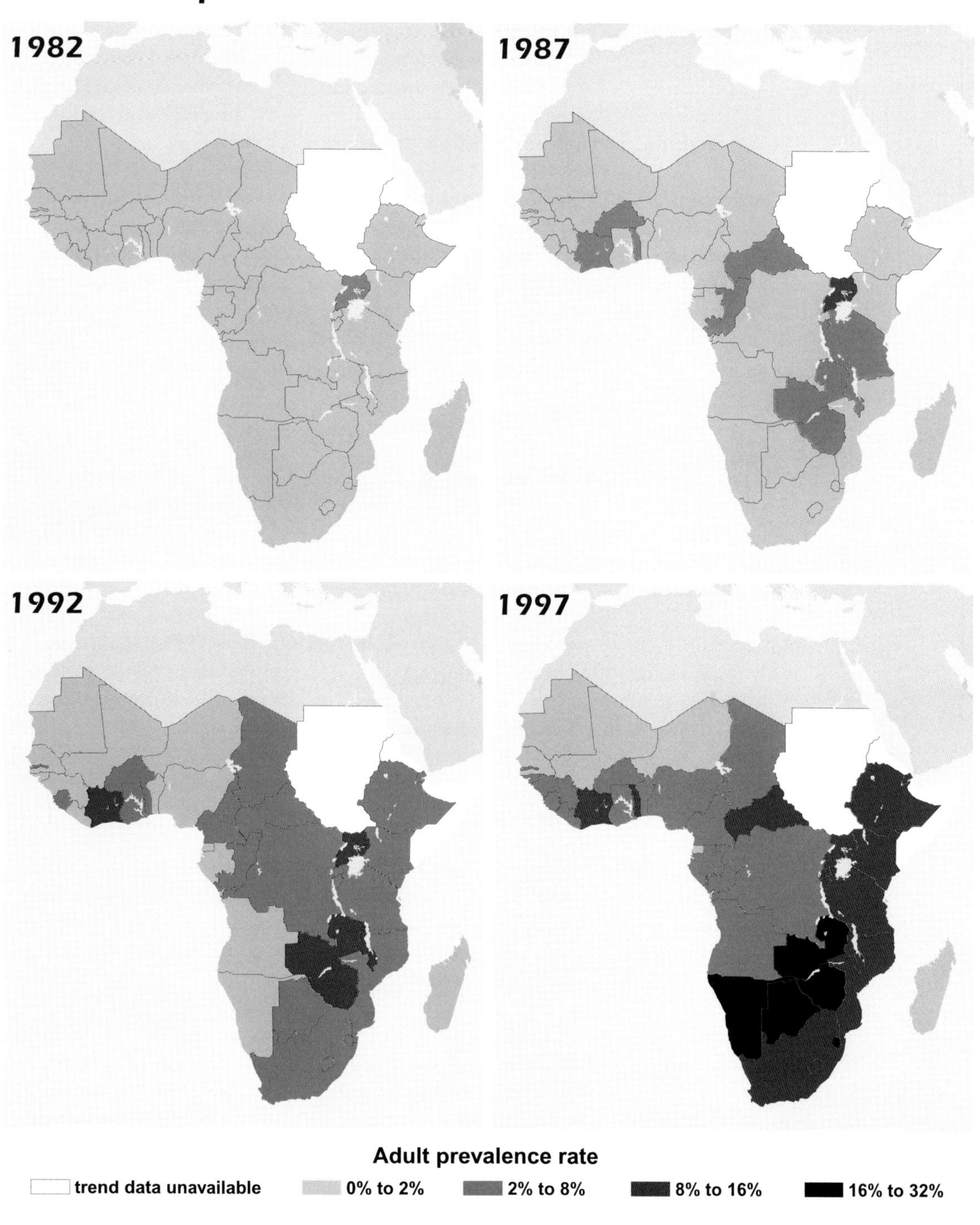

Source: UNAIDS.

A recent World Bank publication, *Intensifying action against HIV/AIDS in Africa*, suggests these moral issues are misunderstood. The assumption that treatment would lead to more orphans is based on the misconception that HIV-infected infants do not survive long enough to become orphans. In fact, claims the publication, "with or without the intervention, more than 80 per cent of the babies born to HIV-infected mothers [risk] being orphaned by the age of five." Use of ARVs to suppress MTCT would reduce the proportion of HIV-infected orphans, and hence the burden of care from the state and family.

Although mother-to-child transmission is the leading cause of HIV infection among under-15s, administering antiretrovirals to pregnant mothers remains a risky strategy. Not only is an efficient primary health-care system needed to identify HIV-positive mothers and control drug use. ARV treatment involves replacing breastfeeding with 'infant formula' powdered milk. As the World Bank publication points out, "promotion of breastfeeding as the best possible nutrition for infants has been the cornerstone of child health and survival strategies for the past two decades". Undermining breastfeeding in developing countries could have catastrophic effects. So protecting young women from contracting HIV and providing family planning services remain the primary prevention strategies.

While the antiretroviral debate causes outrage, the greatest injustice is not the absence of ARVs – it is the fact that millions of people suffer abominably and die because the most basic medical responses, such as ordinary antibiotics, are unavailable to them. Common HIV-related infections such as TB and pneumonia can be treated without sophisticated monitoring – length and quality of life can be increased without ARVs.

And common drugs to treat other sexually transmitted infections (STIs) could contribute greatly to prevention. One of the reasons HIV has spread so rapidly in Africa is that STIs, which provide conduits for the AIDS virus through inflammations and lesions, have gone untreated. Elsewhere in the world cheap cures have been easily available for decades, but not in Africa.

Need for new thinking

In Zimbabwe, where 40,000 babies a year swell the numbers of the HIV-infected, Arjan de Wagt, a nutrition officer with the UN Children's Fund (UNICEF), has another slant on mother-to-child transmission. His primary concern is neither HIV nor AIDS, but growing rates of malnutrition. The most effective single intervention to reduce these rates, he feels, would be to subdue vertical HIV transmission.

"My worry is that the focus is still on the direct effects of HIV and AIDS. The talk is all of prevention, caring for the sick and orphans, as though no one has realized how the virus impacts upon everything we do. It is time for governments, UN agencies, international organizations and NGOs to stop and ask: "What were we planning to do, and are we still able to do it?" Or do we have to make adjustments, not only in our objectives but in our approach? People are calling HIV/AIDS a disaster but we are still trying to do business as usual."

He cited UNICEF education programmes that enable girls to continue education as one example. "Will they still be able to go to school?" he wonders. "Not just because they may be orphaned and no one is paying for them, but maybe they are needed to look after sick relatives. Perhaps there are not enough teachers. In Zambia more teachers are dying than are being trained. Whether it is nutrition, education or water/sanitation, we all have to do some serious rethinking."

Rethinking should include developing long-term policies to respond to the social, cultural and economic factors that fashion sexual behaviour. An orphaned schoolgirl in Kenya or Zimbabwe provides sexual favours for her 'sugar daddy' because her preoccupation is survival. Food, or money for her schooling, override a vague concern for some virus that may kill her ten years from now. UNAIDS's Peter Piot has said that medical and behavioural interventions alone will not halt HIV – economic responses must play a part.

From rhetoric to reality

HIV infects over 14,000 more sub-Saharan Africans every day. The world must face up to the crisis and adequately fund the response. The UN Security Council was told by the World Bank that between US$ 1 billion and US$ 2.3 billion was needed annually for prevention alone in Africa, but official assistance for AIDS was something in the region of US$ 160 million. African nations too must get their acts together. Controversy over drugs and condoms only underlines the absence of direction in the war against AIDS.

"It's easy to despair because of the magnitude of the problem", says Alvaro Bermejo, director of health at the International Federation, "but remember, unlike wars, drought and famine, AIDS is totally preventable. And prevention is affordable, but we need to change our mindset." Limited resources demand clear prioritizing – a policy of the greatest good for the greatest number. Bermejo argues that the best approach to tackling HIV/AIDS is to scale up strategies already proven to work best, such as:

- peer-to-peer education aimed at 12-to-24 year olds, through youth groups, clubs, churches and schools;
- health education targeted at mobile men (such as soldiers, truck-drivers, businessmen) who spread HIV while travelling;
- access to free or affordable condoms;
- better diagnosis and treatment of sexually-transmitted infections;
- better treatment of opportunistic infections, such as TB and pneumonia, which cause unnecessary suffering and premature death;
- screening blood banks to ensure HIV-free transfusions (up to 10 per cent of all infections are through contaminated blood);
- voluntary counselling and testing; and
- home care for HIV/AIDS sufferers, through partnerships with community-based support groups.

A word of caution on home care, however, comes from the International Federation's Hakan Sandbladh: "Home care demands resources that all too often just aren't there," he says, adding: "It needs ongoing long-term funds. A typical family will have lost their breadwinners, leaving the elderly and children. So you give them home care, but that means clothes, food, shelter, education – and before you know it, you are the welfare state. Where do you stop?" Sandbladh's concern is that donor funding peaks and troughs unpredictably, so committing to a widespread and very expensive home-care programme is dangerous if the money to sustain it is not there in, say, three years time. Yet Africa's public health systems are overwhelmed by HIV/AIDS, so home and community-based care are the only options for easing the suffering of millions.

The Red Cross/Red Crescent Movement's strategy in sub-Saharan Africa is to address home care (where the money is available) within the context of community-based first aid programmes. First aid-trained volunteers can identify and then support a 'caregiver' for each AIDS sufferer in their area. Volunteers supporting home care can also inform family members and village leaders of preventive methods and work to reduce the stigma often attached to those living with HIV/AIDS.

Thierry Mertens, former director of WHO's department of HIV/AIDS and other STIs, has observed that "unlike 15 years ago, we know what to do. The challenge now is how to implement what we know works and adapt our interventions to each socio-cultural context." Implementing successful prevention and care strategies means not just improving public health infrastructures. Nor does it simply entail partnerships between governments and international agencies. It means engaging networks of local-level volunteers on a massive scale – a key aim of the African Red Cross/Red Crescent Health Initiative (see Chapter 10).

HIV/AIDS does not exist in a vacuum. Investments made can have long-term development benefits as well as curb Africa's ongoing tragedy. There can be no better investment than in communities themselves, and the community-based organizations that struggle to empower them. In them lie the foundations for strong and effective international partnerships.

Sources and further information

Barnett, Tony and Whiteside, Alan. *HIV/AIDS in Africa: Implications for development and major policy implications.* Fourth SCUSA Inter-University Colloquium, University of East Anglia, UK, September 1999.

Gershon, Martin. A *regional framework for assessment and response to incidence of acute food insecurity in southern Africa.* Harare: International Federation of Red Cross and Red Crescent Societies, October 1999.

Government of Uganda et al. *The National Strategic Framework for HIV/AIDS Activities in Uganda (1998-2002).* December 1997.

National AIDS/STDs Control Programme, Ministry of Health, Kenya. *Aids in Kenya: background, projections, impact, interventions, policy.* 1999.

Rugalema, Gabriel with Weigang, Silke and Mbwika, James. *HIV/AIDS and the Commerical Agricultural Sector of Kenya.* Food and Agriculture Organization (FAO)/UN Development Programme (UNDP), 1999.

Topouzis, Daphne. *The implications of HIV/AIDS for rural development policy and programming: Focus on sub-Saharan Africa.* Sustainable Development Department, FAO/HIV and Development Programme, UNDP, June 1998.

UNAIDS/WHO. *AIDS Epidemic Update.* December 1999.

UNAIDS. *United Nations Strategic Framework on HIV/AIDS in Zimbabwe, 1999-2001.*

WHO. "A new outlook for HIV/AIDS". *World Health.* November/December 1998.

Web sites

Fondation du Present AF-AIDS – http://www.hivnet.ch:8000/africa/af-aids/
Harvard Aids Institute – http://www.hsph.harvard.edu/
International Federation of Red Cross and Red Crescent Societies – http://www.ifrc.org
The Lancet – http://www.thelancet.com
Joint United Nations Programme on HIV/AIDS – http://www.unaids.org
Office of the United Nations High Commissioner for Refugees –
http://www.unhcr.ch/refworld/un/chr/chr96/thematic/44-aids.htm
United Nations Office for the Coordination of Humanitarian Affairs – http://wwwnotes.reliefweb.int/
World Bank – http://www.worldbank.org/aids/
World Health Organization – http://www.who.int/

chapter 4

Section One

Focus on public health

North Korea's public health pays the price of isolation

In an attempt to warm often freezing wards in winter, and in the absence of readily available coal and wood, the director of Huichon City Hospital says his staff heat soot – "coalsmoke pieces" – gathered from local chimneys. To help retain any warmth, cracked glass windows are covered with polythene in spartan wards, fitted out with makeshift beds covered by thin blankets. Windows in the sombre operating area, which lacks effective anaesthetics for all but minor surgical procedures and with only a minimum of instruments, receive the same treatment.

But cold is not the only problem facing the director, Chon Tong Sik, whose 76-doctor hospital is in a northern area of the Democratic People's Republic of Korea (DPRK) – a nation wracked by crippling economic problems following the break-up of the Soviet Union, and ravaged by a vicious cycle of floods and drought since 1995.

"We have about 200 beds but only 50 per cent are occupied," Chon, speaking through an interpreter, told the *World Disasters Report* (WDR) in February 2000. Occupancy in some of DPRK's hospitals during winter is estimated at nearer 15 to 20 per cent according to the International Federation of Red Cross and Red Crescent Societies. Apart from cold, a lack of drugs, food and transport forces some patients to stay at home.

After visiting a variety of hospitals, it was clear to a three-member team from the International Federation that the country's public health system – once the envy of many developing countries – was in serious decline. The decay – mirrored in the pharmaceutical, energy and agriculture sectors – is a manifestation of DPRK's economic decline.

A number of international aid agencies have pulled out of DPRK over the last two years, citing problems with access and accountability. Meanwhile, immediate supplies of essential drugs and equipment, plus longer-term rehabilitation of public health infrastructure and training of staff, are becoming high-priority needs. Staying on in DPRK may help meet those needs – and may bring unexpected benefits.

Floods threaten food security

Huichon was hit badly by flooding. Substantial flood protection embankments are now in place along the Chongchon River and the area, surrounded by jagged snow-clad peaks, has many new homes. One hundred and fifty of the small bungalow-type homes were funded by the Canadian Red Cross Society for flood victims after the devastation of 1995 and 1996.

"At the time of the floods, there were lots of families in the valleys. There were five or six days of rain followed by a heavy downpour for five hours, which just carried away dwellings," said Kim Chol Hup, director of the social and medical services department of Huichon's Red Cross branch. "We had no time to save any materials from the homes. We were just lucky to save our lives," he said.

Photo opposite page: DPRK health workers prepare traditional 'Koryo' medicines. Derived from roots, they comprise 70 per cent of drugs used in some hospitals – essential Western drugs are in very short supply. Tuberculosis and malaria, previously under control, are making a comeback.

Photo: Omar Valdimarsson/ International Federation, DPR Korea 2000.

Kim was sitting in the new home of Han Jong Sun, whose husband died in the floods. Mrs Han, aged over 50, now works on a cooperative farm producing maize and beans in an area almost denuded of trees by post-storm landslides and people in search of firewood. Coal mining is the other main industry in the region but officials said some local mines were working only at about one-third of capacity because of flooding suffered since 1995.

Speaking beneath the gaze of wall pictures of Kim Il Sung, DPRK's late leader who laid the foundation for what is perhaps the world's most tightly controlled state, and his son, Kim Jong Il, Mrs Han said her two sons, aged 15 and 10, worked on the farm during school holidays.

Mrs Han is one of many hungry people who supplement their daily diets with so-called substitute foods – noodles and hard cakes, made from a mix of nutritional plants, such as soybeans and sweet potatoes, combined with indigestible fillers, including grasses and corn husks. Officials say the average amount of such foods taken by a person each day is around 600 grammes, to supplement rations doled out by DPRK's creaking public distribution system. But doctors believe these substitutes form up to 40 per cent of total food intake. Ensuing stomach aches and diarrhoea are seen as the side-effects of assuaging hunger.

DPRK, which has never been self-sufficient in food production, suffered what some commentators referred to as a 'famine' during the mid-1990s. The widespread floods of 1995-96 ruined many hectares of farmland, destroyed dams and damaged mines. Since then, the country has been the recipient of the longest sustained United Nations (UN) food emergency programme in history.

Some of the hospitals the International Federation team visited in February 2000 acknowledged that they had treated cases of malnutrition but, uniformly, they said there had been no deaths. Many close observers of DPRK put deaths caused by the series of floods and malnutrition at between 800,000 and 1.5 million. Some estimates for the period 1995-98 have been as high as 3 million lives lost.

Figures given by a DPRK official during a visit to Pyongyang by major donors in May 1999, taking into account a drop in the rate of population increase from 1.5 per cent to 0.9 per cent a year, suggested 222,000 had died in addition to 'natural wastage' since 1995. "We think this is on the low side," said David Morton, the UN representative and resident coordinator in Pyongyang.

And there is more bad news in the pipeline for DPRK's hard-pressed 22 million people. Since 1995, say officials, essential livestock have been eaten because of a lack of staple foods. This, in turn, has reduced the amount of natural fertilizer needed to ensure satisfactory crops.

Li Jae Rim, a senior official with the country's Flood Disaster Rehabilitation Committee (FDRC), which oversees and coordinates the work of relief agencies, said the amount of rice – or its equivalent – for office workers, labourers and officials was being reduced. Li told WDR in Pyongyang that amounts of 300 grammes per person per day between November and January, 250 grammes in February and 200 grammes in March and April, would be further reduced to 150 grammes for May and up to June 23, the last day for food distribution.

These reductions are despite an improved harvest during October-November 1999 of 4.28 million tonnes of grain and rice – around 700,000 tonnes more than the previous year – which reverses a downward trend seen since the 1995 floods. But DPRK officials say the country needs around 6.5 million tonnes a year to be self-sufficient.

Scant drug supplies reverse past public health progress

Huichon City Hospital's director Chon says traditional *Koryo* medicines, produced mainly from roots, comprise about 70 per cent of drugs used in his hospital, which caters for about 50,000 people in Jagang Province, some 200 km north of Pyongyang. Basic Western drugs, such as penicillin, make up most of the rest. Some are supplied by the DPRK government and others by the International Federation. Some drugs have labels in Russian.

"We use antibiotics for extreme emergencies. It is very difficult for doctors to know who to give treatment to and who not to treat. I don't think the conditions are good. Because of malnutrition, people can get some diseases immediately," Chon said, adding that common colds, bronchitis, pneumonia and cardiovascular complaints were regular problems.

Similar conditions were seen and spoken of in other city, county and *Ri* (district) hospitals and clinics during separate WDR visits to Anju and Kujang, north of Pyongyang, and to Kaesong, about 180 km south of Pyongyang, near the heavily fortified frontier between DPRK and South Korea.

Our party, including six members of DPRK's Red Cross society, travelled in two white Land Cruisers emblazoned with the International Federation's red cross and red crescent emblem. Frequently, groups of children and adults at roadsides acknowledged our waves, as did some soldiers crammed into the backs of military lorries or at checkpoints.

At Kaepung County Hospital, near the southern frontier city of Kaesong, the lilting strains of a Korean folksong directed at South Korea by loudspeakers were clearly audible. Hospital director Dang Cheol Muk said up to 10 per cent of outpatients suffered from malnutrition. There were also instances of diarrhoea caused by poor water.

Water is a major problem. Ralph Ek, the International Federation's water and sanitation delegate in Pyongyang, said some local *Ri* hospitals were particularly bad. "They have nothing, absolutely nothing. At the moment, they have to collect water from wells and carry it into the hospitals in buckets. As for sewers, everything just goes out from the wall. They need septic tanks and sewer pipes but they have no materials for this," said Ek, mandated to try to repair water and sanitation in 36 ordinary hospitals and 111 *Ri* hospitals. Ek has a budget of only 5,000 Swiss francs for each hospital.

The Kaepung Hospital conducts between 15 and 20 operations weekly, with appendicectomies the most common. "We use local anaesthesia, usually a spinal anaesthetic. Our anaesthetic machine is out of order. The tubing [for gas] has decayed," Dang said.

Corinne Baas, a Dutch-born clinical nurse with 18 years' field experience for the International Federation in countries such as Afghanistan and Iraq and now DPRK, said: "Anaesthetics? This is really, really shocking. There is no gas. They don't have the equipment, including masks," she added. "They can give local anaesthetics and a very few county hospitals can do spinal anaesthetics – morphine and pethedine are supposedly available. But if you only think how stressful it must be for the patients. This causes, for some people, a lot of problems," Baas said in Pyongyang.

Underlining equipment problems, Paek Sam Kuyu, director of Kujang's county hospital in North Pyongan province, was asked what equipment he needed. He said: "Operating equipment, diagnostic equipment, X-ray machine, ECG machine [electro-cardiograph] and a greater selection of drugs for cardiovascular disease and other problems, as well as an ambulance and transport for staff."

Infectious diseases once under control in DPRK are making a comeback. The World Health Organization (WHO) says that while tuberculosis (TB) remains one of the most serious public health problems in DPRK, with an estimated 40,000 new cases a year, malaria has re-emerged in southern provinces during the past three years, with a "significant increase" in the number of cases in 1999. Without giving figures, Kaepung Hospital's director Dang confirmed a rise in the number of malaria patients in 1999. "Before 1998 there were no malaria sufferers here," he said. Dang, who even contended that the malarial parasite had come from South Korea, said there had been no deaths from the disease to date.

As for TB, which was once eradicated in DPRK, an official with the Ministry of Public Health in Pyongyang told WDR: "There were quite a number of cases of TB before 1995. But, unfortunately, since 1995 the number of TB patients has increased. The present figure is 50 patients per 100,000 people. It has not been updated [since 1998] but my information is that it has increased a little more."

While DPRK's public health system is stretched alarmingly, foreign experts with first-hand knowledge do not believe the situation is yet desperate. WHO's coordinator in Pyongyang, Eigil Sörensen, said: "If you compare DPRK to some other countries, it has advantages. The general education level is very high. There is even access to health care in remote areas. But the country has been fairly isolated. Many of their principles in public health are based on the 1950s and 1960s."

Foreign doctors say that DPRK, in principle, has a good health infrastructure with 616 general hospitals, 13 TB institutes, 60 sanatoria and more than 10,000 beds to cater for just over 22 million people living in 212 counties and 4,700 *Ri*, although the problems in recent years have severely affected the health sector.

The official from the Ministry of Public Health said his country, with 29 doctors per 10,000 people, operated a cradle-to-grave 'section doctor' system. Such doctors were in charge of primary health care. "Our section doctors each look after, on average, 134 families."

During the peak years for public health in North Korea 30 to 40 years ago, foreign doctors say there were major medical achievements. An effective health-care system, with plenty of human resources, devoted considerable attention to, for example, the control of communicable diseases, and increased the longevity of DPRK's people.

But, added Sörensen, "The problem is that for the past 10 to 15 years they have suffered from a degradation of the health-care system, with basic problems with water, electricity and heating. Then there is a lack of reserves and an economic decline."

'Rogue state' may be ready to engage

The general decline in health care over the past few decades has a close correlation with political and economic developments in DPRK. With the world's largest military after China, the United States, Russia and India, DPRK has been accused by the US Congress of boosting the range of its missiles in line with the substantial growth in foreign aid since 1995. Washington branded DPRK a 'rogue state' with a capability of hitting the mainland US with missiles.

Dominating DPRK is a reclusive personality cult, now with Kim Jong Il at its head. The virtue of *Juche*, or self-reliance, has replaced Marxism and Leninism (see Box 4.1). The leadership's declared aim is reunification with South Korea. The Korean war ended in 1953 but North and South did not sign a peace treaty. China and the Soviet Union supported the North against the South and a US-led force acting under a UN mandate.

Amid a flurry of recent diplomatic activity as well as cultural and business contacts, there are signs that DPRK has, at least for now, adopted an engagement policy. South Korea's President Kim Dae-Jung said in December that North-South ties should see major improvements in 2000.

A suggested policy of US engagement with DPRK was underlined in October 1999 by former Secretary of Defense William Perry, a special advisor on DPRK to President Bill Clinton. His proposal was for a two-pronged approach. The first prong would be engagement. If DPRK chose this route, it could expect increased trade and the gradual elimination of sanctions. But if Pyongyang chose the path of confrontation, Perry recommended that the country be met with firmness and resolve.

In September 1999, DPRK pledged to freeze testing of long-range missiles for the duration of negotiations to improve relations and Clinton agreed to the first significant easing of economic sanctions against DPRK since 1953. In 1994, DPRK and the US signed a nuclear agreement, under which DPRK pledged to freeze and eventually dismantle its nuclear weapons programme in exchange for international aid to build two power-producing nuclear reactors.

Box 4.1 'Juche' – ideological cornerstone

One of the highest landmarks in Pyongyang, DPRK's capital, is the tower to the 'Juche Idea', capped with an artificial flame. The first year of the 'Juche Idea' is now regarded as 1911, the year of the late Kim Il Sung's birth. June 2000 is June, 'Juche' 89.

'Juche', or 'Kimilsungism', is a cornerstone of DPRK society. It superseded Marxism and Leninism and was designed to promote independence as well as self-sufficiency at national and individual levels.

North Korea, which has considered any reliance on the outside world as a sign of weakness, was the only communist state to remain neutral – amid a determination to avoid satellite status – in the Sino-Soviet disputes of the 1970s and 1980s. It was also an active member of the non-aligned movement.

The 'Juche Idea', which has been called an autarky raised to the level of a philosophy, is accredited to North Korea's late leader Kim Il Sung. This philosophy, according to the 'Pyongyang Times', embraces the idea that "Man's essential qualities indicate that he is a social being with independence, creativity and consciousness."

However, the nation's food crisis since 1995 and subsequent humanitarian interventions have cast 'Juche' in a new light. DPRK's military opposed the initial food aid programme in 1995 and forced a temporary shutdown in operations the following year. In a speech delivered in June 1997, Kim Jong Il, who succeeded his father to the leadership in 1994, publicly criticized the aid programme as imperialistic.

But recently, DPRK's Flood Disaster Rehabilitation Committee, which coordinates international humanitarian donations and programmes, has expressed gratitude for the UN's Consolidated Inter-Agency Appeal, which totalled US$ 331.7 million for 2000. The committee called the appeal an "expression of interest and goodwill of the international community to continue support to the North".

Now, in an interesting twist, the US is the biggest relief donor to the DPRK relief operation. Based on current trends, aid from the US alone between 1995 and 2000 is likely to total over US$ 1 billion. In 1999, the UN Consolidated Inter-Agency Appeal for North Korea totalled US$ 292.1 million, and achieved 63.8 per cent funding by November 1999. The figure for 2000 totals US$ 331.7 million, of which 92 per cent is earmarked for food assistance and promotion of food security. Traditionally, the biggest providers are the UN's World Food Programme (WFP) – the main channel for official US food aid – and the UN Development Programme (UNDP), followed by the UN Children's Fund (UNICEF), WHO and voluntary relief organizations.

Funds are needed to keep the relief operation in business, but there are signs of donor fatigue, which could cause some problems in coming months. This fatigue was acknowledged in DPRK. "The percentages of [our] appeals are slowly going down. They were initially between 85 and 80 per cent [covered]. I don't think it is anything to do with the way things are done in this country," said Choe Chang Hun, deputy secretary general of the Red Cross Society of DPRK.

WFP, which has provided more than 1.5 million tonnes of food worth US$ 650 million since 1995 and now feeds more than 6 million people in DPRK, had donor support in February 2000 for continued shipments until the end of April, according to WFP sources.

Do humanitarian needs and principles collide?

DPRK officials and a growing number of foreign medical and aid experts generally agree that current relief operations, largely 'band-aid' developed under the food parcel mentality, are insufficient and that there should be a move at least into medium-term development assistance. Such assistance would involve refurbishing hospitals with equipment and drugs, bringing medical staff up to date on medical techniques and ensuring that as many ordinary people as possible have a working knowledge of personal health care. The amounts of money needed inevitably would be in the billions of dollars – too much for donors and most governments. This indicates the need for approaches to the World Bank, the Asian Development Bank or similar institutions.

For international non-governmental organizations (NGOs) considering assistance to DPRK, there are moral questions based on humanitarian values. How far should agencies go in meeting the humanitarian needs of people living in a country run along tight military lines? Does restricted access to beneficiaries and to distribution networks threaten transparency and accountability enough to justify agencies pulling out? Can an NGO policy of advocacy survive and, if so, how can it be operated?

Some of the NGOs that entered DPRK during and after 1995 found a world they had never experienced before (see Box 4.2). They were in a country about which they knew little – a strong, authoritarian government was firmly in place, dictating all aspects of relief work from shipping goods into the country to distribution and contacts with aid beneficiaries. Also, there was, and is, little room for the types of advocacy espoused by many relief agencies. It is a far cry from dealing with disaster-struck African countries where, sometimes, there is little or no government control and aid workers have a virtually free rein to go about their business, sometimes without consulting local populations.

Several NGOs have already left DPRK, most notably Médecins sans Frontières (MSF), the 1999 Nobel Peace Prize laureate, in a blaze of publicity in 1998. MSF's departure has been referred to by one commentator as "outing and shouting". Other NGOs who have left, mainly over issues focusing on access and monitoring, include Médecins du Monde, Oxfam and Action contre la Faim (see Box 4.3).

Box 4.2 "Nothing prepares you for North Korea"

"Nothing compares. Nothing prepares you for North Korea because nobody really knows," says Marie-France Bourgeois, a Canadian who spent four months in the country as an assessor for the European Community Humanitarian Office.

On boarding a Soviet-built Ilyushin-62 of DPRK's Koryo Airline at China's Beijing airport for the 90-minute flight to Pyongyang – temporary home for some 100 aid workers – you begin an adventure and a challenge. Some people thrive, some fail and others just muddle through.

Security is no problem, says Bourgeois. "You are never going to get attacked in DPRK but there are people watching you...you don't need to lock anything. Nothing is going to disappear."

Most foreigners know they will be watched closely in DPRK. But surprises include knowledgeable conversations instigated by your hosts about one's own country, frequent reminders of the North's yearning to be reunited with the South and the more than occasional eye-contact, and smiles, from ordinary people in streets.

"It is very hard and very challenging here," said Roberto Christen, long-time resident and chief technical adviser to the UN Development Programme in DPRK. "There have been changes since 1995. There are more cars, especially BMWs and Mercedes, in the city and more foreigners. There is also more tolerance of outsiders."

David Morton, the UN representative and humanitarian coordinator in DPRK, says life in the country "is bearable and that local authorities tried to ensure as much comfort as possible. We are a very small [international aid] community. We are actually very close. There is a good exchange of information and ideas."

The majority of aid workers live and work in guarded diplomatic compounds, which, like elsewhere in Pyongyang, often lack water and electricity. They have access to shops, restaurants and a gym in the compound. Outside, a favoured restaurant is a Japanese-type establishment, where a substantial meal for four will total US$ 30 – payable in dollars.

Friday nights are party nights for the aid and diplomatic community at the WFP building. Unwinding takes place at a well-stocked bar and on the dance floor. Some people will be saying farewell, some will have just arrived. Others will be ready for the Saturday flight to Beijing for one week of rest and relaxation.

Life is less relaxed for the locals. "I've seen malnutrition elsewhere, but in North Korea the whole population has been suffering a lack of food," says Rea Noponen, who left Pyongyang in 1999 after one year there as a health delegate for the International Federation of Red Cross and Red Crescent Societies. "It's usually children under five", she added, "but even young men in their twenties are malnourished. I have never seen that anywhere else."

James Orbinski, MSF's international president, told WDR: "In large measure, we found it impossible to deliver humanitarian assistance in an impartial, independent fashion and we found that it was impossible to target the most vulnerable people that we knew to exist but were unable to access." Orbinski alleged that Western foreign policy was using humanitarian assistance as a form of political leverage. He denied allegations that MSF had criticized North Korea and shrugged off criticism that it had broken ranks with other international relief organizations.

MSF's departure, more than any other, has raised the issue of whether humanitarian organizations should stay on and quietly work to continue making valuable inroads – or whether leaving should be the path. Most agencies appear to have opted for the former.

The issues of access and monitoring have been debated widely in the relief community. The UN's David Morton, in Pyongyang for nearly two years, believes the situation has improved. "It has been very difficult," he said. "I think our knowledge and understanding has increased very dramatically from zero in 1995 to what we know today. We think we have a fairly good idea of what the situation is and what is going on. We have access to 75 per cent of the area, which is 85 per cent of the population."

International impressions of what is happening in DPRK depend largely on what people are shown, almost always under strict supervision. Of DPRK's 212 counties, 48 are normally off-limits to humanitarian workers, and aid agencies in the country have jointly agreed that, without monitoring, they will not deliver aid to these areas. An estimated 15.6 per cent of the population lives in these 48 counties, mainly in mountainous land with limited farming possibilities – and it is in such regions that some aid workers believe the worst malnutrition may exist.

Another problem area with some aid suppliers has been allegations that some international aid has been diverted to the army. This has been denied as "a lie" by DPRK's official KCNA news agency. "We will never be able to be absolutely sure where the aid goes. But we know that... at least a very high proportion of it goes to where we think it has been going, where it is supposed to go," Morton said.

"We have never seen anything that would indicate a systematic diversion. Of course, it would be very easy for them to pull the wool over our eyes. Certainly, stuff is going to be taken as in any [relief] operation but we can see the condition of our beneficiaries has visibly improved. Also, the Koreans, especially the army and the elite, eat rice. How attractive is American yellow maize going to be to them? The Chinese give them untied aid with which they can do what they like – they can feed the army with it if they want," Morton added. US food aid, and some from the European Union, has been yellow maize, wheat and smaller quantities of beans and oil. But there is no rice.

Box 4.3 'Outing and shouting': NGO departures underscore problems

Several major NGOs have left DPRK since 1997, underscoring multifaceted problems faced by relief groups working there. The most notable, and controversial, departure was in September 1998 when Médecins sans Frontières (MSF) – which later went on to win the 1999 Nobel Peace Prize – pulled out. Others to leave include Médecins du Monde, Oxfam and Action contre la Faim (ACF).

The departures have intensified debate on the NGO role in DPRK, especially on how far they should go within the confines of humanitarian ideals. Most of those remaining opted for the quiet approach amid signs that their efforts are worthwhile.

ACF left in February 2000. Their director-general, Jean-Luc Bodin, said in a letter to DPRK's Flood Disaster Rehabilitation Committee that the move was linked in part to "the humanitarian context in the country and the difficult operating conditions imposed on humanitarian agencies."

But according to Eigil Sörensen, WHO's coordinator in Pyongyang, "If you are going to work in DPRK you have to accept the framework for agencies. I understand why agencies take that decision [to leave]. On the other hand, we have to look at what we can achieve in both the short and long term."

Announcing its decision to leave, MSF said that since June 1998 there had been a clear policy to further restrict and limit effective humanitarian aid and called on donor governments to review aid policies towards DPRK to ensure, among other things, free and impartial access and monitoring.

Commenting on MSF's departure, North Korea's KCNA news agency reported on 8 October 1998, that the NGO had been asked "to offer the pharmaceutical raw materials needed for increasing pharmaceutical production."

But James Orbinski, MSF's international president, told WDR: "According to our assessment, this was not the primary need at the time. The primary need was appropriate nutrition programmes for people who were suffering from malnutrition." MSF had been running 64 therapeutic feeding centres for around 14,000 children in DPRK.

Asked if relief organizations in DPRK in some way might have been 'used' by outside countries, he said: "Western foreign policy and...largely American foreign policy, is in fact using humanitarian assistance as a form of political leverage. And, in so doing, is making humanitarian assistance conditional on political and not humanitarian objectives."

Orbinski said humanitarian action "must be completely separated" from political objectives, both internal and external. "In the vast majority of situations where humanitarian need arises out of political turmoil there is, obviously, an inherently political context you have to operate in. This does not, however, mean you have to succumb to the desire of the various political forces to influence your choice and your delivery of humanitarian action," he added.

Margareta Wahlström, an under-secretary general at the International Federation, said: "I think the MSF position here is more the democracy, advocacy side rather than the humanitarian side. They say it is more important for us to test this government's willingness to let us go everywhere than to deliver to a very small group of people in the country.... It is their choice."

Jon Bennett, in a paper on DPRK published by the 'Relief and Rehabilitation Network' in March 1999, said the country had been opened up to aid agencies in an unprecedented way, adding that it was "incomprehensible and unforgivable" that MSF should have publicly criticized its host "based on universalist notions and the tenets of self-proclaimed 'advocacy'."

Orbinski said: "I would say that we did not criticize our hosts. We simply stated the facts and we simply, honestly and honourably stated our experience in North Korea. We have, obviously, through our actions made it very clear what our perspective is. And if that runs counter to the herd, then so be it."

Humanitarian dialogue could aid 'soft landing'

A 'hard landing' for North Korea could have disastrous humanitarian consequences. There is a need to keep avenues of dialogue open, to avoid any sudden and major political upheaval in DPRK that could provide chilling parallels with other crises, such as followed the break-up of the former Yugoslavia.

Speaking of DPRK and underlining a need to be politically aware, Margareta Wahlström, under-secretary general for disaster response and operational coordination at the International Federation, said: "For us, this is an extremely important part of the world for peace and stability. If we cannot keep our attention on north-east Asia, we are making a major mistake. Humanitarians are but small-fry actors here. We may be important during a period of time but what is important here is the attention that the world community – the political decision-makers – can give."

But is there not a risk that relief agencies in DPRK are pawns of countries such as China, Japan and South Korea, as well as the US, in a political power game in that part of Asia? "Of course, we may be, but there is a compelling humanitarian need here," the UN's Morton said. "The North Koreans took this very unusual step in 1995 of inviting us in. I think that is because the situation was quite desperate then. I think the peak of the crisis, in terms of food at any rate, was in 1996-97. But the whole country was affected, of course, by the break-up of the Soviet Union and the loss of that export market, as in all the other Eastern European countries at the end of the 1980s.

"Basically, all of a sudden, they had no more fuel imports. All of their imports and supplies, like oil, were suddenly cut off. Then, neighbouring China and other countries demanded hard currency for these [imports]. That affected their industry, and that affected their fertilizer plants... They went into serious economic decline, which has affected everything from health downwards," Morton said.

The International Federation's Wahlström said she did not believe her organization was being used as a political pawn. "I think you are used as a pawn only if you allow yourself to be used as a pawn. We have a strategy and we know why we are working there. I believe also that colleagues in the UN system know why they are working there. The system might be utilized but I must say I think it is for a good purpose because you cannot create stability in this part of the world without creating a bridge.

"The humanitarian agencies, be it the UN, the Red Cross or NGOs, in my view have made an incredible contribution to creating that bridge because they have been there in an almost non-conditional manner. The conditions we have imposed are the conditions that belong to the humanitarian agenda. But we have not said that in order to give food we need something else from you. I believe our presence has greatly assisted in making possible the continuation of a dialogue," Wahlström added.

The Red Cross has provided what has been the sole official link between the two Koreas, sometimes through contacts between the respective national Red Cross societies. "The two societies talk to each other by phone across the border occasionally. I think, basically, they [the two Koreas] are ready to lift the phone and talk to each other," said Wahlström.

Public health sector rehabilitation a priority

There is almost unanimous agreement among major relief and medical organizations working in DPRK that aid should continue, but in a more sustained fashion to help reinvigorate the country's public health service. At the same time, DPRK has said a priority is to rehabilitate its pharmaceutical and health industries, with help from the UN and other international organizations, and this year it is looking for a combination of emergency and what it called mid-term assistance.

"The goal was to have the pharmaceutical industry up-and-running in 2000. We were not so sure it could be achieved by 2000 and we decided to continue assistance to 2001," said the DPRK Red Cross's Choe. He said the duration of international assistance with drugs would depend on how long it took to rehabilitate the local industry. "It is only a matter of years before it comes to an end, I think," he said.

The Public Health Ministry's spokesman said: "We have big expectations [for the work] of NGOs and charity organizations to be continued. Simultaneously, our goal is to make the people live in a peaceful state... We are expecting more outside assistance." And Li, from the FDRC, referring to WFP's plan to go for mid-term assistance to help increase agricultural production, said: "DPRK is very attentive to this assistance. This year, it wants mid-term and emergency assistance to be combined to a certain extent." Aid officials in DPRK view this attitude as a big shift away from the difficult days of 1995-97, when it appeared that the country would allow such foreigners in for only short periods.

Malnutrition still afflicts both children and adults in DPRK. Estimates of the number killed by hunger and floods between 1995-1998 range from an official 222,000 up to 3 million. WFP now feeds more than 6 million North Koreans.

Photo: Nigel Chandler/International Federation, DPR Korea 1997.

In the short-term, WHO's Eigil Sörensen sees the public health system remaining handicapped. "For the time being most funds are emergency funds. Very few donors are willing to promote assistance for development because development assistance is based on potential collaboration. These conditions are not right and, thus, the focus will remain on band-aid in the near future," he said.

Sörensen believes, however, that there is a role in long-term health development. He has advocated to WHO the need to highlight the significance of the public health perspective in relation to the problems affecting DPRK. "The health sector requires stronger priority from the international community as well as the government," he said in a recent position paper, adding: "The difficult situation at the county and *Ri*-level needs more attention and resources."

He said humanitarian assistance for the sector had been focused mainly on providing essential drugs, vaccines and basic medical supplies brought in from abroad, adding that this was not sustainable. He said in the present short-term phase, between emergency and recovery, continuation of external health sector support was essential to avoid a deterioration in the health situation and increased mortality.

"In the long run," argued Sörensen, "the recovery of the health sector will depend on the national economy. The government has the aim and commitment to revive the economy but the revival of the economy is likely to take time and will depend on many external factors."

So, in the meantime, external support should orientate itself towards rehabilitation activities. "Donors may be reluctant to provide assistance for rehabilitation activities. It is therefore important that WHO actively seek cooperation with donors and partners willing to support rehabilitation activities and see how extra-budgetary resources...can enhance recovery of the health sector," said Sörensen, adding: "Government priorities put agriculture, energy, and science and technology above health."

WHO, meanwhile, plans to emphasize training and human resources in the health sector and is looking to sending some doctors from DPRK to attend master of public health courses at a university in Bangkok. "Hopefully, we will be sending three people for epidemiology and other courses in Bangkok. They will have to take exams, and this is important. Also, the Australians are offering training in Australia for doctors," Sörensen said.

Staying on pays off

The International Federation, which works in concert with the DPRK Red Cross Society and supports 1,678 hospitals, has reiterated that it has no intention of leaving the country and will stay there for as long as necessary.

"I think DPRK has accepted and understood the existence of humanitarian aid, how it is given and I think we can talk directly to donors. What we would like to facilitate is even more openness on development aid from the rest of the world," said Margareta Wahlström, adding: "It is the most tightly woven public health service I have ever seen. They have a lot of well-trained medical staff. It is just that they have no medicines...or access to modern medical science."

Maybe the world is looking too much for obvious results from humanitarian relief going to DPRK. There is another side, usually noticed only by people who have worked in the country. "I think the people are suffering so much that some of them will take the risk to tell you how difficult it is for them. The situation is so bad that some of the people will start speaking. That, already, is one of the reasons you have to stay here," said the International Federation's Corinne Baas, a health delegate in DPRK. Simply being there may be the best form of advocacy.

Box 4.4 Chronology of key events, 1950–2000

1950

June: Korean war starts.

1953

July: DPR Korea and South Korea sign ceasefire. No peace treaty signed.

1956

February: Japanese Red Cross Society's (JRCS) vice president visits Pyongyang for first time to agree on repatriation of 36 Japanese remaining in DPRK after the Second World War.

1959-1984

The JRCS, together with the Red Cross Society of the Democratic People's Republic of Korea (DPRKRC), implements repatriation to DPRK of 93,340 Koreans residing in Japan.

1972

August: Seven rounds of full talks between the Republic of Korea National Red Cross Society (RoKRC) and the DPRKRC continue in Seoul and Pyongyang until August 1973.

1974

February: Kim Jong Il appointed as Kim Il Sung's successor.

1984

September: The DPRKRC sends relief goods (rice, cloth, cement, medicines) to the RoKRC to assist flood victims in the South.

1985

September: As a result of Red Cross talks, 30 North Koreans and 35 South Koreans are reunited with family members in South Korea and North Korea respectively.

1989

September: Eight rounds of working-level contacts between South and North Red Cross societies continue until November 1990.

1991

September: DPRK and South Korea join United Nations.

December: Soviet Union collapses.

1992

Undated: North Koreans cut down on eating amid diminishing food supplies.

1993

February: DPRK refuses inspections by International Atomic Energy Agency of two undeclared nuclear sites.

June: DPRK holds missile tests over coastal waters. First talks between high-ranking US and North Korean officials.

1994

January: DPRK allows international monitors to inspect declared nuclear facilities.

July: Kim Il Sung dies of a heart attack.

October: DPRK and US sign nuclear agreement. DPRK pledges to freeze and eventually dismantle nuclear weapons programme in exchange for international aid to build two power-producing nuclear reactors.

1995

March: Korean Peninsula Energy Development Organization (KEDO) set up under October 1994 agreement to promote cooperation with North Korea.

July-August: Floods affect estimated 5.2 million people in DPRK, destroying crops.

September: DPRK appeals for UN assistance and reduces some grain rations. The International Federation of Red Cross and Red Crescent Societies launches its first appeal for DPRK.

.../

"You must let the people know that you will not forget them," adds Baas; "they know you can tell the world. It is not for us to interfere in politics but at least we can make the world aware that people are suffering."

/...

1996

April: US and South Korea propose four-way talks with DPRK and China for permanent Korean peninsula peace treaty.

July: Rains damage grain-producing area of DPRK.

1997

April: UN requests cooperation for emergency humanitarian aid of US$ 120 million to ease starvation in DPRK. Drought hits agricultural areas.

May: Inter-Korean Red Cross talks in Beijing agree that delegates from the South should visit the North to deliver 50,000 tonnes of relief goods. Further agreements for the RoKRC to deliver relief goods to the North follow in July 1997 and March 1998.

1998

January: DPRK says families now responsible for feeding themselves.

April: Vice president of the JRCS visits the DPRKRC to discuss relief and repatriation issues between the two Red Cross societies.

August: DPRK fires Taepo Dong 1 missile that flies over Japan and lands in Pacific Ocean. Pyongyang says it successfully launched its first satellite.

September: MSF withdraws from DPRK.

November: US and DPRK hold first round of high-level talks over suspected construction of underground nuclear facility. US demands inspections.

1999

February: DPRK allows US access to the site in exchange for promises of food. US finds no evidence of any nuclear activity during site visit in May.

April-June: The RoKRC sends 155,000 tonnes of fertilizer to the North.

May: US says it will provide additional 400,000 tonnes of food aid.

July-August: Floods hit eight provinces in DPRK.

August: Reports say DPRK ready to launch improved version of Taepo Dong 1 missile. Floods damage more than 50,000 hectares of crops.

September: DPRK pledges to freeze testing of long-range missiles for the duration of negotiations to improve relations. President Clinton agrees to the first significant easing of economic sanctions against DPRK since the Korean war ended.

October: Former US Secretary of Defense William Perry, acting as special adviser to President Clinton, proposed two-track engagement policy over DPRK.

November: Total US aid to DPRK since 1995 set to exceed US$ 1 billion by end-2000. Report by a US North Korea advisory group says DPRK can hit US with missile. UN Inter-Agency Appeal for North Korea seeks US$ 331.7 million for 2000. Total of 63.8 per cent of needs met for 1999 appeal of US$ 292.1 million.

December: Oxfam withdraws from DPRK.

2000

January: Italy establishes diplomatic relations with DPRK – the first of the G7 nations to do so.

February: Action contre la Faim withdraws from DPRK.

March: Japan says it will give DPRK 100,000 tonnes of rice as precursor to reopening of normalization discussions. DPRK hosts visit by Italian foreign minister to Pyongyang.

The extent to which DPRK has opened up since 1995, when the country requested aid for the first time, must not be underestimated. "The people are seeing foreigners from an array of countries. People know they are here and trying to assist them. In 1997, they ran away. The presence has a major impact," said WHO's Sörensen. "Look at the respect for the red cross emblem on the International Federation's vehicles. There is a strong humanitarian message here."

But change in the DPRK government's attitude to the way relief is delivered will not be fast. "I think there will be little changes slowly but surely," said one long-time Western resident with a relief organization. "This is a place where there is no significant overnight change. You are not going to suddenly wake up one day and find a McDonalds."

Sources and further information

Bennett, Jon. *North Korea: The Politics of Food Aid.* Relief and Rehabilitation Network (RRN) Paper. March 1999.

Food and Agriculture Organization (FAO). *Food Outlook.* September 1999.

FAO/World Food Programme (WFP). *Assessment mission.* June 1999.

Foster-Carter, Aiden. "DPRK". *Asia Year Book 1999.*

"Mortality in North Korean migrant households". *The Lancet.* 24 July 1999.

Natsios, Andrew. *The Politics of Famine in North Korea.* 9 August 1999.

Pyongyang Times. Various articles.

Reese, David. *Prospects for North Korea's Survival.* Adelphi Paper, 1998.

Snyder, Scott. *Mistrust and the Korean Peninsula: Dangers of Miscalculation.* United States Institute of Peace, 1999.

"The Koreas' Survey". *The Economist.* July 1999.

University of Dublin. *Emergency Nutrition Network.* Trinity College, Dublin, October 1998.

Web sites

European Community Humanitarian Office (ECHO) – http://www.europa.eu.int/en/comm/echo/
International Federation of Red Cross and Red Crescent Societies – http://www.ifrc.org
KCNA (DPRK news agency) – http://www.kcna.co.jp/
Relief and Rehabilitation Network (RRN) – http://www.oneworld.org/odi/rrn
Reliefweb – http://wwwnotes.reliefweb.int
United Nations Development Programme – http://www.undp.org
United States Central Intelligence Agency – http://www.odci.gov/cia/publications/factbook/kn.html
United States Institute of Peace – http://www.usip.org/
World Food Programme – http://www.wfp.org
World Health Organization – http://www.who.int/eha

chapter 5

Section One

Focus on public health

Chernobyl: a chronic disaster

At 01:23:40 on 26 April 1986, as winter edged slowly into spring, an alarmed nuclear power plant operator in what is today northern Ukraine reached for an emergency shutdown button. He was too late. In a few seconds, power surged and the heat in reactor no. 4 of the Chernobyl nuclear power plant skyrocketed to 2000°C. Engineers had been testing the RBMK-1000 – the type of reactor used at Chernobyl – at low power. It failed the test and two explosions blew off its metal seal, releasing an estimated 150-200 million curies of radioactivity into the air – at least 100 times the combined impact of the bombs dropped on Hiroshima and Nagasaki, or as much as a medium-sized nuclear bomb. Some 155,000 square kilometres, an area home to over 7 million people, were contaminated. Chernobyl had become the world's largest nuclear catastrophe.

A deadly mixture floated across the northern hemisphere's skies. The most threatening source of radioactivity immediately after the accident was iodine-131, which has a half-life of eight days and is at the root of much of the thyroid cancer triggered by Chernobyl. Next was caesium-137, which will take another 300 years to disappear. Caesium has crept into food chains and could be concentrated in wild food such as mushrooms and berries. Strontium-90, which will be decomposing until 2266 and could affect bone marrow, ranks third. Perhaps least understood and therefore most alarming is plutonium-239, the most toxic of Chernobyl's wastes, which will be around for 244,000 years and is believed to produce lung cancer when inhaled as a dust.

Abandoned in need

Nearly a decade and a half later, Chernobyl has fallen off the media radar screen – but a huge caseload of needs remain. Radioactive materials have wreaked havoc not only on the bodies of those exposed, but on their minds. Most people expected physical ailments to develop in Chernobyl's wake. Few expected that psychological trauma would affect literally millions still living in the shadow of contamination. Economic and institutional crisis have wracked the region since the former Soviet Union dissolved, making the burden immeasurably worse.

Scientists are still debating the causal connections between radioactive isotopes and the birth defects and cancers widely reported in the affected region – and this will improve our understanding and response when the next nuclear disaster strikes. But immediate humanitarian needs are being largely overlooked. Ivan Kenik, chairman of the Chernobyl consequences committee of the Belarus Ministry of Emergency Situations, claimed recently that no adequate medical supervision was being provided for about 2 million people affected by the accident, including 500,000 children. Inside many of these children, thyroid cancers may be slowly growing unnoticed. Rates will not peak for another five years – and without systematic screening and treatment, such cancers can be fatal.

Those who suffered the worst exposure came to be known as 'liquidators' – the 600,000 plus soldiers and civilians who cleaned up the Chernobyl site over several years. Out of these, the most exposed were the 50,000 who worked on top of the reactor to bring the fire under

Photo opposite page:
Around 50,000 'liquidators' fought Chernobyl's reactor fire and entombed it in concrete. Of the 237 hospitalized, at least 45 died. Research suggests 30 per cent now suffer reproductive disorders. Workers, pictured here in summer 1986, proclaim: "We will fulfil the government's order!"

Photo: Volovymyr Repik/AP, Ukraine 1986.

control and build the sarcophagus which now entombs it. “They were supposed to stay on the roof to fight the fire for only 90 seconds then be replaced,” said Jean-Pierre Revel, senior health officer at the International Federation of Red Cross and Red Crescent Societies. “One can easily guess this did not happen.”

Their radiation doses varied. Some 200,000 liquidators were irradiated with about 100 millisieverts (mSv), five times the limit for nuclear plant workers in one year; 20,000 received 250 mSv; and dozens suffered a potentially lethal dose of several thousand millisieverts. In total, 237 liquidators were admitted to hospital, of whom up to 187 developed acute radiation syndrome. Thirty-one died as a direct consequence of the accident and at least 14 more died over the next ten years. The evacuees were the second most-affected group – 400,000 people were relocated, up to 135,000 of them from within the *Zona*, the 30-km radius exclusion zone surrounding the power plant. Under 10 per cent of adults registered at 70 millisieverts, and nearly 5 per cent received more than 100 mSv – equivalent to having more than 1,000 chest x-rays.

That millions of people were put at risk by Chernobyl is undeniable. What is harder to ascertain is just how badly their health was damaged by the accident, since it happened just as the Soviet Union was beginning to crumble. It has become difficult to distinguish whether illness is caused by radiation, or from poor health due to the region's economic and social collapse.

A link established

The challenge of medicine has been to find direct links between illness and the accident at Chernobyl. Since the mid-1990s, thyroid cancer is the only disease visibly traceable to the accident. Before Chernobyl blew up, Belarus, Ukraine and south-west Russia registered 0.5 to 1 cases of thyroid cancer annually in every million people. After the accident, in some areas the figure shot up 100-fold. Children were hurt the most, some receiving radiation doses in their thyroid glands as high as 10,000 mSv.

Belarus, which caught two-thirds of the fallout, recorded only eight thyroid cancer cases in children under 15 from 1974 to 1985. But between 1986 and 1999, 664 cases were identified, according to the World Health Organization (WHO). In early 1999, Igor Zelenkevitch, Belarusian health minister, stated that the incidence of thyroid cancer among the children of contaminated areas was 24 times higher than in other parts of the country.

Skyrocketing thyroid cancer rates should come as no surprise. The region around Chernobyl has traditionally suffered from an iodine deficiency, so children's bodies were quick to absorb the runaway iodine-131. The most vulnerable were embryos and children under four at the time of the accident, who together make up 42 per cent of thyroid cancer cases. They were contaminated through milk passed on by cows grazing on contaminated grass. Contamination was compounded by the initial scarcity of uncontaminated food and inadequate stocks of iodine tablets for prevention. Had raw milk consumption been halted immediately after the accident and iodine tablets distributed as a preventive measure, thyroid cancer rates would probably have been much lower.

When thyroid cancer first appeared around Chernobyl in 1991, the radiological community was highly sceptical of its link to the accident. Iodine-131 was thought to be low in carcinogenic potential, so assistance to hard-hit populations came slowly. Yet thyroid cancer in children is relatively uncommon so its rapid increase should at least have raised an alarm. Today, it most certainly would.

Thyroid cancer can usually be caught in time but diagnosis is expensive and money becoming harder to raise. "If you detect it early and treat it, you have a 95 per cent chance of success. The enemy is time. If you detect it too late, a child can die," said Pierre Pellerin, a leading authority on radiation and Chernobyl, during an International Federation fact-finding tour of the area. Much of the work undertaken by the International Federation and national Red Cross societies in the Chernobyl area has dealt with screening and treating children and adults for thyroid cancer (see Box 5.1).

Box 5.1 Thyroid gland cancer: who cares?

Nearly a decade and a half after the world's worst nuclear accident, thyroid cancer cases among the people of Belarus, Ukraine and Russia are still rising. Yet despite such evidence, the legacy of secrecy from Soviet times continues to throw long shadows. Many Belarusians refuse to believe anything the authorities say – some would rather remain ignorant of their contaminated condition than face the consequences.

Mogilyov is one of Belarus's biggest cities, in a region covered by the International Federation's Chernobyl Humanitarian Assistance and Rehabilitation Programme (CHARP). The city itself is relatively 'clean', but all is not what it seems.

"It is the unexpected that always happens," says Valery, a 47-year-old factory worker, who was one of many manual labourers checked by the Belarus Red Cross mobile diagnostic laboratory (MDL) in February 1999. "Before, I didn't believe it could happen to me," he adds. "It's been 13 years since the accident in Chernobyl and I thought it was already too late to worry about anything. So when the MDL came to our factory, I had my doubts. 'Is it worthwhile to have a check-up?' I asked myself. Well, it costs nothing. So I'll go."

When the doctors showed Valery a picture of his thyroid gland taken by the scanner, he could not believe it. Even to his untrained eye it was clear he had a serious problem. A month later, Valery was operated on in Minsk, and his cancerous thyroid gland surgically removed. He now has to take the drug levothyroxine for the rest of his life, otherwise he could die of organ or immune system failure. But as Valery admits, he is one of the lucky ones: "I live in a big city and could get an examination. What about people living in remote areas who have almost no chance of knowing about their real health situation? The only chance is the Red Cross."

According to Arthur Grigorovich, head of one of the mobile lab teams: "Living conditions have generally been deteriorating in recent years – especially for people in the rural areas. When you can hardly afford to buy food," he adds, "even a bus ticket to the nearest city is too expensive. People who don't feel sick don't spend money on transportation for a medical check-up."

After the operation, Valery returned to his factory and suggested to his colleagues that they have a check-up too. "I knew that only a third of the 800 people working at my factory decided to be examined, so I said them: Doesn't my situation speak for itself? But one of them replied: 'The less we know about our illnesses the less we worry'."

The world's worst nuclear accidents

1. December 1952: Canada
First major reactor accident in Chalk River, Toronto. Technician's error nearly demolishes reactor core.

2. November 1955: USA
Partial meltdown during tests in experimental breeder reactor near Idaho Falls.

3. October 1957: UK
In the UK's worst nuclear accident, a fire at the Windscale reactor kills 32 people.

4. March 1958: USSR
Explosion at Kyshtym nuclear plant devastates hundreds of km^2; scientists say hundreds killed.

5. October 1975: USA
Near Detroit, partial meltdown at Enrico Fermi experimental breeder permanently disables reactor.

6. December 1975: East Germany
Fire at Lubmin nuclear power complex causes near meltdown.

7. March 1979: USA
Human and mechanical failures cause partial meltdown at the six-month-old plant, Three Mile Island, in the USA's worst nuclear accident.

8. April 1986: USSR
World's worst nuclear accident: explosion and fire at the Chernobyl reactor spews radiation over Europe; 31 people die instantly, millions are affected.

9. March 1992: Russia
Near St. Petersburg, loss of pressure in reactor channel releases radioactive iodine and inert gases into atmosphere.

10. November 1995: Japan
Reactor accident leaks three tons of sodium from cooling system.

11. March 1997: Japan
At least 35 exposed to radiation after fire and explosion at a Tokai-mura reprocessing plant.

12. September 1999: Japan
At another reprocessing plant in Tokai-mura, workers trigger a nuclear reaction. One worker died and over 400 were exposed to radiation.

It is still too early to tell whether thyroid cancer will be the only cancer to increase significantly as a result of Chernobyl. The same goes for leukaemia, which scientists have been trying to link to Chernobyl for years. After all, leukaemia was the first cancer to appear at Hiroshima and Nagasaki. Looking for it here makes sense.

In Hiroshima's footsteps

The leukaemia trail is confused. One study carried out in 1996 by a team of Belarusian doctors found that leukaemia rates among registered liquidators who spent more than 30 days in the 30-km zone were four times higher than the national average. But state registration of Belarusian liquidators only began in 1990-91, by which time some could already have died of acute leukaemia.

In other nuclear incidents, such as at the Sellafield Plant in Great Britain, excess leukaemias were reported for radiation doses equal to or higher than 500 mSv. But fewer than 5 per cent of adults resettled from the Chernobyl area received more than 100 mSv of radiation, so the low overall numbers of leukaemia cases should not come as a shock. In Hiroshima and Nagasaki, the number of new leukaemia cases peaked five to ten years after the explosion so, if leukaemia hasn't increased by now, experts say, the chances are it won't anymore.

Still, efforts continue to try to establish the link. According to Arthur Michalek, dean of the graduate division of the Roswell Park Cancer Institute, "We expected to find and have found increased levels of cancer of the thyroid... We do not know what other cancers may result, but we may look at bone, breast and testicular cancer and infertility issues in this region in the future."

Horrifying expectations?

In addition to leukaemia, a growing number of studies are trying to establish solid links between Chernobyl and increases in other cancers, congenital abnormalities, problem pregnancies and other radiation-induced diseases. But this is difficult, as they remain inconclusive and uncorroborated.

One controversial study which re-analysed the Chernobyl data found that children's malformations – cleft palate, Down's syndrome and deformed limbs and organs – had increased 83 per cent in areas heavily contaminated by Chernobyl, 30 per cent in mildly contaminated areas, and 24 per cent in 'clean' areas. Another study found immune system damage in young people from Belarus who, as children or unborn babies, were exposed to radioactive iodine from Chernobyl.

In the Gomel region of Belarus, the hardest hit by Chernobyl, cancers in children have gone up by more than 60 per cent, blood diseases by 54 per cent, digestive organ diseases by 85 per cent, and psychological disorders have doubled since the accident. Some evidence coming to light also suggests that lung, heart and kidney problems are also linked to radiation from Chernobyl.

While solid scientific evidence is weak, anecdotal indications of other Chernobyl-related diseases are widespread. According to Vladimir Chernousenko, a former member of the Ukraine Academy of Sciences, there is hardly a child in Ukraine today who is not suffering from some immune deficiency disease, whether cardiovascular, lymphoid or oncological. In the Ukraine's three largest provinces, a 1989 medical investigation indicated that the health of every second resident was damaged. In the most contaminated provinces, the incidence of immune deficiency diseases has doubled or tripled since 1985. However disputed their increase, the possibility of further congenital malformations (CM) – such as harelip, cleft palate and polydactylism – among newborn children of Chernobyl survivors should not be dismissed.

At the same time, scientists continue to investigate the possible impacts of Chernobyl on liquidators. They were, after all, the closest to the source. One survey found they suffered from fatigue, apathy and a drop in the number of their white blood cells. A number of other studies

Box 5.2 Red Cross volunteers key to psychosocial recovery

Irina* lives in Gomel, Belarus, on the doorstep of the forbidden zone. But she only heard about the Chernobyl accident days after it happened. Rumours about possible health effects were circulating, but it took years before she realized what kinds of effects. Short of cash, her main worry is her young son's health as she can hardly provide him enough food. A schoolmate's thyroid gland was recently removed when cancer was diagnosed – he now has to take drugs for the rest of his life. Irina's secret fear is that the same fate will befall her son.

Recently, she attended a Red Cross training programme for psychosocial support – the first time ever she could share her anxiety with others the same age. She discovered they had the same concerns, the same fears and the same ignorance about what exactly happened. Several participants burst into tears, but were assured this was normal and that there was nothing and nobody to blame. Irina left feeling very relieved – and convinced of the importance of such sessions. She is now actively involved, providing advice, helping and counselling those who, like her, seek a life free from fear.

Widespread anxiety was reported soon after the disaster among those living in contaminated areas. But due to a shortage of resources, it was only in February 1997 that the Red Cross initiated a psychosocial programme. Its aim is to help people resolve their anxieties and thereby restore their ability to take control of their lives again. Several thousand local people have attended lectures which provide simple, reliable and easily understandable information on radioactivity, its causes and health consequences. Some are counselled by telephone and many more are reached through newspaper articles, radio programmes and TV interviews.

Unlike most humanitarian programmes, psychosocial support does not involve highly visible relief distributions. Relying on person-to-person relationships, it may take some time before results are noticed, as better understanding slowly leads to improved quality of life. Since emotions expressed are so culturally specific, local facilitators volunteering for the Red Cross are involved from the needs-assessment stage onwards. And close cooperation with mental health professionals is critical both for training and supervising the volunteers, and to ensure the referral of more traumatized survivors to specialist care.

* false name

in Sweden and Finland are ongoing but are so far not conclusive. Research by Ukrainian and Israeli scientists suggests that one in three liquidators suffers from sexual or reproductive disorders, and that the number of pregnancies with complications has been on the rise.

For scientists, the basic question remains: are these developments directly traceable to Chernobyl or is the erosion of the health system to blame? But some of those in the humanitarian community find such debates a sidetrack. "We are not interested in proving the connection between radioactive fallout and congenital malformation," said the International Federation's Revel. "We are interested in the humanitarian impact." And that impact may be even more invisible than the causal connections scientists seek.

An unexpected scourge

Imagine a nuclear accident near your home. Then turn on the radio or TV only to find near-silence. Imagine breathing the air and gazing anxiously at the horizon, not knowing whether your lungs are pumping oxygen or poison. And imagine being bundled onto a bus and carted away to a distant city. For hundreds of thousands of people, that's exactly what happened at Chernobyl.

Radioactive rain fell for three months following the accident, while children played in the streets. Yet some villages were only told they had been contaminated more than two and a half years after the event. Official silence surrounded the accident, breeding an attitude of distrust. Although, according to the International Atomic Energy Agency (IAEA), the Soviet authorities acted as well as they could under the circumstances, the lack of communication with victims only made things worse. At the time the Soviet government argued that providing information would lead to mass panic. Yet withholding it eventually caused even more damage.

Silence and stonewalling were accompanied by official apathy. In the West, campaigns, political drives and lobbying for post-Chernobyl safety arose even though the accident was distant. But in the stultified Soviet Union, people had been trained to follow instructions and ask no questions. So they didn't.

"In our street," said one witness, "I went up to a vendor and told her to stop selling her sausages, as radioactive rain was falling. But she just said: 'Be off, you drunkard! If there'd been an accident they'd have announced it on radio and TV'."

Displacement and lack of information fueled what is perhaps the greatest long-term health impact to emerge from the accident: psychological trauma. In contaminated areas, up to 90 per cent of people thought they had, or might have, an illness due to radiation exposure. In 'clean' settlements the figure was 75 per cent. Throughout the region, people feared they might die or at least become very ill (see Box 5.2).

And as people worried about their health and survival, their world crumbled. In the 'old days', people – pensioners, veterans and liquidators – knew life was hard in the Soviet Union, but anxiety was not part of their daily experience. The State would take care of them. Suddenly everyone had to fight for survival, but with inadequate tools. No one in the Soviet Union had been trained for survival as individuals.

The partition of the Soviet Union into independent republics in 1991 shocked people who lost a lifetime of familiar references. The cradle-to-grave guarantees of the hammer and sickle had suddenly become obsolete, replaced by the unfamiliar trappings of a free market system. Political change brought few benefits for the victims of Chernobyl, just more hardship for those less and less able to cope. "What will our future be?" they asked.

According to Pellerin, as many as 3 million people may be suffering from chronic stress disorders as a result of Chernobyl. One researcher claims children evacuated from the reactor zone have suffered a 10- to 15-fold increase in neuropsychiatric disorders. As for adult victims of mental trauma, he compares their state to that suffered by veterans of wars in Viet Nam and Afghanistan.

Two groups were most affected. Topping the list were the liquidators, who included soldiers from throughout the Soviet Union. For the first few days they fought the fire, then they cleared away the debris and finally they built the 'sarcophagus', the concrete casing which protects Chernobyl's radioactive leftovers. In the first few years after the accident they were compensated. Today, their payments – US$ 3 a month in the Ukraine, or the cost of ten loaves of bread – can no longer keep pace with inflation. They call it 'coffin money'.

The other group most affected by psychological stress was the local population. Thirty-six hours after fire broke out at the plant, all 45,000 inhabitants in the neighbouring town of Pripyat were taken away. In the following days, another 20,000 were moved from within the *Zona* and nearby villages. Eventually, some 400,000 would be forced to leave their homes, and over 4 million, three-quarters of them children, would continue to live in areas with some contamination. A staggering 7.1 million would eventually require some kind of special health care.

The elderly suffered doubly. Memories of being forced from home by the Nazi invasion in 1941 came flooding back. Some cling to their contaminated villages, preferring empty houses on deserted streets to foreign suburbs in distant cities, perhaps acting out a desire not to be shifted anymore.

Misunderstanding the stress factors and perhaps in an effort to disclaim complaints, some scientists initially branded the public reaction 'radiophobic', a term no longer in use. This alienated people even further, implying their reactions were irrational or abnormal. Yet there was nothing abnormal about reacting negatively to what was the world's worst nuclear accident, which in turn forced a complete disruption of social and family networks, traditional ways of life, and for some, permanent uprooting from home.

Today, that mistrust remains. Having been betrayed already, people in the contaminated areas no longer believe what they are told – including assurances that the food they eat is as safe as the labels say. Often, they are afraid to have children. This distrust, combined with our continuing ignorance about radioactivity's effects, makes it easy for rumours about genetic mutations to spread, prolonging panic among millions of people.

Land of empty

First their bodies. Then their minds. And on top of that, Chernobyl poisoned the very land which fed them. In the most radioactive areas, the people were moved. But nearly half a million remained in areas still considered contaminated.

Much of the land is barren and some of it downright dangerous. The heart of contamination lies within the *Zona*, whose 30-km radius encompasses nearly 3,000 square km of land. Officially it is devoid of all human activity – but some people never left. They continue to use the forests. They cut timber to build homes, hunt and fish for game, and pick mushrooms and berries. They are never far from danger. Equally alarming is the influx of refugees from Chechnya and other parts of the former USSR, arriving in their hundreds, looking for subsistence in the belief that invisible threats must surely be better than a bullet wound.

The land's contamination will reach far into the region's future. In Belarus, the poisoning of farmland has all but shut down agricultural production, severely undermining human nutrition. Some 20 per cent of forests are still contaminated and 6,000 square km of arable land lie disused. Onto a land of food scarcity, land scarcity has been imposed.

Contamination also killed trees, polluted water and drenched the earth with toxic substances. Some trees next to the plant, in what is called the 'red forest', were so irradiated they had to be destroyed as radioactive waste. Should contaminated forests catch fire, clouds of smoke carrying radioactive materials could waft far beyond national borders.

With the water-table at risk, drinking water remains dangerous and monitoring will be needed for a long time. Authorities are keeping an eye on floods, and planning huge works to keep the contaminated Pripyat River from overflowing into the Dnieper River in the Ukraine, which supplies water to 35 million people. Flooding could also wash contamination from waste dumps into groundwater, further contaminating rivers and drinking water.

A land which could have provided plentiful food and shelter for transitional nations struggling to emerge from behind the Iron Curtain has been soiled and mortgaged, some of it stripped of life forever.

Scientific squabbling

Action on Chernobyl has been hamstrung by disputes over numbers and proofs. One of the most disputed figures is Chernobyl's death toll, which some observers call absurdly low. Vladimir Chernousenko, for example, pegs the figure at between 7,000 and 10,000 volunteers dead from high-intensity exposure right after the accident.

Future or potential deaths are also in dispute. According to some scientists in the former Soviet Union, an additional 30,000 to 40,000 deaths from cancers can be expected over the next 70 years. For many Western experts, on the other hand, these figures are extremely overestimated. Scientists do not even agree on who was hurt by what. With the exception of iodine-131, to which people were acutely exposed, some scientists argue that the radionuclides released by Chernobyl have added little to our natural radiation exposure.

In the end, most people who pronounced opinions on Chernobyl at the time got it wrong. The optimists believed the Chernobyl issue would simply evaporate, while the pessimists expected massive deaths, unspeakable mutations and blankets of unbreathable, irradiated air. "Everyone was taken by surprise, the optimists as well as the pessimists," concluded the International Federation's Revel.

But disputes about numbers and predictions should not stand in the way of action – there are enough tangible facts to warrant immediate response. Outside the moribund reactor, tens of thousands of tonnes of contaminated materials have been stored in some 800 hastily-built sites dotted around the exclusion zone – partly buried in trenches, partly sealed in containers isolated from groundwater by clay or concrete screens, and often, simply stored above ground. The potential hazards posed by these time bombs remain to be addressed.

The sarcophagus, a towering mass of 300,000 tonnes of concrete covered with 50,000 tonnes of steel plates, is leaking. It was built, according to the Organisation for Economic Co-operation and Development (OECD), "as a provisional barrier pending the definition of a

Box 5.3 International assistance programmes for Chernobyl

The International Federation's Chernobyl Humanitarian Assistance and Rehabilitation Programme (CHARP), which began in 1990, may be the oldest programme operating in Chernobyl, but the United Nations is also extensively involved:

- WHO helps diagnose thyroid cancer in children and provides health care to liquidators;
- FAO removes strontium-90 and caesium-137 from milk with a magnetic separation technique;
- IAEA rehabilitates waste-disposal sites and provides safety and management training;
- UNESCO oversees social-psychological centres;
- UNICEF provides iodized salt to people living near Chernobyl;
- the UN Development Programme studies soil and water for contamination;
- the International Labour Organization helps workers laid off and resettled because of gradual plant closure;
- the UN Industrial Development Organization assists in economic rehabilitation and modernization of enterprises; and
- the UN's Office for the Coordination of Humanitarian Affairs administers the UN Chernobyl Fund and is involved in research and training.

Non-UN groups are just as active:

- the European Union (EU) has extensive programmes in nuclear emergency preparedness, nuclear safety and radiation protection;
- the G7 through the EBRD is raising funds to seal the sarcophagus and help find alternative sources of energy; and
- the World Bank runs technical and econo-mic rehabilitation programmes in energy development.

The US government has allocated US$ 550 million since 1991 for the safety of east European reactors.

more radical solution for the elimination of the destroyed reactor and the safe disposal of the highly radioactive materials." Its walls were actually designed to be permeable in order to air-cool the melted reactor. But the roof is cracked and the metal which supports it is corroding. Rain and snow can get inside. If it were ever to collapse, large amounts of radioactive dust would probably be released.

Dealing with these leftover radioactive wastes is one of the highest priorities among those involved in Chernobyl's cleanup. Through the European Bank for Reconstruction and Development (EBRD), G7 nations have already raised US$ 450 million of the US$ 1 billion needed to seal the sarcophagus and find alternative sources of energy.

Science is being applied to making life liveable in a post-Chernobyl world. Experiments are attempting to remove caesium-137 from food or trying to keep it from entering the soil. And after succeeding in removing it from water, another experiment is trying to remove it from milk. Some relatively simple, inexpensive and successful agricultural measures are being tested: deep ploughing of surface contaminated soils; adding fertilizers or other chemicals to agricultural lands; changes in crop types; shifting feeding regimes and slaughtering times of cattle; using impregnated 'Prussian Blue' salt licks to limit the transfer of caesium to cattle; and relocating animals to uncontaminated pastures. Other international assistance programmes are outlined in Box 5.3.

Even some institutional advances have emerged out of the disaster. Chernobyl's transboundary nature spawned global efforts to further cooperation in understanding and dealing with emergencies. A number of treaties were improved or elaborated, including international conventions on early notification and assistance in case of a radiological accident by the IAEA and the European Community; an international nuclear emergency exercises programme by the OECD's Nuclear Energy Agency (NEA); an international accident severity scale by the IAEA and NEA; and an international agreement on food contamination by the Food and Agriculture Organization (FAO) and WHO.

Outstanding needs

But beyond the immediate technical fixes lies a plethora of humanitarian needs. Some, though not all, are being addressed, mostly through international aid. CHARP, the Chernobyl Humanitarian Assistance and Rehabilitation Programme, is the International Federation's approach to helping Chernobyl victims. When it started in 1990, CHARP screened food supplies for contamination but, as the radiation situation stabilized, its work spread to diagnosis and screening of local inhabitants. Today, the programme provides extensive assistance for up to 4 million Belarusians, Ukrainians and Russians living in contaminated areas, to help them overcome radiation-related stress. Six mobile labs focus on children or on those who were children at the time of the accident, screening for thyroid cancer and accumulated radioactivity in the body. But it would need 20 such labs to do the job properly.

The ongoing nature of the Chernobyl disaster demands that humanitarian assistance develop into a long-term programme, yet efforts remain hamstrung by insufficient funds from short-term aid budgets. CHARP is slated to continue working around Chernobyl until 2006, but officials wonder whether this is realistic. In a statement to the plenary of the 54th United Nations (UN) General Assembly in November 1999, the International Federation's permanent representative to the UN said: "There is a real danger that our involvement will have to be discontinued." There is little money available and what there is goes on the technical fix, not the humanitarian need. Only a fraction of aid appeals for Chernobyl are funded. Yet humanitarian needs – principally psychosocial counselling, food monitoring and mobile screening labs – could be covered until 2006 with less than 5 per cent of the total budget being sought by the G7 for technical work.

Nor can the cash-strapped economies of the former Soviet Union resolve things on their own. Ukraine is already spending more than 5 per cent of its annual budget dealing with the fallout from Chernobyl, and has introduced a special income tax of 12 per cent to raise the necessary revenue. It provides benefits to Chernobyl survivors – free housing to 3 million people officially recognized as suffering from the catastrophe, including 356,000 liquidators and 870,000 children. Belarus and the Russian Federation are struggling to help. But with a third of all Russians living on less than a dollar a day, funding requests for Chernobyl's survivors must compete with other pressing priorities.

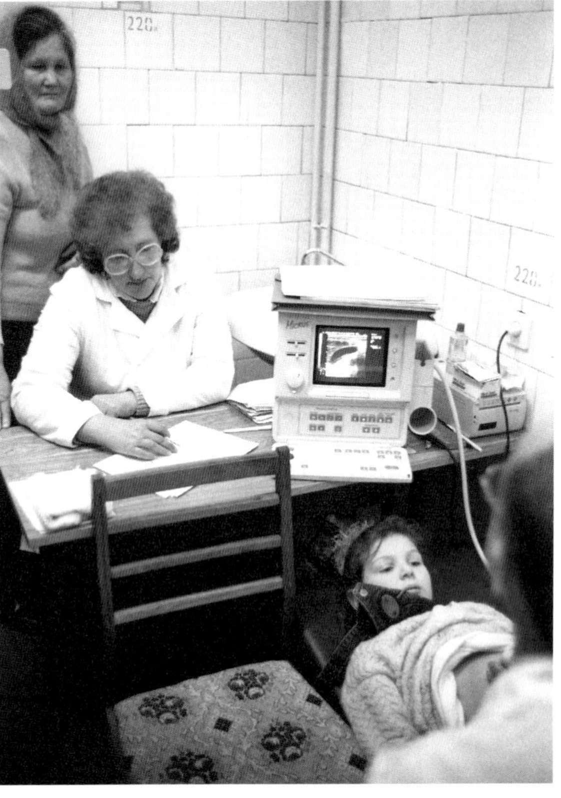

A Ukrainian girl is tested for thyroid cancer, caused by radioactive iodine-131 and fatal if not treated. In some areas surrounding Chernobyl, thyroid cancer rates shot up 100-fold after the accident. Cases are forecast to peak around 2005.

Photo: Jean-Pierre Revel, Ukraine 1998.

The accident's own invisibility defies attempts to focus attention. Some effects were tangible, such as thyroid cancer. But much of the accident's health impact lies in its psychological repercussions. Mobilizing action and money is difficult enough for visible disasters. Doing so for immeasurable damage from unseen particles is harder still. As international aid budgets continue to shrink and donors move on to the next emergency, the hundreds of thousands of Chernobyl survivors are in severe danger of being forgotten. Keeping Chernobyl on the agenda of donors will remain a challenge for the foreseeable future.

Next time?

The threat of more nuclear accidents looms large at the 60 or so Soviet-designed reactors currently operating in the newly independent states and central and eastern Europe. Fifteen of them are RMBK reactors as at Chernobyl, and some will never reach international safety standards. Is this really the right time to scale back assistance?

Box 5.4 Flaws at Tokai-mura look familiar

A blue flash on 30 September 1999 heralded Japan's worst ever nuclear accident. In a nuclear facility at Tokai-mura, some 90 km north of Tokyo, three workers bypassed normal procedures and poured seven times too much uranium oxide into a steel tank. The ensuing chain-reaction or 'criticality' released enormous amounts of energy in the form of neutron and gamma radiation. The micro-nuclear reactor they had created took some 20 hours to bring under control, by which time hundreds of people, both workers and members of the public, had been contaminated with dangerously high levels of radioactivity.

Almost immediately, the worker closest to the steel tank collapsed and began vomiting. Having received lethal doses of radiation, he died three months later, despite exhaustive medical attention. While the emergency services began removing the workers from the accident scene within ten minutes, they were not immediately informed about the high levels of radioactivity. Consequently they too received dangerous doses of radiation.

Are there any lessons to be learned from Japan's accident which reinforce those learned from Chernobyl? Technically, the two accidents greatly differed – Tokai-mura is a nuclear fuel-processing facility, not a nuclear power station. But, as at Chernobyl, inherent dangers of nuclear technology, combined with human error, weak regulations and poor public information exacerbated the human tragedy dealt by Tokai-mura.

Poor safety guidelines for handling medium-enriched uranium were further weakened by the operating company. Workers were poorly trained and unaware of the potentially explosive materials they were handling. Worse still, Tokai-mura had received inadequate official onsite inspection in the past which could have uncovered such shortcomings.

The consequences of the accident were aggravated by a slow emergency response in the critical first hours when radioactive emissions were at their highest. It was over seven hours before neutron radiation measurements were taken at the perimeter of the site, confirming that the criticality was still under way. And given that neutron radiation travelled at least 2 km, the 350-metre exclusion zone was inadequate.

Health checks were initially restricted to external body examinations, even though radiation received was deep-penetrating gamma and neutron doses, causing only limited external contamination. But it is possible to take simple blood salt measurements within the first few hours which would have given reasonably accurate readings of actual radiation doses.

As at Chernobyl, lack of accurate and timely public information unnecessarily endangered local people. Many remained unaware of the accident or the need to evacuate an area around the plant (located in a semi-residential area). The evacuation zone itself was poorly policed with many people passing within 100 metres of the building when radiation readings were still high. After the criticality was stopped the following day, emergency workers received significant gamma radiation doses while building protective concrete and aluminium fluoride walls. And the decision to allow people back into the exclusion zone was made while radiation remained at least five times above background levels.

Initial government claims that no members of the public received a radiation dose proved inaccurate. By February 2000, the authorities had acknowledged that 439 people were affected, some receiving more than 100 times the maximum recommended annual radiation exposure. Long-term health monitoring, initially not considered necessary, is now likely.

Japan operates 52 large-scale nuclear reactors, as well as hundreds of nuclear-related facilities. New safety and emergency regulations rapidly passed by the Japanese government, while welcome in principle, will not significantly reduce the risk of further serious accidents in Japan.

Chernobyl forced authorities and experts around the world to radically review their approach to radiation protection and nuclear emergency issues. Many countries established nationwide emergency plans in addition to existing local ones, and Chernobyl gave new impetus to nuclear safety research. The accident renewed efforts to expand knowledge on the harmful effects of radiation and its medical treatment, and led to soul-searching on the issue of public information. Chernobyl has already taught us many things – but we still have more to learn.

Given its horrifying impacts, known and not yet known, can anything be done to prevent future Chernobyls? And if there are no guarantees, can we at least ensure that if they do happen, their effects are not as catastrophic?

In retrospect, the walls of institutional silence which surrounded the Chernobyl catastrophe caused unnecessary levels of radioactive contamination and psychological trauma. If people had been better informed and moved more quickly during those crucial first few days, radiation doses might have been lower, the crisis less lengthy. Silence intensified people's fears about their health and especially that of their children.

Fourteen years later, officials remain uncomfortable with transparency and efforts to obtain information are still clouded in controversy and confusion. It is perhaps unreasonable to expect major changes in attitude. After all, many of those making decisions today are the same ones who made them on 26 April 1986. But greater openness could yield numerous benefits – it could encourage even greater technology sharing between East and West, modernization, better preparedness and training, improved early warning and response mechanisms. It could also help comfort the millions who still live in Chernobyl's shadow.

Humanitarian agencies were slow to reach the disaster zone. In truth, few had experience of nuclear disasters – while many were trying to deal with the fallout from famine in the Horn of Africa. Nor was it part of the mindset of the Soviet Union in 1986 to call in international support. The first international team to visit the disaster zone arrived two years after the accident. And while local Red Cross branches distributed relief goods early on, it was not until January 1990 that the International Federation made the first humanitarian assessment of the situation. The role of humanitarian agencies, a dedicated radiation response team, and rapid evacuation measures could all form part of a government plan to deal with future nuclear emergencies.

Greater preparedness would clearly alleviate suffering. New evidence suggests some thyroid cancers can be prevented if potassium iodide tablets are distributed within three hours of the accident. Dilwyn Williams runs a thyroid cancer research unit attached to Cambridge University: "One of the major lessons we have learned is the extreme sensitivity of the youngest children… They should have done more to make sure potassium iodide was available." The use of preventive iodine is now widespread in Western countries with nuclear facilities.

Key to avoiding future accidents would be an increase in vigilance and upgrading the safety of installations, with regular rehearsals and evaluations of mistakes made. One would have hoped that Chernobyl had instilled a culture of greater caution into the nuclear industry. Yet repeated accidents – even in countries that have experienced nuclear catastrophe before, such as Japan – show this has not happened (see Box 5.4).

Hope denied?

It happened in an instant, but Chernobyl's effects will survive far longer than we will. No longer an emergency, it is worse – a chronic disaster, a rehabilitation problem that has dragged on so long it has exhausted donors. In a sound-bite world of short attention spans and media-driven impatience, sustaining donor interest takes more than mere need or urgency. It takes instant, vivid video, and Chernobyl has little to offer in terms of exciting footage. The accident is old, at times too old to be remembered by the young journalists who cover such things. Their attention shifts quickly – to earthquakes in Turkey, to floods in South Asia.

Yet ongoing work at Chernobyl is essential and, if anything, response should be strengthened, not diluted. Waiting for all the scientists to agree may cost lives. Uncertainty should not be used as a cover for inaction. Chernobyl remains a desperate situation, where millions are still suffering – whether physically, psychologically or economically. Add to the woes of forced displacement and invisible diseases the additional burden of post-Soviet economic and institutional collapse – and the case for strengthening humanitarian action is compelling.

If some have relegated Chernobyl to the slag heap of history along with the Soviet Union, the truth is that the catastrophe continues to devastate the populations of three countries a decade and a half after it happened. In fact, the worst may be yet to come. If we have learned one health lesson from Hiroshima and Nagasaki, it is that cancers caused by radiation can take many years to detect. Thyroid cancers, for example, are expected to peak around 2005 – and will continue to appear until those who were children in 1986 grow old.

Chernobyl still has lessons to teach both nuclear industries and humanitarian agencies. "The expertise we are gaining in how to deal with the aftermath of nuclear accidents is unique," said the International Federation's desk officer for the region. Chernobyl is an ongoing public health disaster for those living in its shadow. But it is also an opportunity for richer nations – not just to learn how to avoid future mistakes, but to lend a helping hand to millions of people on whom flawed technology and fractured politics have inflicted decades of continuous suffering.

Sources and further information

Health and Information: From Uncertainties to Interventions in the Chernobyl Contaminated Regions. Papers presented to the 2nd International Scientific Conference on the Consequences of Chernobyl Catastrophe, 1997.

Darby, Sarah. "Radiation Risks." *British Medical Journal,* 16 October 1999.

Dufay, Joanne. *Ten Years After Chernobyl: A Witness to the Devastation.* Greenpeace Canada, 1996.

Edwards, Rob. "Too Hot to Handle." *New Scientist,* 5 June 1999.

Guterman, Lila. "Back to Chernobyl." *New Scientist,* 10 April 1999.

Henshaw, Denis L. "Chernobyl 10 years on." *British Medical Journal,* April 1996.

International Atomic Energy Agency (IAEA). *Booklet.* Conference: One Decade After Chernobyl: Summing Up the Consequences of the Accident. Vienna: IAEA, April 1996.

International Federation of Red Cross and Red Crescent Societies. *Coping with Crisis.* Geneva: International Federation, 1996.

International Federation of Red Cross and Red Crescent Societies. "Insight: Chernobyl." *Emergency Report.* Geneva: International Federation, 1996.

International Federation of Red Cross and Red Crescent Societies. "Chernobyl Humanitarian Assistance and Rehabilitation Programme (CHARP): Evaluation." *Mission Reports,* Geneva: International Federation, 1996 and 1999.

Josefson, Deborah. "Childhood thyroid cancers rise 10-fold in the Ukraine." *British Medical Journal,* 1999.

Knight, Gary. "Where is the next Chernobyl?" *Newsweek.* October 18, 1999.

Maconochie, Noreen. "The Nuclear Industry Family Study: Linkage of Occupational Exposures to Reproduction and Child Health." *British Medical Journal,* 1999.

Mitchell, Peter. "Ukrainian Thyroid Cancer Rates Greatly Increased Since Chernobyl." *The Lancet,* 3 July 1999.

Roman, Eve, et al. "Cancer in Children of Nuclear Industry Employees: Report on Children Aged Under 25 Years from Nuclear Industry Family Study." *British Medical Journal,* 1999.

Roswell Park Cancer Institute. "Health Effects of Chernobyl Accident after 13 Years." *News Release,* Buffalo (USA), 1999.

Shcherbak, Yuri M. "Ten Years of the Chernobyl Era." *Scientific American,* April 1996.

Williams, Prof. E. D. "Thyroid Effects." *Report to the Chernobyl Project.* Vienna: IAEA, 1990.

World Health Organization (WHO). "Health Consequences of the Chernobyl Accident: Results of the IPHECA Pilot Projects and Related National Programmes." *Scientific Report.* Geneva: WHO, 1996.

WHO. "Health Consequences of the Chernobyl Accident." *Summary Report.* IPHECA Pilot Projects and Related National Programmes. Geneva: WHO, 1995.

Web sites

British Medical Journal – http://www.bmj.org
Chernobyl – http://www.chernobyl.com
Environmental News Network – http://www.enn.com
Greenpeace – http://www.greenpeace.org
International Atomic Energy Agency – http://www.iaea.org
International Federation of Red Cross and Red Crescent Societies – http://www.ifrc.org
Kurchatov Institute – http://www.kiae.ru
OECD Nuclear Energy Agency – http://www.nea.fr
Radiation Health Effects (RadEFX) – http://www.radefx.bcm.tmc.edu
UN Office for the Coordination of Humanitarian Affairs – http://www.reliefweb.int/ocha
Uranium Institute – http://www.uilondon.org
US Department of Energy – http://www.ne.doe.gov
World Health Organization – http://www.who.org

chapter 6

Section One

Focus on public health

Kosovo – the humanitarian Klondike

Many observers believe that Kosovo in 1999 constituted the worst humanitarian disaster in Europe since the end of World War II. NATO bombardments against the Serb-dominated government of Yugoslav President Slobodan Milosevic – indicted of war crimes against Kosovar Albanians – represented a magnitude of military assault not witnessed on the continent for almost half a century. The conflict also culminated in the forced exodus of over 1 million refugees. Many fled to neighbouring countries such as Albania, Macedonia and Montenegro, while others sought refuge within Kosovo itself.

Yet the initial humanitarian response in many ways failed to match the needs of a modern European refugee crisis. Intense media coverage led to hundreds of aid agencies swarming into the region, which, added to NATO member states' own humanitarian and political agenda, made coordinated action virtually impossible. "It was a bit like a humanitarian Klondike [gold rush] with everyone trying to set up projects," said Folke Lampen, health coordinator of the International Committee of the Red Cross (ICRC) in Pristina.

Too much short-term aid hampered local efforts at recovery. Longer-term strategic vision and commitment of resources are needed to address the ongoing rehabilitation of Kosovo's public health infrastructure and chronic needs such as psychosocial support for mentally traumatized Kosovars. Yet ethnic tensions and violence throughout the region continue to frustrate efforts at rehabilitating both services and society.

Immediate impact on public health

The initial refugee crisis did not provoke any dramatic public health disasters, such as epidemics of cholera or typhoid. For the majority of Kosovars, the immediate refugee plight was less than three months. Only those displaced among the mountains of Kosovo with little food or shelter suffered from overt signs of malnutrition, fatigue and other ailments. In no manner did the situation reflect the humanitarian disasters associated with large-scale refugee crises such as in Somalia, Afghanistan or Central Africa. Kosovars' demands were quite different – having just fled their homeland, for example, many wished to contact family members by mobile telephone.

Most immediate health problems were the result of chronic or acute medical needs from pre-existing conditions, such as diabetes, dehydration or war injuries. Mines and unexploded ordnance (UXO) such as cluster bombs – including many dropped by NATO – caused up to 170 casualties during the first month of refugee returns, according to the World Health Organization (WHO). Personal safety remains threatened by 425 minefields identified by the Kosovo Peacekeeping Force (KFOR) throughout the province.

In reality, many Albanian Kosovars, who had fled their homes fearing for their lives during winter 1998-99, survived on their own without substantial outside assistance. When Serb

Photo opposite page:
Over a million refugees were forced to flee Kosovo during 1999, many at gunpoint. The assault, rape and murder of thousands of Kosovars, plus the destruction of 90,000 mainly ethnic Albanian homes, have taken a heavy psychological toll.

Photo: Boris Grdanoski/AP, Macedonia 1999.

intimidation forced more to leave in spring 1999, most refugees fled in relatively good physical condition and remained so throughout their period of exile.

Over two-thirds of the estimated 450,000 refugees who fled to Albania, one of Europe's poorest countries, were taken in by host families in an extraordinary show of solidarity by their fellow ethnic counterparts. Similarly, in Macedonia, where nearly a third of the overall population are ethnic Albanian, locals took in some 150,000 out of more than 250,000 arrivals. The rest lived in tented camps or 'collective centres'. Only as sanitary conditions deteriorated in the camps with the warm weather in May and June 1999 did aid agencies report a rise of 30 to 40 per cent in health problems, such as diarrhoea. Many refugees, notably children, also suffered from skin irritations due to increased dust and water shortages.

While Kosovo did not suffer a public health disaster, the repression leading up to the crisis and the way the crisis was handled by the international community, had – and still have – a crucial bearing on public health. Yugoslavia's own socialist-influenced welfare past, with its overwhelming focus on tertiary health care, has also been critical in shaping Kosovo's health-sector needs.

Legacy of repression

The traumatic dislocation at gunpoint of hundreds of thousands of Kosovar Albanians coupled with the long-term, negative influence of Serb repression over the previous decade, has taken more of a psychological than physical toll. According to leading medical aid organizations, mental trauma represents a principal health concern in Kosovo today (see Box 6.1).

"The refugee crisis was the first emergency to deal with psychosocial trauma from day one," noted Stefan Baumgartner of the International Federation of Red Cross and Red Crescent Societies in Pristina. "We were fully aware of the problem based on earlier assessments so there was clearly an urgent need to assist communities under stress, even if the Kosovars have proven to be a very resilient people."

Since 1989, many Kosovars have lived in a state of constant fear and insecurity in the face of repression from Belgrade. Politically ostracized, ethnic Albanians also found themselves ousted from their jobs as teachers, journalists, engineers and civil servants. Their shops, businesses, schools and clinics were also shut down. Many, including qualified medical personnel, simply left the province in search of employment abroad.

Doctors and nurses were specifically targeted by the Serb effort to destroy institutionalized medical care for Kosovar Albanians. The parallel medical care system which arose to care for ethnic Albanians (supported by the local Mother Theresa Foundation) was shattered when Serb forces began to drive people out. But now it will form a significant part of any restructured health system in Kosovo.

Repression of Kosovo's ethnic Albanian community climaxed in 1998-99 with the destruction of 80,000 to 90,000 mainly Albanian houses. Some were ruined during the NATO bombardments, but most were burned, ransacked or booby-trapped by Serb military and paramilitary actions aimed at forcing ethnic Albanians to leave. Wells were left polluted by debris including human or animal corpses.

An issue still being investigated by international human rights organizations is the hunting down of thousands of men, women and children by Yugoslavia's security forces, sometimes with the alleged collusion of local Serb and Roma (gypsy) populations. Many were beaten, murdered, raped, kidnapped, tortured or assaulted. Hundreds of thousands were forced to abandon their homes by foot and by car, or jammed into buses, trucks and tractor trailers, to seek refuge in the mountains or across the border. Even bedridden hospital patients were forced to leave.

While the Serbian regime in Belgrade argued that the refugee flight was caused by NATO bombing, various studies carried out by Human Rights Watch, Physicians for Human Rights and other monitoring groups have clearly determined that the bulk of Kosovar Albanians had fled the country as a direct result of Serb repression. All this has contributed to the stress and anxiety now found among so many Kosovars.

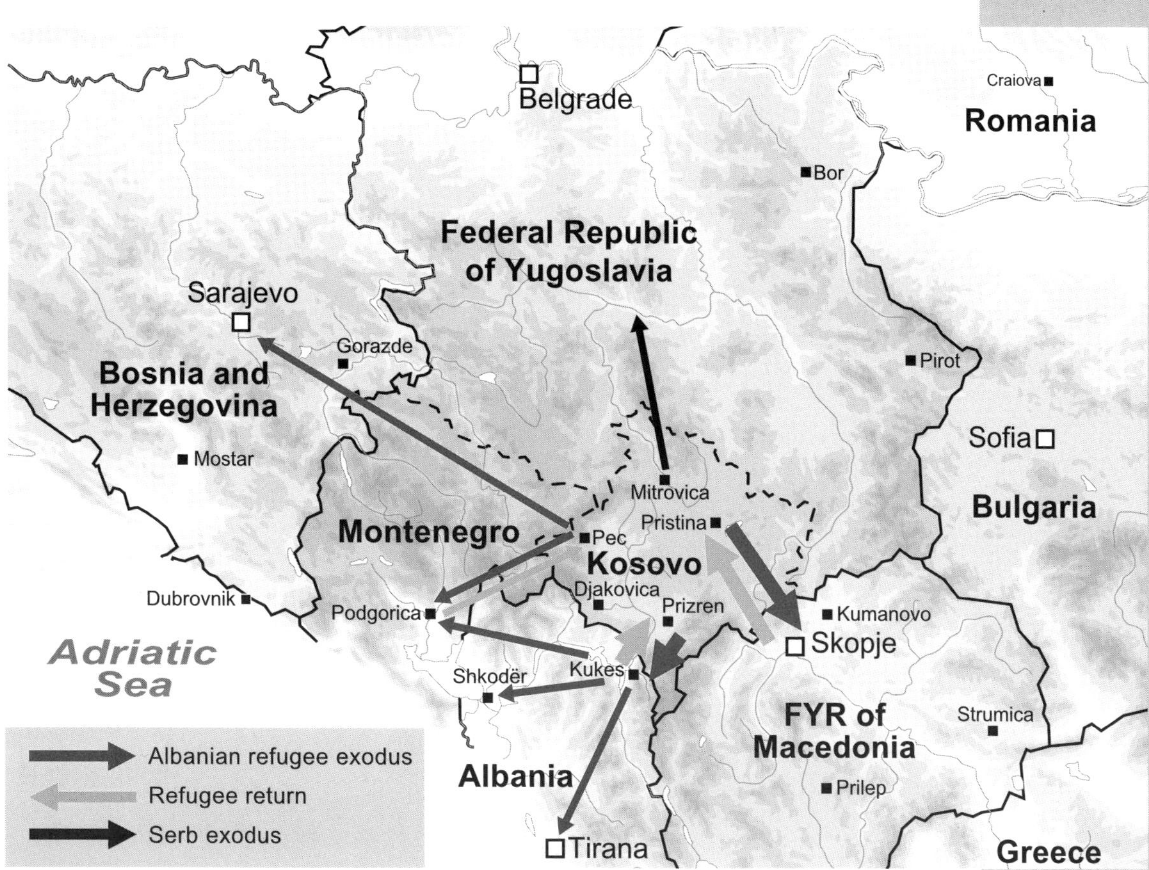

Source: UNHCR.

Refugee crisis wrongfoots humanitarian response

The humanitarian intervention in Kosovo demonstrated remarkably few lessons learned from the Somali or Rwandan experiences, even though, as one regional coordinator for the non-governmental organization (NGO) International Rescue Committee (IRC) pointed out during the early stages in Albania, "this is the last chance for the international community, and above all the NGOs, to get it right." If not, he warned, the mandate for helping refugees and other victims of war would be gradually assumed by the military and, increasingly, the private sector (see Box 6.2).

Box 6.1 Ten tons of darkness

"I have ten tons of darkness to unload," confessed Flutra, a 19-year-old Albanian Kosovar from Prizren. Her home town, nestled at the foot of snowcapped mountains in Kosovo's south-east corner, smouldered as she spoke. A month after NATO had finished bombing the province in June 1999, ethnic Albanians were busy setting Serb homes alight in vengeance attacks, despite the presence of peacekeeping troops.

An hour up the road, in Gjakova (known in Serbian as Djakovica) we had met Agim Byci, editor of Radio Gjakova and chairman of the local cultural union. He was lucky enough to escape when masked men came to burn ethnic Albanian houses. One of them shouted at Byci: "You have a minute to get out to Albania," before shooting dead a neighbour in front of him and his wife. Instead, Byci dug a hole in a friend's garden and hid.

Over 1,000 men, women and children were killed in Gjakova alone, claimed Byci. He showed us the photos of 20 women and children murdered, so he said, on 26 March 1999 by Serb paramilitaries and tossed into a mass grave. One five-year-old boy played dead and was being guarded as a witness to war crimes.

In Gjakova and the neighbouring town of Peja (Pec in Serbian), thousands of houses lay in ruins – burnt reminders of a black chapter in Balkan history. A month after the bombing stopped, unclaimed, unburied bodies still littered the rubble. How were Kosovars trying to deal with the trauma of such desperate, recent memories? Down in Prizren, the local radio station had started to broadcast a daily programme entitled 'We are looking for the people we know'. The programme worked with the ICRC in trying to locate some of the estimated 2,000 young men abducted from Kosovo and taken prisoner in Serbia. The station also broadcast information on humanitarian activities – reconstruction, health, aid deliveries.

What, if anything, can international agencies do to mitigate mental suffering? "We must train locals in the basic principles of psychology: how to listen and talk, how to give skills and reassurance, how to use gifts and activities with kids, how to organize support meetings," argues a senior mental health official with WHO.

"Stimulate suffering people by returning a sense of normality, busy-ness and routine to their lives. Sufferers must forget, then talk, then forget – forgetting is their oxygen. Talking should be within local groups, so train local doctors, nurses or teachers within an existing social group to guide the talking," adds the official. "But mourning is the first phase, that of denial and silence – so don't push people to talk too soon."

"Now I feel nothing," Agim Byci told us in July last year. "I am talking as a robot. Every minute I am waiting for a paramilitary soldier to come to my house. I was waiting for bullets and bombs for three months. I don't know exactly if I am in freedom or not. Perhaps this job helps me forget the time of war." Only Byci can be the judge of when he is ready to remember again.

Logistically, many agencies thought the crisis would be straightforward given that it was on western Europe's doorstep and included the direct intervention of NATO forces. Yet when tens of thousands of refugees began pouring into Albania, Macedonia and Montenegro in early 1999, the initial humanitarian response could not cope with the scale of the crisis. From 24 March 1999, when the NATO bombing first began, until early June, when the peace agreement was signed, over half the country's ethnic Albanians – originally 85 per cent of Kosovo's 2 million people – fled.

Certain agencies, some of which had been operational in Kosovo during the 1990s but were forced to leave as Serb repression worsened, were on hand within days to assist the refugees. Medical groups such as Médecins sans Frontières (MSF), Médecins du Monde (MDM), International Medical Corps and the Red Cross Red Crescent Movement were in the forefront. For the most part, however, there were often no aid workers to meet the refugees at the border.

Refugees had left the bulk of their food supplies behind in Serb-controlled areas, and little was readily available in Albania and Macedonia. But only ten days after the start of the bombing did NATO create relief areas in the affected countries and begin to divert its resources towards the humanitarian effort. Some observers, however, argue that such humanitarian relief is beyond NATO's mandate.

International aid agencies and donors, including the United Nations (UN), took as long as NATO to begin delivering effective assistance to this hapless exodus of people. This was despite the fact that ample early warning of a massive crisis in the offing had been provided by journalists, human rights groups, select aid agencies and military intelligence.

In what has become a characteristic reluctance to respond with foresight to a possible if not probable humanitarian crisis, many international donors refused to contemplate the need to take pre-emptive measures. The Office of the UN High Commissioner for Refugees (UNHCR) found itself strapped for both cash and equipment, such as tents and communications support. As a result, UNHCR literally had to beg for appropriate funds or was obliged to borrow off humanitarian operations from other parts of the world in order to cope. Donor pledges for health, food and other forms of refugee relief and humanitarian assistance were often drawn from programmes already committed to Africa and Asia. As one European Union official noted: "Some governments are simply reshuffling aid to the detriment of victims elsewhere."

Coordination vacuum

Perhaps most shocking of all was that, as in previous emergencies, there was no effective coordination of humanitarian relief, neither by the UN nor the NGOs. Notwithstanding the numerous evaluations that emerged following the humanitarian crises of the earlier 1990s strongly recommending firmer coordination of international aid activities, it took weeks for any such direction to be implemented.

To aid organizations and observers outside the UN system, it was not clear which UN agency had been assigned the role of overall coordinator. During the first three weeks of the humanitarian response in Albania in April 1999, the UN Office for the Coordination of Humanitarian Affairs (OCHA) was nowhere to be seen. In fact, most aid agency representatives interviewed by the *World Disasters Report* during this period had little if any idea of what OCHA was doing, or whether it was indeed active. Nor did anyone have any clear idea who was supposed to be responsible for coordination, whether NATO, the Albanian government or the UN. One senior UNHCR official in Tirana said: "I think OCHA is around somewhere, but I think we're the ones supposed to be doing the coordination." Only later in Kosovo did OCHA begin to adopt a higher profile.

It took about a month for UNHCR to assertively assume the coordinating role and sign a general protocol with the Albanian government creating the Emergency Management Group (EMG). This spelled out respective roles and responsibilities within the international aid effort. Meeting daily, the EMG sought to provide overall coordination through operational desks for food, shelter, health, logistics and security.

Despite initial UNHCR reservations, for the first time ever in a humanitarian operation involving the military, NATO granted access to a specialized – and editorially independent – media representative to gather critical background data of relief operations. Officially incorporated as part of the EMG, the journalist sought to assess and, through radio programming, meet the information needs of refugees – such as news on issues ranging from emergency medical assistance to food distribution and vaccination campaigns (see Box 6.3).

In early May, a Humanitarian Information Centre was set up in Tirana for local and international NGOs, the UN, NATO and support governments. Relief representatives discussed the need to monitor performance, provide accountability for their actions along the lines of the Sphere Project's minimum standards, assess the impact of aid on local communities, and establish an ombudsman function. Whether such aims were actually achieved remains debatable.

So how could coordination have been improved? The independent evaluation of UNHCR's role in Kosovo argues that:

- prioritizing shared resources such as warehousing, transport and communications could provide a bridge between assistance packages of different actors;
- the exact role of the lead agency needs to be better defined, to avoid variable expectations and interpretations;
- 'surge mechanisms', such as temporary loaning of staff from other agencies to enable a more effective response to sudden-onset crises, should be examined;
- pre-arranged contractual and funding obligations with other humanitarian actors could ensure a more authoritative coordination role;
- credible leadership is more likely to come from staff well-trained to coordinate;
- joint contingency planning with the military could lead to more sharing of information; and
- UNHCR can only coordinate those willing to be coordinated. Responsibility for weak coordination in the Kosovo response is shared equally between UNHCR, other humanitarian actors and donors.

Box 6.2 Military and private sector challenge established aid providers

Rising involvement of the military and private sector in the humanitarian response to Kosovo's refugee crisis contributed overwhelmingly to a confusion of roles in health assistance. Never before have military disaster relief operations been of such size. In many instances, theirs was the first emergency medical assistance available – something which military public relations departments covet. There is nothing like media images of military helicopters, vehicles or medical teams helping refugees or bringing assistance to old-age pensioners too scared to leave home.

In Macedonia, the German military operated a camp for 3,200 refugees, including an eight-tent hospital with operating and emergency rooms, separate wards for men and women, and a staff of 20 medical professionals, among them four doctors. Italian, Spanish, French, and other NATO military components (including the Israelis, not members of NATO) were also involved in providing health care to refugees.

The International Federation refused to rely on the military for support as did other relief agencies. However, the Austrian, Belgian, German and Italian Red Cross Societies worked individually beside the military – but not without problems. International Federation representatives said they had advised National Societies only to accept security from the soldiers.

Toby Porter, emergency programme coordinator for Oxfam in Albania, pointed out that NATO forces tended to establish camps without the input of experienced site planners. Latrines were often poorly sited and tents placed too close together. Such mistakes could have been avoided had aid agencies been involved earlier. And, maintained Porter, the "guiding principle for many donor governments was to pour as much money as possible into 'their' camp, and to try and attract the maximum number of refugees there." This exacerbated coordination problems as camps were often prepared without informing UNHCR.

There is no doubt the military are far better equipped than most aid agencies to cope rapidly and effectively with war injuries under certain circumstances. But their facilities are not fully geared to deal with civilian requirements. In Albania and Macedonia, for example, they had no incubators to handle newborn babies, but this did not prevent them from improvising.

NATO forces eventually handed over their camps and medical responsibilities to aid organizations such as the Red Cross Red Crescent Movement. NGOs were often selected and funded by NATO country donors based on shared nationality with the camps. While the military, with vast and costly logistical resources at their disposal, performed a remarkable job, the involvement of uniformed NATO personnel in humanitarian assistance has raised some very pointed and uncomfortable questions for the aid community.

Leading aid representatives have repeatedly pointed out that the military cannot be considered impartial. The presence of uniformed NATO personnel acting as aid workers in refugee camps or clinics, while their forces were also caught up in military action, threatened the neutrality of aid workers, they warned. "The two need to be kept clearly separate," said James Orbinski, president of MSF International. If not, he warned, belligerents may regard civilian relief operations, such as aid convoys or medical teams, as legitimate targets.

Both during emergency and reconstruction phases, private business has been seeking contracts for everything from medical kits and sanitation facilities to the setting up of refugee camps, mobile communications centres and even fully equipped mobile hospitals.

Some may find commercialism within humanitarian relief unethical, but many analysts consider it inevitable that private business will adopt a higher profile in such humanitarian interventions. Not only will companies seek to perform more competitively and efficiently than NGOs, but the lines between charity-based organizations and corporations will become steadily blurred as donors look to bottom-line efficiency of delivery.

While profits may be made, the private sector is probably more interested in the good will and high-profile publicity to be gained. When Nokia and other companies distribute their merchandise free to refugees, it not only looks good in the annual reports, but also when broadcast on the television news.

WHO seeks more effective coordination role

During the Kosovo crisis, WHO tried to coordinate the public health response to the emergency, building on a forward-planning assessment of health needs in Kosovo made prior to the NATO bombing by WHO's emergency and humanitarian action department. In April 1999, a WHO humanitarian office – set up in Macedonia – began to jointly chair health coordination meetings with UNHCR three times weekly.

Concerns that WHO was not appropriately structured to deal with emergencies beyond its normal institutional activities are now reportedly being addressed by the administration of the director general Gro Harlem Brundtland. Following the Rwandan crisis, where WHO was criticized for having played a largely ineffective and tardy role in the relief effort, certain officials argued their organization should become more decisively involved in the field, and not just in an advisory capacity.

"Health needs to be coordinated very early on in a crisis but I am not sure WHO is the right organization to do it," noted the late François Jean of MSF, speaking in autumn 1999 and expressing a view shared by other aid agency representatives. "At present, WHO simply does not have the respect or the means to do so."

By the end of May 1999, some 150 agencies had registered with UNHCR in Albania, most of them involved in one way or another with health projects. Like other NGOs, many medical relief organizations had deployed without waiting for UN directives. This, together with what some observers saw as a lack of firm leadership from WHO during the early stages of the crisis, led to an unclear division of responsibilities, particularly among newcomers, and often resulted in duplication of efforts and wasted resources.

Determined to hit the ground running with a close eye on what was expected to be a limited window of opportunity for large-scale funding, certain agencies indulged in well-meaning but often inappropriate, short-term projects. Many have stayed on but it is clear that the entire operation could have been done on a more modest basis. Far too many expatriate medical teams were brought in. As WHO officials have pointed out, Kosovo probably has more of its own doctors than it needs. "Kosovo represents a group of people with lots of capabilities and a great deal of self-reliance, but there have been considerable problems in trying to adjust to the high influx of aid agencies," noted Dean Shuey, WHO policy coordinator in Pristina.

Some agencies refused any form of coordination and would not even register their medical personnel with the Albanian or Macedonian governments. According to medical relief analysts, it took four to six weeks before WHO began to assume its role. "The lesson to be learned here", admitted one senior WHO official, "is that there has to be a rapid action blueprint if WHO is to assume a more effective coordinating role of health activities."

Poor coordination among aid agencies has hampered the long-term humanitarian effort in Kosovo. By late summer 1999, when most refugees had returned, some 400 international aid organizations had established themselves in the province. Of these, WHO estimated as many as half were focusing on health assistance – two or three times more organizations and programmes than were actually needed.

Another key failing – repeated in disaster after disaster – was the ad hoc manner in which drugs (often inappropriate) flooded in from companies and other donors. Strict guidelines, developed by WHO with other leading medical groups, were not enforced. A June 1999 audit by WHO of drugs received by Albanian authorities revealed that 400,000 tablets and 1,200 large-volume intravenous fluids had already expired on receipt. Two million tablets, 85,000 injection vials and 16,000 tubes of creams were to expire by the end of the year. And less than one-third of the donations were packed according to international guidelines. According to Indro Mattei of the Swiss Disaster Relief unit seconded to WHO in Tirana, an estimated 50 per cent of drugs donated by non-medical organizations were "inappropriate or useless" and would have to be destroyed. WHO expressed concern at pharmaceutical companies apparently using humanitarian crises to get rid of unwanted stockpiles.

For some critics, including representatives within WHO's own ranks, the Geneva-based organization urgently needs to adopt a more forceful stance in order to regulate such abuses. When the relief effort moved into Kosovo, for example, different donors loaded the health system with all sorts of sophisticated equipment, much of which is incompatible and will require spare parts, replacements and maintenance from numerous different sources. "In the long run this could prove incredibly costly," said one ICRC representative in Pristina.

While certain WHO officials are aware of the drawbacks and the need to prevent similar problems from arising in future humanitarian crises, much will depend on the willingness of the international community, particularly the donors, to allow WHO the mandate – and the flexibility – it requires to play a more effective coordination role.

Strategic vision needed amid emergency

In Albania and Macedonia, many medical organizations focused on traditional relief responses to the crisis with the creation of clinics, mother-and-child health care and other high-profile projects in refugee camps. More experienced organizations recognized this could not be the only response. With the majority of refugees living among host families, health support would also have to be directed towards locally available facilities. Not only would this help the refugees, but also would enable host nations to overhaul their own infrastructures.

Since the end of the communist era, Albania's rundown health system has been barely capable of assisting its own people. An ongoing economic crisis has prevented development of a proper infrastructure. Salaries remained low and many trained staff emigrated. Health centres, already suffering water and power shortages, were left in disrepair.

While the Albanian government may have cooperated closely with NATO and international agencies in the hope that the aid intervention would benefit them, many observers have commented on the extraordinary hospitality they have shown to their Kosovar brethren to the north. Medical groups such as the Red Cross Red Crescent Movement, MSF, MDM and MERLIN have helped key areas of Albania, such as Tirana and Kukes, attain a far higher level of health care than before the crisis, with scores of clinics rehabilitated, pharmacies restocked, equipment replaced and new health centres opened.

Other organizations have focused on more specialized forms of assistance, such as the French Red Cross's rehabilitation of the Elbasan psychiatric hospital. And the International Federation has helped strengthen the Albanian Red Cross with vehicles, warehouse support and equipment, leaving it in far better shape today to help meet health needs.

In Macedonia, many ethnic Albanians sought to assist the Kosovars seeking refuge in their country. The Skopje government, on the other hand, was far more reluctant. More than anything, it worried about upsetting the delicate ethnic balance (ethnic Albanians accounted for 30 to 40 per cent of the population). It tolerated, and still tolerates, the international presence while trying to glean as much as possible from the intervention. As in Albania, certain medical NGOs sought to help upgrade local facilities given that they were being shared with refugees.

Box 6.3 News you can use

Media involvement during the Kosovo crisis went far beyond anything aid agencies had witnessed previously. Certain agencies actively courted the media for high-profile, 'look good' coverage, or as a means of attracting donor funding. But what the international community neglected to do – notably prior to the NATO bombing – was to lay the groundwork for credible mass information initiatives focusing on the humanitarian needs of refugees and victims of war.

Efforts to persuade donors several months prior to the exodus to help furnish local journalists from Kosovo and neighbouring countries with a better understanding of humanitarian operations and how to provide health and other needs-based information aimed at refugees – a vital component of any emergency response alongside food, shelter and medical relief – fell on deaf ears. Even when the international relief operation was in full swing, numerous aid organizations and donors were more obsessed with the need to court the international media, particularly television, rather than trying to communicate with the very beneficiaries they were supposed to be helping.

Many failed to understand the crucial importance of allocating resources for working with locally-based media initiatives aimed at broadcasting reliable – and credible – humanitarian information to victims on both sides of the border. It was only after initial criticism that UNHCR, which had dropped its mass information department months earlier for budgetary reasons, agreed to support needs-based radio programming aimed at helping keep refugees informed of humanitarian operations as well as security conditions inside the country.

This included programmes such as the humanitarian news broadcasts of Media Action International (MAI), a Geneva-based NGO established in 1998 by a group of international journalists and broadcast producers to support media-based humanitarian and development initiatives. MAI set up editorially independent teams of local reporters in Albania, Macedonia, and eventually Kosovo which produced daily half-hour programmes of impartial humanitarian 'news you can use' for broadcast on local and state radio stations covering the entire region. MAI worked closely with international agencies ranging from the ICRC and MSF to WHO, UNICEF and IRC producing lively reports and public service announcements on topics such health care in the camps, vaccination programmes, psychosocial trauma, family tracing and food distribution. In Kosovo, MAI established two teams of Albanian and Serb journalists with each producing similar but separate programmes.

Nevertheless, humanitarian organizations have complained about obstructive and corrupt Macedonian bureaucracy. Aid representatives privately admit to being blackmailed by local officials for assuring the quick movement of relief goods, such as refrigerated vaccines, and discussed the possibility of transferring logistical operations to Tirana, even if less convenient.

The transfer of medical relief operations from neighbouring states back into Kosovo, as refugees returned, has had a profound impact. Many aid agencies completely pulled out from Albania and Macedonia, removing almost overnight substantial aid benefits from host countries. And the massive influx of outside organizations into Kosovo itself may postpone much needed health reforms. Aid analysts fear that too much aid will only encourage greater reliance on outside support.

International NGOs tend to soak up well-qualified local people to work on emergency projects, potentially hampering long-term recovery. "Many Kosovars trained in areas important for economic and political reconstruction, from electricians to professors, are employed as drivers or interpreters rather than using and developing their skills", wrote Oxfam's Elizabeth Sellwood in late 1999. "They earn far more performing relatively unskilled work for the international community than they would if they returned to public service as teachers or health professionals or if they tried to set up or restart businesses," she added.

"Few lessons have been learned. Once again, we have seen everything dominated by an emergency mentality," said the International Federation's Baumgartner. "This will have far-flung consequences if we don't adopt more effective strategic thinking, which is not what the donors have been doing. We need to respond to emergencies but we must also think of the future."

At present, so much is geared to the rehabilitation of Kosovo that international aid has produced a severe imbalance. "While there appears to be enough funding and commitment to Kosovo, we are forgetting about other parts of the region, such as Serbia, which has a public health crisis of its own for lack of funding," said ICRC's Folke Lampen. Focusing extensively on the tracing of lost relatives, the ICRC has the advantage of being able to operate throughout the region and pinpoint the gaps where assistance is needed.

Reforming Kosovo's public health system

In Kosovo, the international medical effort is now focused not only on rehabilitating health infrastructure, but on radically reforming the system in a sustainable and regionally appropriate manner. While health care in Kosovo has suffered from Belgrade's anti-Albanian policies, the war and the flight of Serbs from the province, it must also cope with the top-heavy legacy of a welfare state imposed by the Yugoslav communist government under Tito.

Prior to the crisis, Kosovo had an annual gross domestic product of US$ 350 per person and suffered from problems similar to those found in parts of the developing world. This included the highest infant mortality rate in continental Europe (51.2 per 1,000 – compared to Germany's rate of 5 per 1,000) and nearly 75 per cent unemployment. An estimated 62 per cent of Kosovars lived in rural areas, often in remarkably backward conditions when compared to other parts of Europe.

The local population is not in a position to undertake reforms alone. At the same time, some aid representatives believe that external players should not impose reforms but encourage transformation in partnership with the local population. And it should take place without delay. "It is probably best for the Kosovars to take this bitter pill now rather than later," noted one International Federation representative.

According to WHO, now the de facto Ministry of Health under the UN Mission in Kosovo (UNMIK), far too many organizations are involved in the present reforms – no fewer than 17 Red Cross national societies and dozens of NGOs. This is a direct result of the way international agencies flocked to Kosovo at the end of the bombing without any form of real coordination. "We all have bad consciences coupled with a certain arrogance that enables us to plunge into crises certain that we know what's best and how it should be done," observed one UNMIK representative.

Since the end of June 1999, WHO had begun to establish guidelines for projects to support longer-term initiatives. It also implemented regular coordination meetings with NGOs in the five operational regions of Kosovo. Originally, areas of responsibility were allocated by UNHCR which sought to accommodate any organization that came in and wanted to do something. This resulted in an exceptional number of aid agencies focusing on child-based projects or psychosocial trauma programming. Since autumn 1999, all projects have had to go through UNMIK. Now no NGO may receive donor funding unless it has met WHO requirements as part of the overall development approach.

By the end of 1999, WHO – having completed the emergency health-care phase – was well into its second stage of relief and rehabilitation planning. This represented a more organized six-month interim period in which to prepare for possible disease outbreaks (such as cholera, measles, influenza, typhoid, dysentery and tuberculosis) and to develop the basics for a new health-care system. But by spring 2000, the international community was still debating whose job it would be to reform the system and how – in the long term – it should integrate itself within the region.

Overall, aid analysts say, Kosovo needs to rid itself of its heavily subsidized welfare system, and develop health insurance schemes – a move that may not prove popular. Under the previous Yugoslav system, health care was based almost wholly on a top-heavy tertiary rather than primary approach. "There is a strong need to spread and rationalize responsibilities through the deployment of more generalists and primary health-care providers," added WHO's Hilary Bowers. Virtually every form of medical assistance was carried out by a doctor who was also a specialist. No doctor, for example, could deal with an infant between zero to six months unless 'specialized' in this domain. Midwives could not deliver babies and nurses had very limited, subservient roles.

Currently, most primary health care is provided by NGOs but some are downgrading their roles and implementing exit strategies. Many emergency-oriented organizations are unlikely to remain beyond 12 months. There also appears to be greater readiness among the NGOs, many of whom lack experience of longer-term humanitarian initiatives, to accept WHO guidance, such as help with training Kosovar doctors and nurses. Privatization is expected to become a principal focus of the reform process with Kosovars themselves contributing towards its costs.

"Sadly, many people are unrealistic about the changes needed," noted Shuey. "They remember the days when everything was provided for."

The big question, however, is sustainability. As health analysts stress, the system needs to be in a position to support itself. It will also have to change medical customs, for example, lessening dependence on injections as a way of dealing with everything from the common cold to diarrhoea. Alternative sources for donated blood are needed. Previously, the army provided blood; now only family members give. No one is paying for blood, but it means the system will need to find new, voluntary groups to keep hospitals supplied. For the moment, unlike other parts of central and eastern Europe, there is no significant problem with HIV/AIDS.

Psychosocial support needs long-term commitment

Aside from reforming the public health system, Kosovo's principal health predicament is how to coordinate acceptable, professional ways of dealing with psychological trauma.

Psychosocial support programmes for Kosovars set up by various aid groups in Albania and Macedonia only began to come into their own when the refugees started to return en masse. "It was a weird situation with the train moving faster than we could cope," noted the International Federation's Baumgartner. "So all our efforts had to be transferred to Kosovo." He and others expect more psychological problems during the months and years ahead – especially while levels of ethnic tension and violence in and around Kosovo remain high.

The International Federation is working with local Red Cross branches to reach the psychologically vulnerable. In December 1999 alone, over 1,000 Kosovars of all ages – with an almost 50:50 gender split – received psychosocial support through special Red Cross centres and mobile outreach teams, located in the five most adversely affected areas of Kosovo.

Some NGOs, however, are suspected of pursuing psychosocial projects for publicity or funding purposes – something concerned aid organizations consider a blatant abuse of human rights. They argue that there needs to be tighter oversight of what agencies can do, particularly if the mental health of people is involved. "The press picked up and suddenly everyone was talking about 'psychosocial trauma'," noted Kris Hurlburt, psychosocial coordinator for the International Federation, based in Pristina. "The expression is flung around a lot but no one really

Military spending dwarfs aid flows. For example, one B-2 stealth bomber carries a fly-away tag of US$ 997 million. Funding requirements for the UN's consolidated appeal for humanitarian operations in the whole of south-east Europe during 2000 totals US$ 660 million.

Photo: U.S. Air Force.

Box 6.4 Returning to normal: the role of radio in traumatized societies

In July 1999, as hundreds of thousands of Kosovars returned home from weeks of exile in neighbouring countries, a needs-assessment was carried out to determine the information requirements of the population. Hundreds of Albanian and Serb Kosovars were asked to choose potential radio programming topics. The organizers of the survey assumed that security or land-mines awareness would lead the results. They were wrong: Kosovars wanted more information on post-conflict mental health issues.

Making sense out of situations which are seemingly senseless and helping individuals re-establish control over their lives are essential components of mental health work in post-conflict societies. Educating populations about the symptoms of trauma is a necessary step in helping individuals overcome those symptoms. Popular forms of communication, such as radio programming, could play an important role in helping facilitate this process. But the use of radio and other forms of mass communication to disseminate mental health education programming is proving controversial.

When approached with the concept of 'trauma recovery' radio programming, many health professionals instinctively recoil in suspicion. Trauma and mental health issues are far too complicated, they argue, and need personal attention to have any impact. One physician, representing an international organization working in Kosovo, maintained that a year-long research project designed to identify causes and symptoms of trauma in the society, followed by a second year of individualized counselling was first needed before any educational programming on a mass level could be envisaged.

But this lengthy, clinical approach is hardly likely to be the only effective approach in post-conflict situations such as Kosovo where hundreds of thousands of people may have been mentally disturbed by murder, torture and social upheaval in their homeland. The most realistic option is a mass approach, and mass media is the best vehicle for such a campaign. Why then is the international community reluctant to undertake such programming?

Trauma and mental health field projects are a popular new component in complex humanitarian emergencies and dozens of organizations operated such projects in Kosovo. But to develop a coordinated approach to psychosocial education through the media requires a consensus on the best approach to trauma counselling which is currently lacking.

There is, furthermore, a thorough lack of understanding about the potential role media can play in informing local populations about their humanitarian plight. Communications in conflict situations – 'humanitarian reporting' – is still in its infancy and often restricted to transmitting simple facts rather than more complex messages.

Thirdly, potential donors and sponsors have difficulty conceptualizing programming which may not be quantifiable. Misunderstanding how professionally produced education programmes can impact on the well-being of listeners is the root cause of such attitudes.

Anecdotal evidence, however, indicates that local populations affected by conflict have a more pragmatic view. "The more I know about why I am feeling the way I am, the more likely I am to understand myself and my family's reaction to what is happening to us," said one Kosovar interviewed in Albania. There are also examples in Afghanistan and Rwanda which indicate that local audiences affected by traumatic upheavals benefit from innovative radio programming about mental health issues.

Even so, developing mass media as a vehicle for mental health work is still very much in a conceptual phase. Communication professionals and mental health experts must work more closely together to develop an appropriate methodology for crisis areas. But the few programmes that have been successfully produced so far offer hope that, in the future, the international community will respond with a more open mind to the desire and right of affected populations to find out more about trauma reactions to crisis situations. Media will have an important role to play in disseminating that information.

knows what it means. Yet everyone wants to become involved with it and not everyone is qualified to do so."

Much to the horror of specialists, one American NGO operating in northern Albania during the refugee crisis wanted to interview raped women and other victims of war and then rebroadcast the interviews in camps as part of the 'healing' process. But the media can be used creatively to promote mental health (see Box 6.4).

Other agencies set up haphazard one-on-one counselling with no systematic or long-term approach in mind. Some, too, have elected to focus only on women and children, projects which are often far more easily funded, but neglect to deal with men.

"One needs to understand the Albanian culture," added Hurlburt. "Kosovo is very much a family-oriented society and you cannot simply take short-term approaches on a one-on-one basis. You need to involve the whole family and do so with sensitivity." For organizations such as the International Federation, MSF and other specialized NGOs, it is crucial to use proven techniques that take into account what people have gone through: the horrific killings and torture, the stress of fleeing to a foreign country, the flurry of international activity, the lack of information, the return to a homeland strewn with shattered houses and unexploded ordnance.

According to Hurlburt and other specialists, it takes time for difficult psychological disorders to develop. It also becomes a generational issue with children reacting to what they have witnessed and how their parents deal with things. "Anxiety and stress prevent people from functioning normally," noted Hurlburt. "And if parents do not function normally, there is anger."

Given that most NGOs will move on shortly, it is vital that local specialists are trained properly. The number of young people who have been 'trained' as counsellors and now operate without supervision is "horrifying", maintains Hurlburt. Many are themselves trying to cope with psychological distress. As she and others point out, dealing with stress is not a matter of handing out boxes of food. Nor is it a matter of 'quick-fixes' as one MSF psychologist put it. These only create a sense of abandonment if one does not return. Counselling is a form of assistance that needs to be taken seriously and with the long term in mind.

But psychiatrists are not necessarily the answer that recently returned refugees need. "Refugees are normal people – it is the situation that is abnormal", argues a mental health official with WHO. "The problem for most refugees is one of *suffering*. They don't need psychiatric treatment for this – they need psychosocial support. They need empowering through small, limited daily routines which you can slowly expand. Psychosocial support must cut across all disciplines – education, health, shelter, food. And psychosocial training must be for doctors, midwives, teachers, social workers, development workers, engineers, administrators, volunteers."

Another factor which needs to be linked to the psychological well-being of Kosovars is the way human rights abuses are dealt with. While various groups are investigating massacres and other gross violations, many Kosovars feel that those responsible need to be brought to justice, or at least atone publicly for their actions. As other post-conflict situations have shown, this too is part of the healing process.

Ethnic tensions hamper recovery

Kosovo's six major hospitals were hardly touched by the war. Most Serb doctors and nurses remained when KFOR entered the country. But roles of repression have now reversed. When ethnic Albanians, ousted from their hospital jobs a decade earlier, began clamouring to return, Serb doctors began to leave. By the end of December 1999, no more than 200 were thought to remain. Out of the estimated 200,000 Serbs and Roma who lived in Kosovo prior to the war, some 160,000 have fled, leaving most of those who remain living in isolated enclaves. Many dare not go out, even for medical reasons.

Both ethnic Albanians and Serbs are reluctant to be treated by medical personnel from the opposite ethnic group, although most doctors on either side will do so if asked. While there appear to be enough Serb doctors to deal with the remaining Serb population, it is a matter of ensuring that everyone has access to their services. The ICRC tracing groups have been instrumental in keeping track of medical needs in the enclaves and will send in expatriate doctors to deal with them. Nevertheless, KFOR is often obliged to ferry patients requiring special care under armed escort to the hospitals and clinics where members of their own ethnic group can still be found.

Ethnic tensions and violence during 1999 and the first months of 2000 in the northern Kosovar town of Mitrovica and along the Kosovo/Serbia border have continued to traumatize inhabitants and hamper the restructuring of regional social welfare systems. "It is difficult to see how the public health situation can progress until the wider political and social situation has stabilized," said the Balkans desk officer for the International Federation.

While rebuilding a multi-ethnic health-care system for Kosovo is the long-term aim, even when complete, both Serb and Albanian Kosovars will probably have to travel elsewhere for more specialized care. Regional medical centres such as Skopje, Ljubljana and Sofia will need to be included in health-care planning for Kosovo which, with its own limited population, cannot expect to command similar facilities.

The main challenge facing Kosovo now is how to wean itself off the overwhelming surfeit of international emergency assistance so as to develop a sustainable public health service. Kosovo's health system is having to recover from the triple burden of its history, the war and the well-intentioned aid effort. The system must be rebuilt by those who will have to fund, staff and use it. The role of the international community is to help Kosovars do this in a realistic manner capable of responding to the long-term social and economic needs of the region.

Sources and further information

Glenny, Misha. *The Balkans 1804-1999: Nationalism, War and the Great Powers.* London: Granta, 1999.

Human Rights Watch. "Federal Republic of Yugoslavia: Abuses against Serbs and Roma in the new Kosovo". *Human Rights Watch*, August 1999, Vol. 11, No. 10 (D).

Human Rights Watch. *New Figures on Civilian Deaths in Kosovo War.* Press release, Washington, 7 February 2000.

Malcolm, Noel. *Kosovo, a Short History.* London: Macmillan, 1998.

Office of the UN High Commissioner for Refugees (UNHCR). *The Kosovo refugee crisis: an independent evaluation of UNHCR's emergency preparedness and response.* Geneva: UNHCR, February 2000.

Sellwood, Elizabeth. "Kosovo: Frustration Grows". *The World Today,* December 1999.

UN Office for the Coordination of Humanitarian Affairs (OCHA). *United Nations Consolidated Inter-Agency Appeal for The Southeastern Europe Humanitarian Operations: January - December 2000.* Geneva: UNOCHA, 16 November 1999.

Vickers, Miranda. *Between Serb and Albanian: a History of Kosovo.* London: Hurst & Company, 1999.

World Health Organization (WHO).*Yugoslavia (Kosovo): Main Health Issues.* Geneva: WHO (HINAP), 17 December 1999.

Web sites

European Community Humanitarian Office (ECHO) – http://europa.eu.int/comm/echo/kosovo/index.html

International Committee of the Red Cross – http://www.icrc.org

International Federation of Red Cross and Red Crescent Societies – http://www.ifrc.org

International Medical Corps – http://www.imc-la.com

International Monetary Fund – http://www.imf.org/external/pubs/ft/kosovo/052599.htm

Office of the UN High Commissioner for Refugees – http://www.unhcr.ch/

Organization for Security and Cooperation in Europe – http://www.osce.org/kosovo/

The Lancet – http://www.thelancet.com

United Nations – http://www.un.org/peace/kosovo/news/

UN Office for the Coordination of Humanitarian Affairs – http://www.reliefweb.int

US Committee for Refugees – http://www.refugees.org/news/crisis/kosovo.htm

World Health Organization – http://www.who.int

World Health Organization Health Information Network for Advanced Planning (HINAP) – http://www.who.int./hinap/

chapter 7

Section Two

Tracking the system

Surprise upturn in global aid

For the first time since 1994, total official development assistance (ODA) for the world's poorest nations rose during 1998. The share of spending on emergency assistance also increased. However, the amount of ODA committed to health was the lowest since 1991, and the share directed towards basic health continues to fall. Gains in total ODA were more than offset by falls in private flows to developing countries over the same period.

In 1998, ODA from member nations of the Organisation for Economic Co-operation and Development's (OECD) Development Assistance Committee (DAC) reached US$ 51.9 billion, a rise of 9.6 per cent in real terms on the year before, taking account of inflation and exchange rate fluctuations. The figure's significance, however, is more symbolic than financial. In actual cash terms, the increase on 1997 of just over US$ 3.5 billion still means that ODA would have to go up by the same amount again, just to bounce back to 1996 levels. Put another way, according to figures from the United Nations Development Programme (UNDP), the increase in ODA from 1997 is equal to one-tenth of the amount spent each year on business entertainment in Japan.

The rise in ODA for 1998 among the G7 nations was largely accounted for by increases from Britain, Italy and the United States. Japan's giving recovered slightly after significant decline since 1995, but Canada, France and Germany all gave less.

The top donors in absolute terms were Japan, the US, France, Germany and the UK. But when aid is measured in the accepted way as a proportion of gross national product (GNP), the picture is quite different, with Nordic countries and the Netherlands continuing to outperform the larger economic powers. One of only four countries to meet the United Nations (UN) target of 0.7 per cent of GNP was Denmark at 0.99 per cent, followed by Norway at 0.91, the Netherlands at 0.8 and Sweden at 0.72 per cent. The US remained at the bottom of the overall DAC donor league, with an aid offering of 0.1 per cent of GNP.

The OECD highlights the period between 1992 and 1994 as the beginning of the long-term downward trend of aid. It estimates that if the momentum of the previous two decades had been maintained, total aid from member countries for 1998 should have reached US$ 73 billion – while the actual figure was US$ 21 billion less. The accumulated shortfall of giving from OECD countries between 1992 and 1998 reached US$ 88.7 billion.

Emergency aid gains while basic needs lose

Emergency assistance also recovered in 1998, both in absolute terms and as a share of giving. It climbed from US$ 2.1 billion in 1997 to over US$ 2.7 billion in 1998 – a real terms rise of 31 per cent. But at 7.9 per cent of bilateral ODA, it remains a small slice of the aid cake. In the first half of the 1990s (largely as a result of conflict in Europe) emergency assistance rose by more than three times as a proportion of ODA, from 2.7 per cent of the total up to 8.4 per cent. From 1995 to 1997, the percentages dipped then climbed again in 1998.

Fluctuating and unreliable emergency relief funding from the major donor nations has led some humanitarian organizations to create their own disaster relief funds, on which they can

Photo opposite page:
While donations from OECD countries to emergency and development aid rose during 1998, sums directed towards basic needs continued to fall. Just US$ 578 million (1.3 per cent of bilateral ODA) was committed to supporting basic health in the world's poorest nations.

Photo: Alvaro Hernandez/AP, Venezuela 1999.

draw in order to respond immediately and effectively to sudden-onset crises. But, as UNHCR's experience during last year's Kosovo refugee emergency showed, more money needs to be spent helping agencies to prepare in advance for worst-case scenarios (see Box 7.1).

While 'social infrastructure and services' accounts for approximately 30 per cent of the bilateral ODA cake, ever smaller proportions of aid are being targeted directly to basic needs. DAC nations' commitments to health spending totalled US$ 1.5 billion in 1998 – the lowest cash figure since 1991. Within this total, US$ 578 million was committed to basic health – defined by the DAC as: basic health-care provision, training of basic health personnel and development of basic health infrastructure, nutrition, infectious disease control and public health campaigns. In cash terms and as a share of overall health spending, basic health funding was at its lowest since 1994. It accounted for just 1.3 per cent of all DAC nations' commitments to bilateral ODA.

A greater amount, US$ 2.5 billion, was committed to important health-related services for clean water and sanitation – but again this was the lowest figure since 1992. Meanwhile, commitments to education funding totalled US$ 4.4 billion in 1998 – the lowest amount of the decade so far – of which just US$ 434 million was directed towards basic education.

The above data for social services are only the amounts to which DAC nations made commitments. Data for actual disbursements of aid towards social services are not available,

Figure 7.1
ODA in 1998 from DAC countries – net disbursements US$ millions – current prices and exchange rates

Source: OECD/DAC

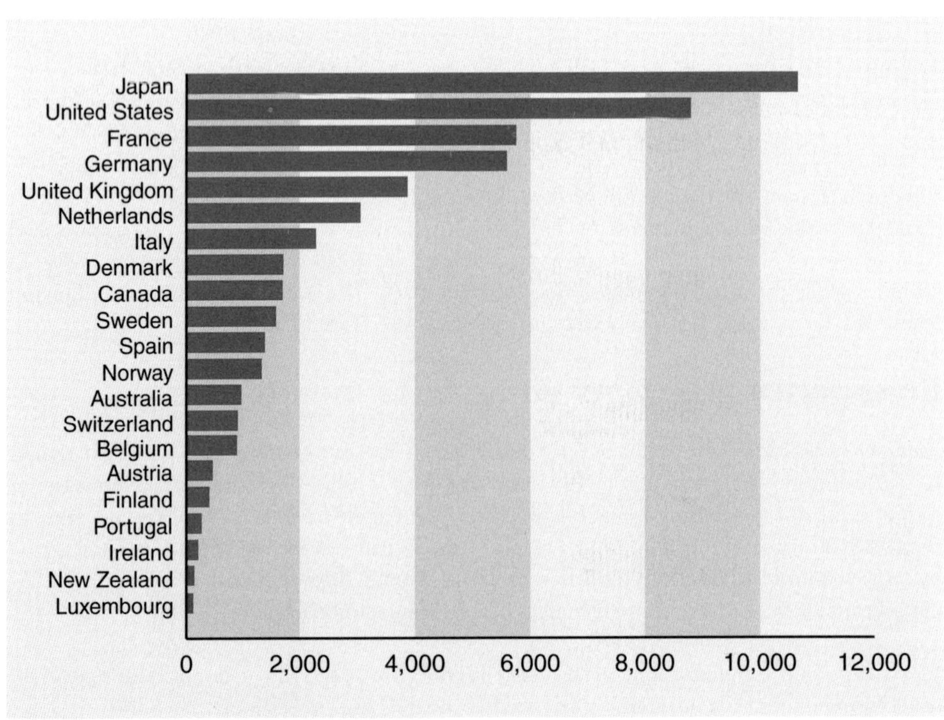

but would be less still. The amount of bilateral ODA disbursed during 1998 was US$ 8.5 billion less than the figure to which DAC nations committed.

Funds from DAC nations spent multilaterally, as opposed to bilateral funds allocated directly from donor state to recipient state, are calculated separately. During 1998, US$ 4.2 billion was donated to UN agencies and US$ 4.3 billion to the World Bank Group, some of which would have been spent on emergency relief and basic needs. And in addition to bilateral and multilateral ODA, expenditure on development assistance and relief to developing countries by non-governmental organizations (NGOs) from DAC member nations totalled nearly US$ 5.4 billion in 1998.

Private capital flows fail to protect poorest

During 1998, as aid modestly recovered, flows of private capital heading into developing countries slumped. For some years, much faith was put into the snowballing increase of private capital to compensate for the long-term downward curve of aid. The trend coincided with, and seemed to support, the economic model of a private sector-led development strategy supported by key creditors like the World Bank and International Monetary Fund (IMF).

But private capital flows have proved highly problematic in developing countries. The movement of short-term, 'hot' money caused havoc in Asia during the financial crisis of 1997

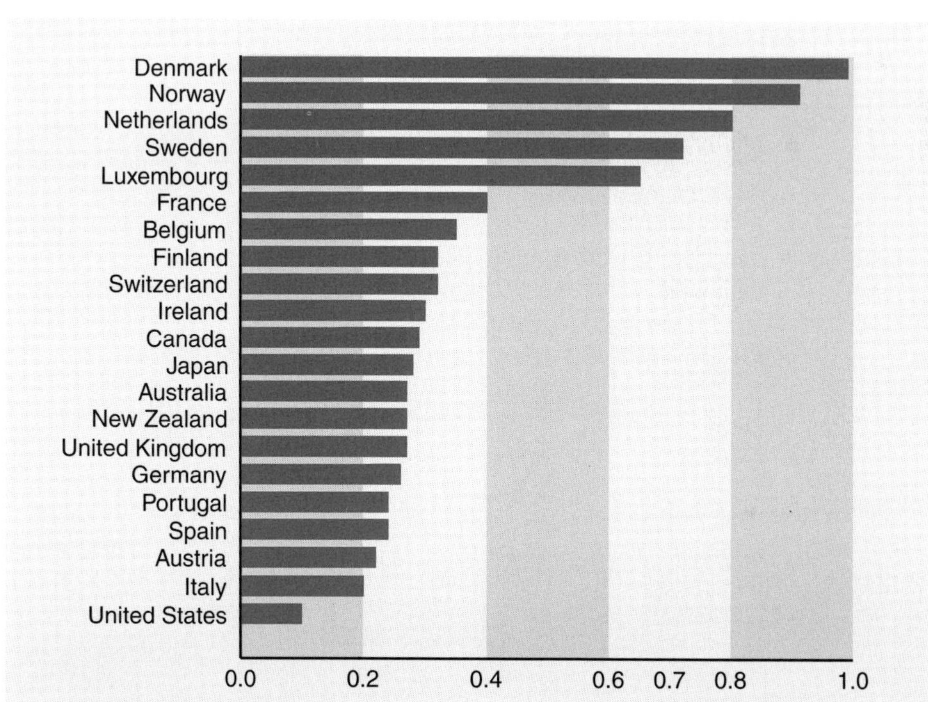

Figure 7.2
ODA in 1998 from DAC countries as a percentage of GNP

Source: OECD/DAC

Box 7.1 Advance funding and contingency planning save lives

Humanitarian organizations trying to develop operational capacity in disaster preparedness are frustrated by the voluntary and unpredictable financing of their operations, and by simultaneous demands to respond to today's crises while preparing for tomorrow's.

As well as emergency response teams, some agencies call on dedicated emergency funds when donors delay or fail to deliver. In addition to its US$ 25 million emergency fund, the Office of the UN High Commissioner for Refugees (UNHCR) can draw on the Central Emergency Revolving Fund (CERF) managed by the UN's Office for the Coordination of Humanitarian Affairs. The International Federation has established a Disaster Relief Emergency Fund (DREF) which was used 48 times in 1999, releasing a total of CHF 5.1 million. Oxfam and the International Rescue Committee (IRC) have created rapid response funds amounting to GB£ 4 million and US$ 1 million a year respectively.

But more access to flexible, advance funding is needed. And post-emergency evaluations indicate that the quality of preparedness structures can help – or hinder – agency performance in emergencies.

IRC: Tanzania (1993). In December 1993, some 250,000 Burundians fled into Tanzania. With a US$ 100,000 allocation from the CERF and drawing on its standby emergency grant from the LeBrun Foundation, IRC was able to deploy a response team rapidly to Tanzania, which also responded to Rwandan refugees flooding into the country in April 1994.

Oxfam: Goma, Zaire (1994). Unable to secure advance donor funding, Oxfam used its standby Catastrophe Fund to pre-position water and sanitation materials sufficient for a population of 50,000 refugees, prior to the Rwandan refugee influx into Goma. Had other agencies or donors acted similarly, access to safe drinking water and the control of cholera among refugees could have been greatly improved.

Oxfam: Afghanistan earthquake (1998). Using its Catastrophe Fund, Oxfam financed a needs assessment and GB£ 500,000 of emergency supplies within 36 hours of the disaster. Formal funding approval from Oxfam's donors took around three weeks.

IRC: Northern Kenya, Walda refugee camp (1992). Poor health conditions in the Walda camp were resulting in high death rates among the population of Somali, Ethiopian and Sudanese refugees. Unable to finance improvements in health, sanitation and nutritional services on its own, IRC applied for donor funding. After delays in the negotiation, approval and allocation process, IRC eventually secured funds. Within four weeks, the number of deaths in the camp declined from 70 to 14 a day.

UNHCR: Uganda/Rwanda (1994). Prior to the Rwandan refugee crisis, UNHCR's North Kivu Contingency Plan had called for the upgrading of the road between Uganda and Kivu. Had UNHCR acted on its plan and had the resources to do so, it would have enabled a much greater proportion of relief supplies to be transported overland from Uganda, rather than through costly air transport. Lack of advance funding not only delayed humanitarian action but ratcheted up costs of intervention.

UNHCR: Kosovo refugee crisis (1999). The evaluation of UNHCR's preparedness and response in Kosovo identified critical weaknesses in early warning, contingency planning and management systems. UNHCR had only 20 emergency response staff available and was prepared for a maximum outflow of 100,000 people when half a million refugees fled Kosovo in the space of two weeks. Official communications warning of possible 'massive outflows' went unheeded. Contingency plans were stunted by the organization's low estimates of potential refugees, and throughout the crisis UNHCR had great difficulty finding and placing experienced personnel.

Complicating factors did contribute to UNHCR's poor preparedness stance, including extraordinarily high levels of politicization and bilateralism in relief efforts. And the size and rapidity of the crisis were of a scale seen only twice before: in northern Iraq/Turkey in 1991 and in the African Great Lakes region in 1994. UNHCR was not alone – few if any agencies were prepared for the scale and scope of the Kosovo crisis. However, given that Kosovo is unlikely to be the last humanitarian emergency of this magnitude, donors and agencies need to invest far more in improving response funds and structures – before the next disaster strikes.

and 1998. In the aftermath, health budgets were cut in the Philippines and Thailand by 10 per cent, and by up to 20 per cent in Malaysia in the early stages of the crisis. Higher suicide rates, street crime and domestic violence were experienced in all affected countries. Reported domestic violence against women during and after the crisis rose by seven times in South Korea, according to UNDP. Less immediate, but equally damaging in the long term, countries ranging from Angola to Venezuela and Zambia were hit by the outward ripples of the financial crisis and its negative impact on the prices of their key exports.

Foreign direct investment (FDI) is a more stable form of private capital and considered more appropriate for less developed countries. But, according to the UN Conference on Trade and Development (UNCTAD), flows of FDI to developing countries fell from US$ 173 billion in 1997 to US$ 166 billion in 1998. This US$ 7 billion drop amounted to double the rise in ODA over the same period.

There are other problems with FDI as a source of capital. It tends to crowd into higher-income countries and a handful of the larger poor countries. Just five nations received 55 per cent of FDI in 1998. China alone attracted US$ 45 billion – over one-quarter of all FDI in developing countries. All the 48 least developed countries combined received less than 1 per cent of the FDI available. Optimism that eventually even the poorest countries in sub-Saharan Africa might benefit significantly from FDI has faded. Flows to Africa fell by over US$ 1 billion to US$ 8.3 billion. Recipients of FDI in Africa are accounted for largely by Nigeria,

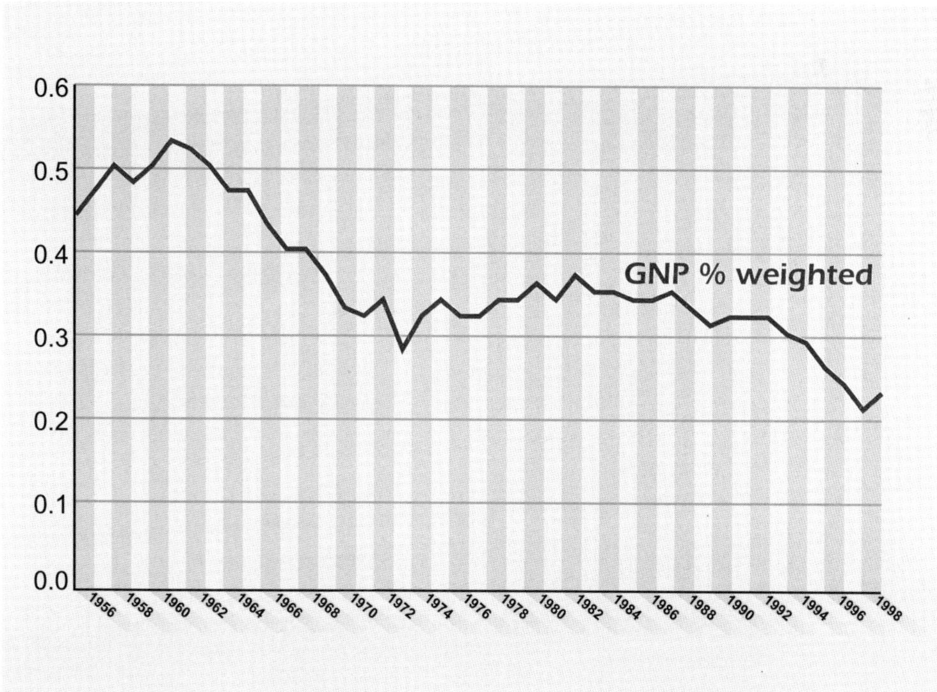

Figure 7.3
The long-term decline: ODA as a percentage of DAC donors' GNP from 1956 to 1998

Source: OECD/DAC

Box 7.2 A climate of debt

On 1 March 2000, the world's media reported a story of hope amid the despair and catastrophe of Mozambique's massive floods. For days, while the international response stalled, just a handful of helicopters plucked a lucky few stranded people to safety. Then a woman was found clinging to a tree to escape the water. She had been there for three days. Extraordinarily, in the minutes before her rescue, she gave birth. There was a ripple of inappropriate self-congratulation in the Western press.

The story diverted attention from the large but unknown number of deaths, the estimated 1 million people displaced, the loss of countless livestock and crops, the immeasurable damage to infrastructure. Typically, poverty had moved large numbers of people into areas highly vulnerable to climate-related disasters.

For a country still recovering from years of conflict and debt, the flood not only wiped out hard-won development gains, but set the country back far into the foreseeable future. In spite of its poverty and efforts towards reform, the servicing of foreign debts had been allowed to drain Mozambique of precious resources for many years.

Even following treatment by the latest improved debt-relief deal, known as HIPC II, current estimates suggest that Mozambique will still have to spend US$ 45 million a year on debt servicing – more than it spends on either primary health care or basic education.

Yet, while highly indebted poor countries are pursued by creditors to service their foreign debts, industrialized countries are themselves responsible for a larger and potentially more damaging ecological debt. A debt for which no accounting system exists to force repayment. And those most responsible for the debt are least likely to suffer the consequences.

Reckless human use of fossil fuels – overwhelmingly by industrialized countries – has helped raise the spectre of climate change, which darkens everyone's horizon. According to a letter co-signed in December 1999 by the under secretary of the US National Oceanic and Atmospheric Administration and the chief executive of the UK Meteorological Office, "the rapid rate of warming since 1976, approximately 0.2 degrees Celsius per decade, is consistent with the projected rate of warming based on human-induced effects...we continue to see confirmation of the long-term warming trend."

But poor people in poor countries suffer first and worst from extreme weather conditions linked to climate change – a fact highlighted in the 'World Disasters Report 1999'. Today, 96 per cent of all deaths from natural disasters occur in developing countries. By 2025, over half of all people living in developing countries will be "highly vulnerable" to floods and storms. Ironically, these are also the people likely to be most affected by the results of financial debt.

Mozambique was just the latest example. Late last year, the coasts of Venezuela and India's Orissa state suffered some of the worst storms and flooding in living memory, killing tens of thousands. Ever-worsening floods in Bangladesh left 21 million homeless in 1998. That same year, the El Niño weather phenomenon left its scars in droughts and floods from southern Africa to northern India, Latin America to the Pacific. Then, ironically, Mozambique had to prepare for drought. When Hurricane Mitch hit Central America, the Honduran president commented, "We lost in 72 hours what we have taken more than 50 years to build." According to the reinsurance giant MunichRe, the number of great weather-related and flood disasters quadrupled during the 1990s compared to the 1960s, while resulting economic losses increased eight-fold over the same period.

Geological history shows the earth gripped by natural cycles of cooling and warming. But now, because of human-driven accumulation of carbon dioxide in the atmosphere, we are moving beyond natural climatic variations.

.../

South Africa and a few north African states. Where the poorest countries succeed in attracting some investment, as with the case of Angola, it tends to be focused on exploiting natural resources such as oil and gas.

Early estimates for 1999 indicated that private capital flows had stabilized and modestly recovered for some countries in the Asian region at the heart of the financial crisis. Although the picture varies greatly between developing countries, and in spite of the recent crises, there has been a consistent decline in the share of aid as a proportion of all money going to developing countries. According to UNCTAD, the shift away from aid to private capital, and

.../

To solve the problem or, at least, mitigate its worst effects, all nations will have to live within one global environmental budget. Emissions need controlling because the atmosphere, seas and forests can only absorb a certain amount before disruption begins. Currently, industrialized countries generate over 62 times more carbon dioxide pollution per person than the least developed countries.

No one owns the atmosphere, yet we all need it. So we can assume that we all have an equal right to its services – an equal right to pollute. On the basis of the minimum cuts in total carbon dioxide pollution needed to stabilize the climate, estimated by the Intergovernmental Panel on Climate Change to be between 60 to 80 per cent of the pollution levels reached in 1990, and assuming that we all have an equal right to pollute, rich countries are running up a massive climate or 'carbon' debt. By using fossil fuels at a level far above a threshold for sustainable consumption, year after year the carbon debts of rich countries get bigger.

Ironically, poor people in poor countries suffer whatever the debt – whether from the smaller, conventional debts their nations owe, or from the larger, more threatening carbon debts being amassed by industrialized nations.

There is a direct link between fossil-fuel use and the economic output gained from overutilizing these non-renewable reserves. Because of this, the carbon debt can be given illustrative estimates in economic efficiency terms. Such sums show heavily indebted poor countries in carbon credit up to three times the value of their conventional debts. G7 nations, however, fall US$ 13 trillion into debt.

Given the policy conditions associated with conventional debt, logic suggests that poor countries should now, in the face of climate change, be able to impose a reverse form of structural adjustment on those most responsible. In 'Caring for the Future: Report of the Independent Commission on Population and Quality of Life', M.S. Swaminathan comments that "what we really need is adjustment to sustainable life styles". The onus is on industrialized countries.

Instead of old-style structural adjustment programmes for poor, indebted countries, a far more critical challenge will be devising sustainability adjustment programmes for the rich. Klaus Töpfer, executive director of the UN Environment Programme (UNEP), has called for a 90 per cent cut in consumption in rich countries to meet the challenge. Töpfer, in UNEP's latest report, 'Global Environmental Outlook 2000', pointed to global warming as one of the main threats to the human race, and added that "a series of looming crises and ultimate catastrophe can only be averted by a massive increase in political will".

Any political solution to climate change will need to be based on reductions in emissions, otherwise known as contraction. As the climate is owned by no one and needed by everyone, we will also have to move towards equally sharing the atmosphere, known as convergence. Our collective survival could depend on addressing both.

the removal of controls on how that money moves around the globe, "has made matters worse." It says that "these new inflows of private capital are not necessarily being put to productive use" in the interests of development. The money tends either to be held in reserve as a safeguard against economic shocks, or to go on buying up local firms rather than on adding new productive capacity.

It has long been assumed that when developing countries can attract FDI, it brings certain benefits. It is the opinion of most creditor governments that aid-receiving countries should manage their own economies to maximize the attraction of direct investment. However, the work of both independent academics and UN bodies is beginning to question this received wisdom. First of all, FDI is fairly random when it comes to meeting social needs. There is no guarantee that it can be attracted to weak areas of social provision, or areas of the economy that need developing. Evidence of concrete benefits from hosting transnational corporations (TNCs) is often weak.

A report on the various kinds of foreign private investment going to developing countries, *Drowning by Numbers,* points out that foreign companies demand high returns on their investment. They do this to compensate for investing in very poor countries that are considered high risk. But the consequences for the countries in question can be high demand for scarce hard currency resources, balance of payments difficulties and new debt problems.

UNCTAD, in its *World Investment Report 1999*, promotes the potential benefits of FDI. But it also describes how the weak negotiating position of many developing country governments

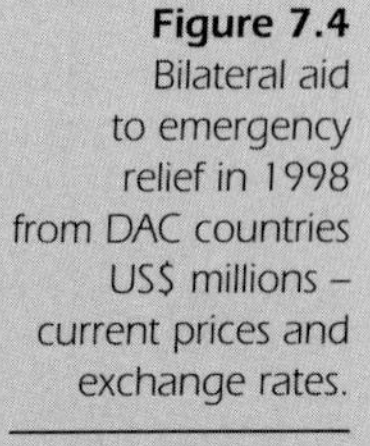

Figure 7.4
Bilateral aid to emergency relief in 1998 from DAC countries US$ millions – current prices and exchange rates.

Source: OECD/DAC

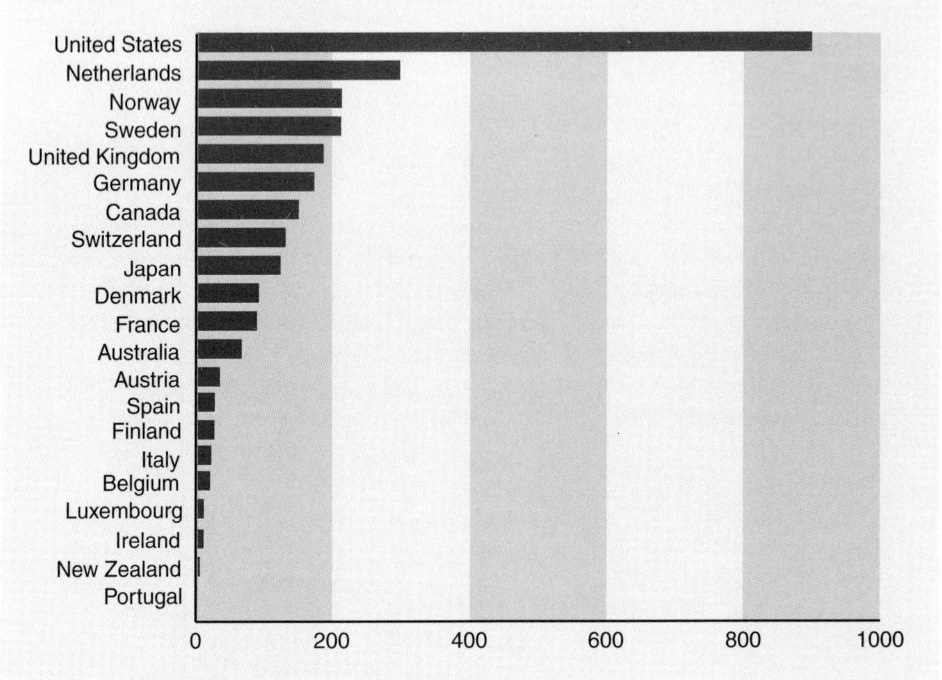

makes it hard for them to strike deals with investors which could guarantee that benefits will flow to their country as well as to foreign companies. UNCTAD's head, Rubens Ricupero, wrote: "The outcome of foreign direct investment depends significantly on how well the host economy bargains with international investors... However, the capacity of developing host countries to negotiate with TNCs is often limited."

Today, a greater realism is beginning to prevail about the potential costs and benefits of private capital in its different forms. This realism would seem to reaffirm the need for increased aid to safeguard development for the world's poorest countries.

However, long-term shrinkage of ODA has led some participants in the development debate to suggest more dependable approaches. They argue that addressing issues of debt relief, international trade and 'carbon debt' could release resources to benefit human development in poorer nations which would dwarf current aid flows (see Boxes 7.2 and 7.3).

Public health suffers under structural adjustment

While allocations of aid towards health, education, water and sanitation are declining, debt relief may not automatically fill the gap left in social sector provision. In 1996, key OECD bilateral creditors, the World Bank and the IMF launched the international debt relief initiative that became known as HIPC. It was supposed to provide a lasting exit from debt for the poorest and most heavily indebted countries.

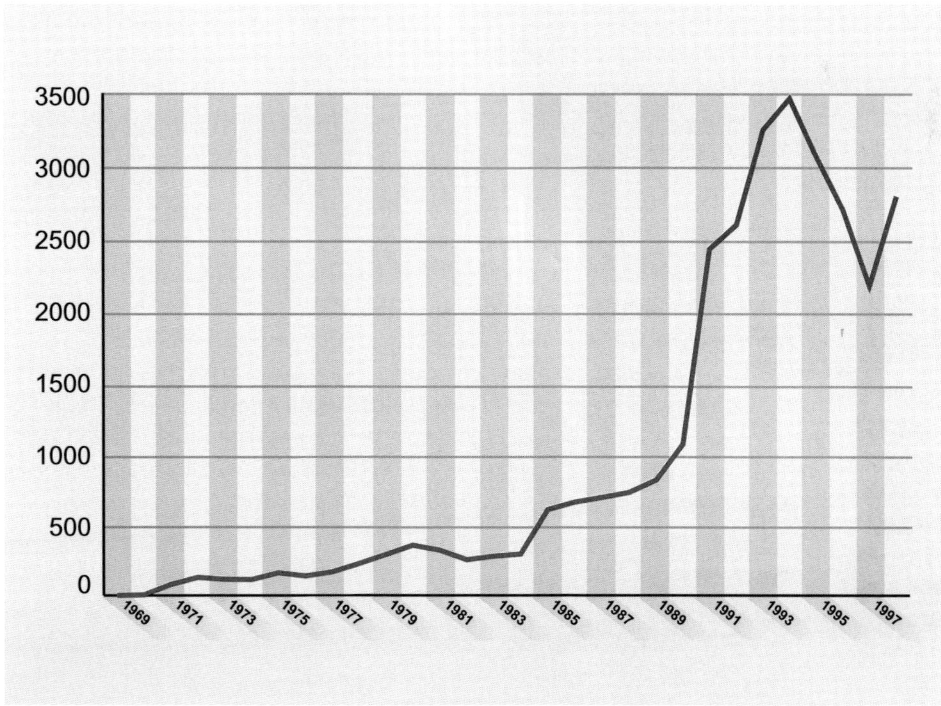

Figure 7.5
Fluctuating allocations to emergency relief from DAC countries (1969–1998) as a percentage of total ODA

Source: OECD/DAC

But the assumed benefit of qualifying for debt relief can be undermined by the consequences of the conditions attached. To receive debt relief, a country must accept an economic plan, known as a structural adjustment programme, designed under the influence of the major creditors and multilateral institutions.

Box 7.3 Aid overshadowed by trade and debt

While global aid giving appears to be making a modest recovery after years of consistent decline, the public perception of its importance has been overshadowed by two other issues which have claimed worldwide attention: international trade and foreign debt.

An inconclusive meeting of the World Trade Organization (WTO) in Seattle in the United States at the end of 1999 drew attention to the way that developing countries are disadvantaged in the current international trade regime. Figures from the specialist United Nations body which addresses trade and development issues (UNCTAD) suggest that rich country protectionism, involving low-technology industries alone, costs developing countries approximately US$ 700 billion per year. A figure that dwarfs both improved aid flows by a factor of nearly 14 to one, and average private foreign capital inflows by at least four times.

Dissatisfaction in Seattle among African and Latin American country groups was marked. Their complaints were both about the undemocratic running of the world trade body and the failure of mostly wealthy OECD countries to fulfil their existing international commitments to open domestic markets to developing countries. Each year, OECD countries subsidize their domestic agriculture by US$ 350 billion – twice the value of developing country exports, and nearly seven times the value of foreign aid.

Around the world, the Jubilee 2000 Coalition campaign for debt relief gained pace and both enormous public and political support. The coalition estimated that for every dollar of ODA going to the least developed countries (LDCs), the same amount was drained away in debt servicing. For all developing countries, the figure rises to around US$ 9 of debt service for every US$ 1 of aid according to the coalition.

US President Bill Clinton chose the closing moments of the World Bank and IMF annual general meetings in Washington DC, in September 1999, to declare a readiness to cancel 100 per cent of eligible bilateral debt owed to the United States by qualifying highly indebted poor countries (HIPCs). The announcement came after the meetings had been told that no further concessions were likely.

The British chancellor, under pressure from campaigners, matched Clinton's pledge two weeks before the end of the millennium. Importantly, the US commitment remained dependent on support from a reluctant Congress. As at April 2000 (amid the run up to US elections), any progress on debt relief remained deadlocked.

It is still unclear whether, when and how the high profile of the issue and its attendant rhetoric will translate into significant new resources being made available to spend on health and education in highly indebted countries. Debts owed to countries like Britain and the US are a fraction of total outstanding debt and remain only part of the picture. Multilateral organizations like the World Bank and IMF also play a big part. The route to eventual debt relief for poor countries is labyrinthine and tangled with myriad conditions, economic uncertainties and political complexities.

Many countries, however, have experienced mixed results from economic adjustment programmes lasting for years or decades. A comprehensive 1995 survey of 53 countries by the World Bank showed an average decline in health spending per person of 15 per cent over the course of structural adjustment. The squeeze on health budgets led one Zambian doctor interviewed by the British NGO Christian Aid to comment: "We have seen things go from being fairly acceptable, where we could admit anybody and be happy to look after them, to actually being scared to look after a patient because we can't even do the very basic things."

A consequence of poor pay and provision in the health sector has been to drive essential qualified staff overseas. World Bank findings suggest nearly half of Zambia's physicians now work abroad. In the same period that spending on health declined, the average spent on servicing debt rose more than threefold as a proportion of gross domestic product, with the World Bank commenting: "In many countries, public expenditure reductions worsened existing biases and inefficiencies."

Equally controversial has been the introduction of charges for health services – an approach known as 'cost recovery', and the result of new policies associated with the economic changes required by creditors. New evidence from research in Africa published in 1999 shows such 'user fees' leading to a significant fall in the number of people using health services. George Alberti, president of the Royal College of Physicians in Britain, has said: "I think user fees have been a catastrophe. I think it's a misguided bit of economics..." And the international health

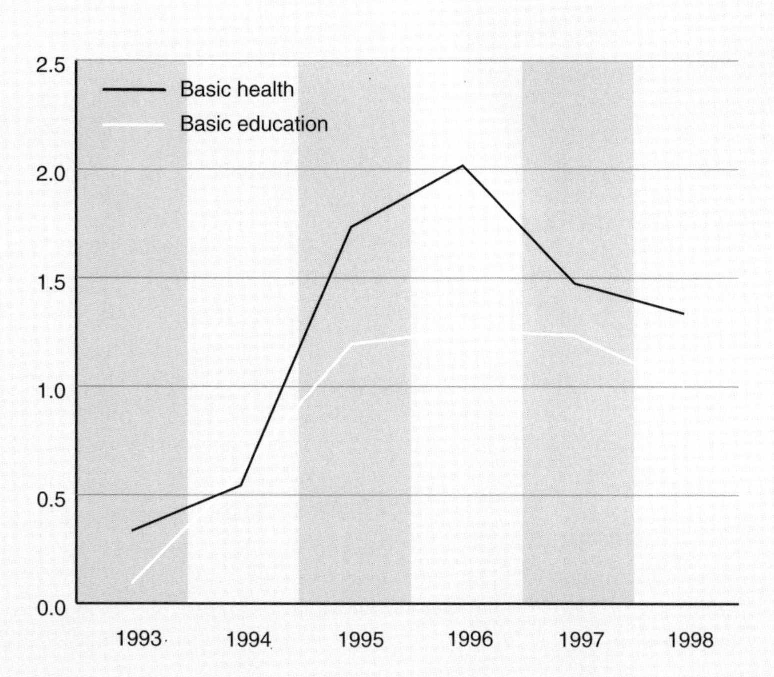

Figure 7.6 Commitments to basic health and education as a percentage of DAC bilateral ODA from 1993–1998

Source: OECD/DAC

organization Medact believes: "Evidence shows that equitable health services are best directed by governments, not by markets."

Over a decade ago, there were wide calls from the aid community for adjustment with a human face. A core argument was the need to ensure social safety nets when radical economic changes took place. The World Bank itself has repeated the priority of protection for the poorest. But it seems that a gap between policy and practice remains.

Disaffection with the policy framework under which assistance is given reached the level of the (departing) chief economist at the World Bank, Joseph Stiglitz, in 1999. He was reported in the *Financial Times* in November last year as saying that the conventional conditions attached to both aid and debt relief had been a failure and needed rethinking. "Was imposing conditionality an effective way of changing policies?" he asked, adding: "There is increasing evidence that it was not. Good policies cannot be bought." Stiglitz went on to question whether the bank's market-based reform strategies had been either sufficient or necessary for economic development. "China, which is by all accounts the most successful of the low-income countries, did not follow many of the key precepts of the Washington consensus," he was quoted as saying.

Can debt relief deliver?

Are recent debt-relief initiatives more likely to serve the public-sector needs of the world's poorest nations? Contrary to popular impressions, the rationale behind HIPC was never directly to make available more funds for health or education spending. It had specific financial goals to halt the necessity for constant future debt rescheduling. Because of the complexity and peculiarities of restructuring debt, it was quite possible that, even after treatment from the initiative, an indebted country could face higher debt-service obligations than it had previously.

There has also never been agreement on what levels of debt are actually 'sustainable.' Debt relief offered to Germany in 1953, as part of a post-war agreement signed in London, was around four times more generous than that offered to poor countries by the initial HIPC initiative in 1996. Pointedly, the logic of the 1953 deal was to lift up a country shattered by conflict, build its economy and prevent further social breakdown and a return to violence.

Today, countries wanting to benefit from the debt-relief initiative updated and improved at the 1999 G8 summit, and now known as HIPC II, are expected to have national 'anti-poverty strategies' in place. The 'necessary' status of the strategies is, however, unclear and they would be in addition to the standard attached economic conditions – these typically include privatization, deregulation and liberalization.

By April 2000, five countries (out of the original HIPC list of 41 countries) were expected to have qualified for partial debt reduction under the new, improved initiative. Its total potential value over the lifetime of the scheme, for the 32 countries most likely to qualify, is projected to be US$ 50 billion in real terms – equivalent to one year's worth of aid giving from DAC nations, or slightly less than half what Europeans spend on alcohol each year. According to debt campaigners, over 50 countries actually need relief and their outstanding debts amount to over US$ 300 billion.

Estimates show that even *after* the latest debt deal, Mali (which is yet to qualify), for example, would be spending on debt service almost the same amount that it needs to spend (additional to its existing health budget) on providing universal basic health care to its population. Zambia would be spending on debt service nearly three times the amount it needs to on health to achieve the same target of a universal basic health service.

Target aid at basic needs

After a long-term decline, aid spending by the world's richest countries modestly recovered in 1998. But the accumulated shortfall during the decline is much larger than the recovery. ODA, which in 1998 amounted to 0.24 per cent of DAC nations' GNP, remains well below the UN target of 0.7 per cent. The DAC, taking a view over the last 30 years of development assistance, says in its 1999 report: "It might well be argued that if more donors had met the ODA target [0.7 per cent of GNP], the mass poverty and humanitarian emergencies which persist in many parts of the developing world today might have been largely avoided."

Aid volume must not only increase. It must be more carefully targeted to meet humanitarian and social sector needs. While aid rose in 1998, the tiny percentages of ODA directed towards basic health and education continued to shrink. Falling allocations of ODA to fundamental needs, and the use of some aid to encourage 'economic liberalization' – so-called policy-based giving – run counter to popular perceptions of the humanitarian purpose of aid, and may even hinder development in the world's poorest nations.

Improvements in ODA during 1998 were more than cancelled out by falling flows of private capital into developing countries. Increased foreign direct investment during 1999 may benefit nations such as China and South Africa, but it does not make up for inadequate aid. There is no guarantee that increases in FDI will translate into extra resources to benefit social services within the world's poorest nations – so it is essential that aid and debt relief are geared to fill the gap.

In terms of the development debate, attention has focused on the potentially massive resource flows which fairer international

Natural disasters have quadrupled since the 1960s, hitting countries least able to cope. As aid funding flows in, debt repayments pour out. Even after debt-relief, Mozambique will spend US$ 45 million a year on debt servicing – more than it spends on basic health or education.

Photo: Christopher Black/International Federation, Mozambique 2000.

trade rules and debt relief could provide. But in spite of numerous promises, significant and realistic debt relief remains a distant promise for nearly all heavily indebted poor countries.

It is possible to work out what it would cost to help all developing countries reach the DAC-endorsed international development targets (IDTs) for poverty reduction, health and education focused on the year 2015. Measuring necessary levels of debt relief and increased aid flows by how they contribute to meeting these targets would be one large step in the right direction.

Sources and further information

Caves, Richard E. *Multinational Enterprise and Economic Analysis.* Cambridge: Cambridge University Press, 1996 (second edition).

Christian Aid. *Millennium Lottery: who lives, who dies in an age of Third World debt.* London: December 1999.

International Institute for Environment and Development, Global Commons Institute and Christian Aid. *Who owes who? Climate change, debt equity and survival.* London: September 1999.

Jubilee 2000 Coalition. *Unfinished Business.* London: September 1999.

Killick, Tony. *Aid and the Political Economy of Policy Change.* London: Overseas Development Institute and Routledge, 1998.

OECD/DAC. *The DAC Journal, Development Co-operation: 1999 Report.* Vol. 1, No. 1. Paris: OECD, 2000.

Oxford Policy Institute. *International Aid: Economics and Charity.* Briefing Paper. Oxford: January 2000.

Simms, Chris. *Adjustment and health in Africa.* Mimeo. London: Christian Aid, 1999.

United Nations Conference on Trade and Development (UNCTAD). *World Investment Report 1999: Foreign Direct Investment and the Challenge of Development.* Geneva: UNCTAD, 1999.

UNCTAD. *Trade and Development Report 1999.* Geneva: UNCTAD, 1999.

United Nations Development Programme. *Human Development Reports.* New York and Oxford: Oxford University Press, 1998 and 1999.

Woodward, David. *Drowning by Numbers: the IMF, World Bank and North-South financial flows.* London: The Bretton Woods Project, September 1998.

World Bank. *The Social Impact of Adjustment Operations.* Washington DC: World Bank, Operations Evaluations Department, 1995.

World Bank. *World Bank Policy Research Report: Assessing Aid.* Washington DC: World Bank, 1998.

World Bank. *Global Development Finance 1999.* Washington DC: World Bank, 1999.

World Bank. *World Development Indicators 1999.* Washington DC: World Bank, 1999.

Web sites

Christian Aid – http: www.christian-aid.org.uk
Global Commons Institute – http: www.gci.org.uk
Jubilee 2000 Coalition – http: www.jubilee2000uk.org
Organisation for Economic Co-operation and Development – http: www.oecd.org/dac
United Nations Conference on Trade and Development – http: www.unctad.org
World Bank – http: www.worldbank.org

Section Two

Tracking the system

Towards an international disaster response law

Natural and technological disasters between 1990 and 1999 affected on average 196 million people annually, and last year alone killed 80,000 people, according to the Centre for Research on the Epidemiology of Disasters (CRED). Disasters are also becoming more expensive. Economic losses from natural catastrophes worldwide during the 1990s amounted to over US$ 600 billion – nearly nine times more than the figure for the 1960s, according to reinsurance giant MunichRe.

On the cusp of the new millennium, earthquakes in Turkey, cyclones in India, and torrential floods in Venezuela and Mozambique devastated hundreds of thousands of lives and inflicted immense damage to property and infrastructure. As poorly planned urbanization and coastal migration push ever more people into the path of natural and technological hazards, the disaster response resources of governments and relief organizations are being stretched beyond breaking point. But humanitarian efforts to meet these challenges have not been matched by commensurate advances in international law.

While an extensive body of law has developed since the 1860s to regulate military conduct in war and provide for humanitarian assistance to its victims, remarkably we enter the 21st century with no similar body of law to help alleviate the effects of natural and technological disasters. True, there have been advances in recent decades in treaties related to environmental threats and some litigation has established that victims of such disasters may seek compensation. But outside of a narrow range of more technological or directly human-enhanced disasters, there has been limited legal progress.

Elements of law that aid our humanitarian response exist in other treaties – on civil aviation, customs regulations and ground transportation. There are legal authorities specific to disaster relief, such as the Tampere Convention covering the use of radio communications in disasters. There are United Nations (UN) resolutions and there is, of course, customary law. But these are all at the periphery of the issue. At the core is a yawning gap. There is no definitive, broadly accepted source of international law which spells out legal standards, procedures, rights and duties pertaining to disaster response and assistance. No systematic attempt has been made to pull together the disparate threads of existing law, to formalize customary law or to expand and develop the law in new ways.

Without a body of international disaster response law, there are no internationally agreed standards for donor and beneficiary government action, and no predictable mechanisms to facilitate effective response in times of natural or technological disaster. While an occasional newsworthy disaster may be flooded with relief, others go unreported and receive inadequate response, whether from the international community or from the affected state. In either situation, objective standards to measure humanitarian needs and action are lacking. Anecdotal pressure to respond should give way to systematic, swift and effective assistance to disaster victims anywhere in the world. In the absence of commonly agreed standards, the

Photo opposite page: Weather-related natural disasters have quadrupled since the 1960s – often hitting those least able to cope. Yet no body of international law exists to guide or facilitate disaster response. Investing efforts now in developing the law will benefit future generations at risk.

Photo: Christopher Black/International Federation, Mozambique 2000.

disaster victim is at the mercy of the vagaries of humanitarian response, political calculation, indifference or ignorance.

This chapter reviews the potential development of international disaster response law against the backdrop of its nearest existing relative – international humanitarian law (IHL). It does not seek to cover all potentially relevant law, particularly that which is rapidly developing in the environmental field, but it does seek to provide a solid platform for future discussion and debate – a platform firmly based upon the needs of disaster victims.

International law – why does it matter?

Disaster response is still too often hampered by procedural confusion, and by policies that do not facilitate effective deployment of humanitarian personnel, equipment and supplies. In the wake of destruction dealt by earthquakes and floods, or contamination from a technological accident, bureaucratic obstacles can loom large as a multiplier of suffering. There are no universal rules that facilitate secure, effective international assistance, and many relief efforts have been hampered as a result.

In the aftermath of the two earthquakes which shattered north-eastern Afghanistan in February and May 1998, for example, Islamabad – separated from the epicentre by one of the highest mountain ranges in the world – became the focal point for the relief effort (see *World Disasters Report 1999*). This was due in part to authorities far more accessible to the disaster failing, for whatever reason, to facilitate relief flights. Vital airlifts of emergency supplies were seriously hampered by the refuelling, time and weather constraints of crossing a 6,000-metre barrier en route to the earthquake zone.

Laws requiring and guiding swift and constructive cross-border relief could have saved lives. But law is never a panacea. No one benefits from rules unenforced and unimplemented – as exemplified by the occasional unwillingness of states to facilitate customs waivers for relief goods destined for afflicted populations; or instances where mariners have failed to honour rules requiring rescue of shipwrecked passengers and sailors at sea. However, one cannot press for better compliance with rules before they even exist.

No one should underestimate the importance of international law. Successes are sometimes invisible to the casual observer. But the humanitarian community could not function at all without the quiet success of a rich matrix of treaty-based rules which govern, for example, civil transportation, civil aviation, telecommunications and postal services. These complex international systems are entirely founded in the routine, well-organized functioning of international legal agreements that work on the basis of voluntary compliance.

Even if international law fails, we should keep in mind that domestic laws are not always followed either. But we need the law to set standards of behaviour for governments and other actors involved. Without standards there are no grounds on which to seek compliance. With them, we have a permanent foundation and frame of reference to seek new or better rules.

States may disagree about some aspects of the law. However, the availability of well-developed rules makes it possible for state, inter-governmental and humanitarian actors to employ a common frame of reference for negotiations and problem-solving. It also makes it possible to distinguish between problems generated by a lapse in compliance with existing law, and those rooted in genuine gaps that need to be closed by establishing new rules.

International humanitarian law and refugee law are the only well-developed, cohesive bodies of international law that apply during large-scale emergencies. Both are invaluable within their sphere. Refugee law protects those in flight from political persecution or upheaval by setting out criteria for them to secure asylum elsewhere. It applies where the claim for asylum is pressed. IHL regulates armed conflict between states, and between governments and insurgents. It is unique in being the world's only attempt at comprehensive rules for response to catastrophic events.

Many civilians, wounded and prisoners of war have been protected under IHL. During the Falklands war between Britain and Argentina in 1982, for instance, both sides carefully observed rules for protection of hospital ships and treatment of the wounded. This adherence to IHL and humanitarian cooperation was, however, overshadowed by other aspects of the conflict.

Violations of IHL draw far more attention than successes, since their consequences can be horrific. The work of journalists, human rights organizations and international criminal tribunals provides important support to prevention and response. However, voluntary compliance by combatants – supported by effective dissemination and training programmes – remains the most important mechanism for implementation, since it is the only sure way to prevent violations in the first place.

IHL as a case study

A brief overview of IHL provides a useful point of comparison with existing legal authorities relevant to international response during natural and technological disaster.

IHL, the body of rules and principles utilized to save lives and alleviate suffering during armed conflict, is rooted in customary battlefield practices that have been evolving over centuries. Over time, such practices became accepted as binding rules for all sides in a conflict. The use of a white flag, to signal surrender or a desire to speak with the other side, is one such customary rule.

The mid-19th century revolution in transportation and communication made possible the first systematic efforts at international cooperation in humanitarian action. In 1863, the International Committee of the Red Cross (ICRC) and the first national Red Cross societies were established, followed a year later by the adoption of the Convention for the Amelioration of the Condition of the Wounded in Armies in the Field.

The value of putting humanitarian standards in treaty form extended even beyond benefits accruing to victims in the field. It provided a frame of reference to identify weaknesses and gaps in the law requiring further development. The Geneva Convention of 1864 was dedicated to the protection of wounded and sick soldiers – then considered the group most likely to suffer in war – and to those who cared for them. With that treaty serving as a catalyst, however, negotiations were already under way by 1868 to extend similar protection to maritime combatants.

The 1864 convention became the foundation for the 'Geneva law' strand of IHL – rules that govern wartime protection for the wounded, sick, captives and civilians; and that identify the duties and status of those who care for them. Geneva law now extends its protection far beyond the groups and circumstances covered by that first convention.

New treaties followed. Based on experience in World War I, a Convention relative to the Treatment of Prisoners of War was adopted for the first time, along with a new and updated Convention for wounded and sick soldiers. The horrors of World War II led to the adoption of four new Geneva Conventions in 1949. The first two conventions expanded protection for wounded, sick and shipwrecked combatants. The third did the same for prisoners of war. Fourth and entirely new was the Convention relative to the Protection of Civilian Persons in Time of War. This was the first time that civilians were singled out as special beneficiaries under Geneva law.

The other strand of IHL is known as 'Hague law', which regulates the means (weaponry) and methods (targeting and tactics) of warfare. The impetus for explicit, treaty-based rules can be traced to 1868, when the Russian government convened a diplomatic conference that adopted the famous St. Petersburg Declaration Renouncing the Use, in Time of War, of Explosive Projectiles under 400 Grammes Weight. This brief declaration paved the way for the Hague Conventions of 1899 and 1907, which marked the beginning of systematic attempts to regulate wartime military practices.

Other important legal guidelines followed, including the 1925 Geneva protocol on chemical weapons, the 1980 UN Convention on Conventional Weapons, and the 1997 Convention on the Prohibition of the Use, Stockpiling, Production, and Transfer of Anti-Personnel Mines and on their Destruction. In 1977, these Hague and Geneva strands came together when a diplomatic conference adopted two protocols additional to the Geneva Conventions of 1949.

IHL treaties provide a readily accessible source of international law. Widely published and disseminated, they are available to anyone with a personal or professional interest in the rules of war. While these rules are not always easy to implement, there is little room for disagreement about the sources of modern IHL.

As these treaties developed, so too did an institutional framework for their enforcement. State-linked armed forces are responsible for implementing these rules. Insurgents are also bound by the IHL treaty-based norms that their state has committed to, even if they are in rebellion against the authorities.

The ICRC has a special duty as guardian of the Geneva Conventions, while other components of the Red Cross Red Crescent Movement also play a role in the dissemination and implementation of IHL. The UN has emerged as a forum for discussion and action on a wide range of IHL-related challenges, and journalists, human rights organizations and non-governmental organizations (NGOs) also play a role in efforts to develop IHL.

International criminal tribunals – such as those following World War II, the 1994 genocide in Rwanda, and recent wars in the Balkans – are emerging as an increasingly important mechanism for enforcement of IHL, and they set a precedent for legal action across national borders (see Box 8.1). The law, its implementing mechanisms and those who watch over both play mutually reinforcing roles.

The effectiveness of IHL sometimes seems to be eroding in the post-Cold War era, with massive violations of the law and growing numbers of irregular combatants lacking the legitimacy and responsibilities of state actors. However, the fact that we have a well-developed body of IHL provides a stable anchor and frame of reference for dealing with new challenges.

International law and disaster response at the dawn of the 21st century

Over 130 years of work to shape and advance international humanitarian law has not been matched by corresponding efforts or achievements in response to non-conflict disasters. No similar body of wide-ranging law exists to regulate or guide international humanitarian action in the wake of natural and technological disasters, although a modest number of rules and guidelines have developed over time. We thus have an imbalance, with significant humanitarian response capacity on one side and sparse legal authority, guidance or standards on the other.

In 1869, the second International Red Cross Conference passed a resolution calling on National Societies to provide relief "in case of public calamity which, like war, demands immediate and organized assistance." At the 1884 International Red Cross Conference, a resolution was adopted to extend the Geneva Convention of 1864 to provide for assistance to victims of natural disaster as well as war – but this was never done. International conferences have addressed assistance to victims of natural disaster ever since, but there has never been another attempt to extend the Geneva Conventions in this manner.

The League of Red Cross Societies was founded in 1919 to further humanitarian assistance in peacetime, and in 1927 a convention was adopted for the establishment of the International Relief Union. This marked the first and, to date, only instance when states attempted to launch a universal, treaty-based structure for disaster response and prevention (see Box 8.2). The Union never fulfilled its promise and perished along with the League of Nations system.

Over 40 years would pass before the issue advanced further. The 1969 International Red Cross Conference adopted the Principles and Rules for Red Cross Disaster Relief. Though these rules did not carry the same authoritative status as a treaty, they were approved by state participants at the conference as well as the Red Cross and thus made an important contribution to the development of international humanitarian practice.

A spate of institutional and legal initiatives followed in the 1980s, reminiscent of events a century earlier when new military manuals and increased diplomatic dialogue paved the way for breakthroughs in Hague and Geneva law. In 1980, the International Law Association offered a model agreement for cooperation in disaster relief, and the International Institute of Humanitarian Law sponsored a path-breaking congress on International Solidarity and

Box 8.1 Sovereignty and assistance – room for reconciliation?

The horrors of World War II prompted the first widespread rethinking of the long-held principle of a sovereign's near-absolute control within national boundaries. In 1945, the allied powers agreed to prosecute major Nazi leaders before an international tribunal at Nuremberg.

Along with crimes committed during the war, the tribunal's charter extended jurisdiction to pre-conflict crimes against humanity. The latter essentially meant crimes committed in territories where there was no armed conflict under way and no application of international humanitarian law (as it came to be called in later years.) This underscored that nations had legal obligations at home, and leaders could be held to answer for grave violations.

The UN Charter was adopted the same year, and under Chapter VII the Security Council can authorize action (including military action) to deal with "any threat to the peace, breach of the peace, or act of aggression". Over the past decade, this authority has been used to respond to war-related famine in Somalia and wartime suffering in former Yugoslavia. This suggests further erosion of sovereignty as a bar to humanitarian assistance.

Some advocates of intervention seem to suggest that sovereignty has been eclipsed and should be no obstacle when other states or humanitarian actors decide to intervene. If one accepts this premise, then there may be a role for assertive intervention in response to natural and technological disaster. Though the law is not well developed in this field, international human rights law may provide some supporting authority.

Article 3 of the Universal Declaration of Human Rights provides that "Everyone has the right to life, liberty and the security of person". Article 6 of the International Covenant on Civil and Political Rights states that: "Every human being has the inherent right to life. This right shall be protected by law. No one shall be arbitrarily deprived of his life." Official indifference, corruption or calculated neglect in the wake of natural or technological disaster may well constitute a de facto death sentence for those in need. This certainly warrants international pressure, perhaps even intervention, to respond to acute needs.

However, sovereignty cannot be treated lightly. States shoulder heavy responsibilities for national security, law enforcement, customs, public health, immigration, civil defence and agricultural quarantine sectors. These need to be respected and taken into account in shaping disaster response law and policy. Other than Chapter VII enforcement action, the UN Charter explicitly discounts an activist approach to intervention in state affairs. According to Chapter I, "Nothing contained in the present Charter shall authorize the United Nations to intervene in matters which are essentially within the domestic jurisdiction of any state or shall require the Members to submit such matters to settlement under the present Charter..."

Though sovereignty has eroded, it is still unclear which issues "essentially within domestic jurisdiction" in 1945 are now subject to international scrutiny and enforcement efforts. However, if states can be called to account for other human rights abuses, then it is reasonable to argue that they should be called to account if they frustrate humanitarian response.

Even where humanitarian efforts are obstructed, though, experience shows that states are reluctant to intervene. And there is presently no international court or similar body to which humanitarian organizations can turn for judgement on state cooperation.

With credible standards of conduct, such as those developed by the Sphere Project, humanitarian responders can now exert a moral pressure on agencies and states to cooperate in disaster relief. But a treaty establishing such specific standards would give the humanitarian community even more teeth.

Humanitarian Actions. In 1981, the League of Red Cross Societies undertook a pioneering analysis of international law and disaster relief. A year later, the UN Institute for Training and Research (UNITAR) issued its *Model Rules for Disaster Relief Operations.* In 1984, the Office of the UN Disaster Relief Coordinator issued its own *Draft Convention on Expediting the Delivery of Emergency Assistance.* Another important milestone was marked in 1985 with publication of a treatise entitled *International humanitarian assistance: disaster relief actions in international law and organisation.*

All of these initiatives and documents remain important resources and form a foundation for future efforts. However they do not constitute binding rules, only an (as yet) underutilized source of insights and experience that can be used to establish them. Other developments followed, but the intellectual momentum of the 1980s was lost, and no treaties resulted.

Some institutional development continued into the 1990s. The UN General Assembly has passed a series of resolutions that underscore its concern with disaster relief, and declared 1990-2000 as the International Decade for Natural Disaster Reduction (IDNDR). The UN Office for the Coordination of Humanitarian Affairs was established to deal with a range of disasters. International standards for disaster relief have been developed, and many humanitarian organizations have adopted the *Code of Conduct for the International Red Cross*

Box 8.2 IDL – precedents for an operational approach

Much can be achieved by developing functional, treaty-based operating procedures in support of international disaster response. By attending to these seemingly mundane details now, and demonstrating that such procedures work in practice, the way will be open later for those who may have more visionary legal goals in mind. We have two precedents available that offer very different lessons for the future.

The Convention Establishing an International Relief Union was adopted in 1927. The IRU was envisioned as an operational organization that would render assistance to victims of disaster and "encourage the study of preventive measures against disasters". This treaty had a notable weakness – it focused on parliamentary and administrative issues and offered no standards or guidance for work in the field. As the IRU never received adequate political or financial support, it could not become an effective operational organization. Even though it would never have been enough by itself, an operational treaty would have provided a useful starting point for anyone who wanted to promote an assertive role for the IRU.

In the telecommunications sphere, a starting point for such action does exist. The Tampere Convention on the Provision of Telecommunication Resources for Disaster Mitigation and Relief Operations of 1998 provides useful procedures when states request telecommunications assistance. Among issues covered are:

- provision of privileges, immunities and facilities for telecommunications functions;
- protection of personnel, equipment and materials brought into the state for that purpose; and
- reduction or removal of regulatory barriers to emergency use of such telecommunications equipment.

It took until the end of the 20th century to produce a treaty offering universal procedures for any aspect of international disaster response. Much remains to be done. The Tampere Convention offers an interesting, even inspirational, starting point.

and Red Crescent Movement and NGOs in disaster relief (see Chapter 10). Ongoing development of the Sphere Project has drawn in hundreds of agencies to establish professional minimum standards in disaster response (see Box 8.3).

The European Union (EU) also pioneered several notable initiatives in the closing years of the century. The Fourth Lomé Convention, adopted in 1989, along with EC Council Regulation 1257/96, establishes some guidance on objectives and standards for humanitarian assistance rendered external to the EU. Beginning in 1990, the Council of the European Union also adopted the first in a series of resolutions designed to strengthen civil protection and mutual aid among member states in the event of disasters.

Although peacetime disaster response has received little attention by way of treaties devoted exclusively to that challenge, there are relevant provisions tucked away among treaties governing air traffic, customs duties, and rail and maritime transport. These treaties were negotiated across a span of almost 50 years and, in every case, the negotiation process was probably unknown to the humanitarian community. Nonetheless, lawyers and diplomats with specialized commercial portfolios took the initiative to incorporate humanitarian provisions in these agreements.

The Convention on International Civil Aviation of 1944 calls upon states to facilitate entry, departure and transit of relief flights "undertaken in response to natural and man-made disasters which seriously endanger human health or the environment...". The Convention on Facilitation of International Maritime Traffic of 1965 provides that "Public authorities shall facilitate the arrival and departure of ships engaged in disaster relief work...". In the Convention on the Simplification and Harmonization of Customs Procedures of 1973 we find provisions to facilitate entry of goods destined for those "affected by natural disaster or similar catastrophes". Less specific but still significant is a provision in the Convention concerning International Carriage by Rail of 1980 that provides for reduction in rail charges for "charitable, educational or instructional purposes". As recently as 1990, humanitarian provision was added in the customs-focused Convention on Temporary Admission, wherein guidance is furnished for temporary admission of goods to be used in relief work.

Over the years, states have made bilateral agreements on disaster relief. Regional initiatives include the Inter-American Convention to Facilitate Disaster Assistance and, from the Council of Europe, an outline model agreement on mutual aid in the event of disasters in border regions. But despite the persistent appearance of humanitarian provisions in treaties negotiated across many years, and occasional initiatives from regional organizations, it is still rare to see an organized effort to adopt disaster-focused treaties with universal reach. Two were quickly adopted, however, in response to the world's worst nuclear accident at Chernobyl in 1986: the Convention on Early Notification of a Nuclear Accident and the Convention on Assistance in the Case of a Nuclear Accident or Radiological Emergency.

Towards the end of the century, another important treaty was adopted. It is the first, since the days of the long-vanished International Relief Union, to establish rules that can be applied in all manner of disaster relief situations. The Tampere Convention on the Provision of Telecommunication Resources for Disaster Mitigation and Relief Operations of 1998 seeks to

Box 8.3 Sphere's Minimum Standards – customary international law in the making?

A ship's captain would be hard pressed to argue he has no obligation to rescue shipwrecked sailors – it is there, with or without recourse to treaty-based rules. Such is customary international law, deriving from a historical pattern of field-based practices enjoying widespread support, which eventually becomes a binding legal norm. And when treaties gain near universal acceptance among states, standards found in them may also become customary international law. Though states can renounce the Geneva Conventions of 1949, they cannot reject their core humanitarian principles and protections.

The Sphere Project's Humanitarian Charter and Minimum Standards in Disaster Response may well be a case study for customary international law in formation. Guidance on standards for humanitarian assistance is sparse within international law. Sphere is the closest we come to a set of comprehensive standards for disaster response. In that respect, Sphere standards resemble guidance that might be found in treaties, legislation or regulations. However, they indisputably lack the force of a treaty or persuasive authority of well-established customary practice.

The Geneva Conventions of 1949 are the authoritative source for guidance on war-zone health standards, as seen in the Geneva Convention Relative to the Protection of Civilian Persons in Time of War, which sets out a public health baseline for the well-being of civilians in occupied zones. "To the fullest extent" of its available means, an occupying power must maintain "the medical and hospital establishments and services, public health and hygiene in the occupied territory... In adopting measures of health and hygiene and in their implementation, the Occupying Power shall take into consideration the moral and ethical susceptibilities of the population of the occupied territory."

A baseline is also provided in regard to civilians who are detained by the occupying power. "Daily food rations for internees shall be sufficient in quantity, quality and variety to keep internees in a good state of health and prevent the development of nutritional deficiencies. Account shall also be taken of the customary diet of the internees... Sufficient drinking water shall be supplied to internees."

For health-care professionals, such criteria are little more than a starting point. How are such standards to be implemented? Sphere offers explicit standards for wartime and peacetime alike. In regard to water, Sphere establishes standards for quality, excreta disposal, vector control, solid waste disposal and hygiene. Regarding nutrition, Sphere establishes standards for analysis of the nutritional situation, nutritional support for the general population and specially targeted needs, analysis of conditions generating food insecurity, and methods for fair and equitable distribution.

Sphere will not be a panacea. Realizing minimum standards in the field requires levels of access, security and resources beyond Sphere's ability to dictate. It could take a long time to demonstrate that these standards have actually attained customary legal status. Those who may want to see the Sphere standards attain that status need to consider some important questions.

How much field use, and state acceptance, would be essential to support a plausible claim that Sphere standards have gained the status of customary international law? If Sphere standards entered into customary international law, would there be a duty to implement them or would they, rather, have an 'aspirational' character? Would such customary standards apply equally in peacetime and in war? Would they apply only to those who are in detention or receiving emergency humanitarian assistance, or would they apply more broadly to development situations or stressed communities which may harbour refugees? If obligatory, how would the duty of implementation fall between states, insurgent groups, international organizations and the humanitarian community? How would a right to claim the benefit of these standards be enforced?

If these daunting challenges are met with convincing practice in the field and compelling, practical legal answers, then Sphere's minimum standards could someday advance into the realm of customary international law. Today they provide standards for professional performance and humanitarian achievement. Someday they may also become the standards required by international law.

facilitate use of such resources, sharing of information, and admission of foreign nationals to assist with communications during relief operations (see Box 8.2).

Even though important individually, scattered limbs of legislation do not form a body of law. In 1994, the UN Department of Humanitarian Affairs had to conduct a survey to determine what sources of law already existed that could be used in support of disaster relief operations. Without systematic organization and analysis, these rules cannot be used effectively. We may be missing many opportunities to advance the law in ways that will benefit victims of natural and technological disasters.

Some possible organizing concepts

'International disaster response law' (IDL) is proposed as a conceptual framework within which to begin shaping this amorphous body of rules and regulations. A broad-based, action-oriented concept will most effectively capture humanitarian action in all phases –

Box 8.4 IDL – areas in need of further legal development

- **Humanitarian standards of professionalism** (e.g., Sphere). Quality assurance mechanisms, impartially applied, would enhance the legitimacy of humanitarian responders seeking access to funds and disaster zones.
- **Humanitarian standards of conduct.** Humanitarian responders should abide by legal norms (e.g., respecting host nation public health and traffic regulations).
- **Transportation, immigration and customs.** A common framework of universally recognized rules granting priority transportation and entry for relief goods and personnel must be built on foundations that already exist.
- **Standards for relief goods.** Current guidelines on appropriate drug and relief donations need strengthening in order to avoid diversion of logistical resources to the delivery of inappropriate assistance.
- **Information sharing.** Rapid sharing of data on unfolding disasters, consequences and responses – internationally and locally – could greatly boost agency coordination and effectiveness.
- **Access and security.** States should cooperate with humanitarian responders and ensure that assistance is not disrupted, nor the security of aid staff threatened.
- **Contingency planning.** Rapid response to sudden disasters saves lives. But to achieve this, responders need a system to train and maintain emergency response teams, prearranged waivers to allow rapid deployment, and perhaps a system for pre-positioning of essential supplies.
- **Interface with IHL.** Complex humanitarian emergencies have blurred distinctions between peace and war. The overlap of IHL and IDL would need clarifying in situations when natural or technological disasters afflict areas where armed conflict is under way.
- **Lessons learned.** Any treaty-based approach to international disaster response should promote information sharing, so as to incorporate lessons learned and hone better rules and regulations for the future.
- **Disaster preparedness and mitigation.** To be truly effective, IDL would encompass disaster mitigation measures ranging from construction codes and environmental planning to early warning systems and evacuation procedures. Rules could facilitate information sharing and technical cooperation between states to achieve these goals.

preparedness, relief and rehabilitation. Thought and debate on the shape of IDL can and should proceed on many levels. Multiple approaches would help the law develop to meet operational and policy needs. Areas in need of further legal development are suggested in Box 8.4, while some compatible organizing concepts for IDL are offered below:

- **Operational approach to build IDL**. Much of international law relies upon an apolitical, systems-based approach to problem solving. For example, long-held customary rules for rescue and assistance at sea have been well established in international treaty law since the Brussels Conventions were adopted in 1910. Though politics play a role in all treaty-making, the world as we know it could not function without profound operational and legal cooperation in fields such as civil aviation, international postal services and commercial transport.

  The Tampere Convention offers model and precedent for an operationally focused approach to international disaster response. Rather than focusing on rights or duties, we could concentrate on establishing IDL standards and procedures. However in the absence of clearly defined rights and duties, there is always a chance that standards and procedures may never make the leap from abstraction into action.

- **Regional security as a framework for IDL.** Regional structures would provide a logical starting place for stronger IDL rules. The secondary brunt of most disasters falls on neighbouring states, and timely lifesaving assistance will often need to come from those countries. Unless and until the civil defence and regional security implications of disasters are given greater consideration in a legal context, the impetus to develop regional agreements may just not be there.

- **IDL as an extension of international humanitarian law.** IHL requires cooperation even transcending armed conflict. Cooperation between Greece and Turkey following the earthquakes of 1999 extends the spirit of IHL into peacetime. Despite long-standing political and military tensions, which have sometimes involved armed conflict between them, these nations moved promptly to assist each other by dispatching rescue teams and other forms of assistance.

  Some IHL rules are easily analogized to disaster response and equally useful in meeting non-conflict challenges. In fact, complex humanitarian emergencies often involve overlays of disaster response during armed conflict. Rules for safety zones ('humanitarian space') could be extended to

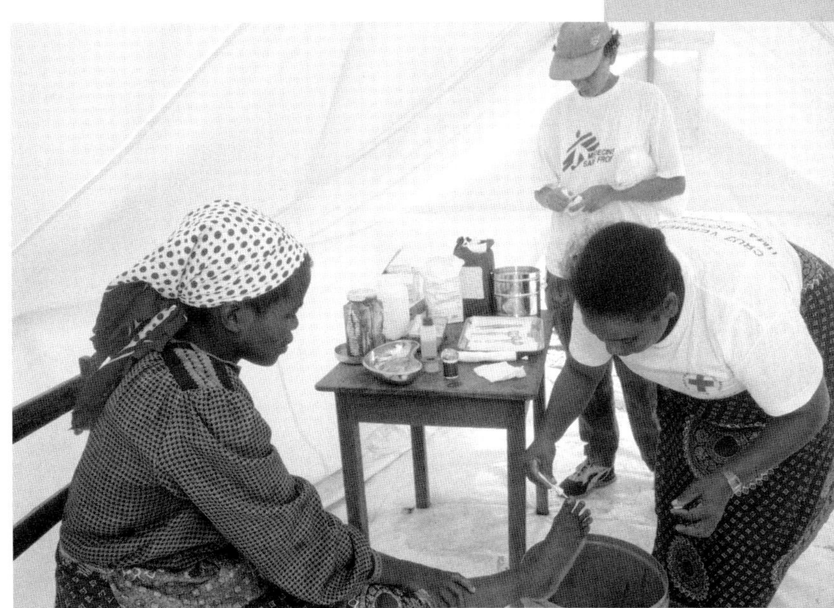

Cooperation between humanitarian agencies is essential in creating a body of common standards for disaster response, as the Sphere Project has shown. Moving towards an international disaster response law will require cooperation between states as well.

Photo: Christopher Black/International Federation, Mozambique 2000.

cover humanitarian response after natural and technological disasters. Rules and principles by which humanitarian organizations are authorized to provide assistance during armed conflict can also be extended, by analogy, to post-conflict and peacetime operations.

Perhaps it is time to revisit the proposal first raised at the International Red Cross Conference in 1884, and look to extend Geneva law to natural and technological disasters. However, IDL would address humanitarian response and needs in peacetime, and would be predicated on cooperation among all parties. On the other hand, IHL is predicated on the need to impose some humanitarian constraints on warring parties. The approaches found in IDL and IHL may be incompatible. To merge them in their entirety in the context of a treaty or other unified source of law may prove to be impractical.

- **International human rights law as a foundation for IDL.** Human rights law has sparked the imagination and support of many in the closing years of the 20th century, and sometimes provoked the ire of others. It has already entered prominently into thinking on humanitarian assistance through the *Humanitarian Charter* outlined by the Sphere Project as the basis for its minimum standards in disaster response.

  Sphere has deliberately approached assistance based on rights, not needs, and its charter draws on key human rights authorities such as the Universal Declaration of Human Rights (1948) and the Convention on the Rights of the Child (1989). A human rights-centred approach could engage a more energetic constituency than any other, but would also be likely to generate the most resistance to further development of the law.

There is some law, then, that applies directly to international disaster response. Additionally, there are legal frameworks that can be applied by analogy. By what process can we move towards systematic development of international disaster response law?

Step forward

While any new growth in IHL remains firmly rooted in the Hague and Geneva Conventions, a similar legal foundation does not yet exist for international disaster response.

But the International Red Cross and Red Crescent Movement, by drawing upon a unique network of operational managers and lawyers specializing in humanitarian issues, could move that day closer. Some of them work domestically with National Societies, which are independent from their governments but also assist them as auxiliaries. Others work with the ICRC and the International Federation of Red Cross and Red Crescent Societies, which are likewise independent of state control, but answer to unique roles assigned them under international law. Drawing upon insights and access readily available through this network, and pioneering legal foundations set in place during the 1980s, they could design practical legal tools to strengthen disaster response around the world.

The Movement could begin a simultaneous dialogue with states, international organizations and the humanitarian community on the formation of a comprehensive, readily usable set of disaster response rules. For presentation at its next International Conference, the Movement could then draft a model treaty or declaratory instrument (and perhaps also a model law for national legislation) that draws together existing law. Approval at the conference of such a declaratory instrument, or draft treaty, would encourage important efforts to develop the law, and could serve as a foundation for negotiating a universal treaty for IDL standards and cooperation. Parallel action within the UN system could also play a valuable role in moving forward this long-neglected facet of international law.

At the dawn of the 21st century, a cohesive approach to international disaster response law is not much further along than it was at the start of the 20th. From earliest days, the Movement has been attentive to peacetime disaster response policy, but has made no sustained effort to meet the legal dimensions of this challenge. It has fallen behind, relative to its own long record of service in the development of international humanitarian law.

Our response capacity grows, even as natural and technological disasters cut deeper and wider paths in the world. The law has grown very slowly, perhaps because earlier generations seldom encountered the same mix of humanitarian needs and means that are spread before us now. That said, it is unlikely that any other challenge looming so large in world affairs has received so little attention in the legal realm. During the early decades of the 21st century, a strong, new international law of disaster response could, and should, be counted among the International Red Cross and Red Crescent Movement's contributions to the world community.

Sources and further information

European Community. *Law in Humanitarian Crises. Volume II.* Luxembourg: European Commmunity, 1995.

International Committee of the Red Cross/International Federation of Red Cross and Red Crescent Societies. *Handbook of the International Red Cross and Red Crescent Movement.* Geneva: ICRC/International Federation, 1994.

ICRC/Henry Dunant Institute (HDI). *Bibliography of International Humanitarian Law Applicable in Armed Conflicts.* Geneva: ICRC/HDI, 1987.

Macalister-Smith, Peter. *International humanitarian assistance: disaster relief actions in international law and organization.* Dordrecht: Martinus Nijhoff, 1985.

Schindler and Toman (eds.). *The Laws of Armed Conflicts: a collection of Conventions, Resolutions and Other Documents.* Dordrecht: Martinus Nijhoff, 1988 (3rd edition).

UNESCO/HDI. *International Dimensions of Humanitarian Law.* Paris: UNESCO, 1988.

Web sites

European Union – http://europa.eu.int/celex/celex-en.html
International Committee of the Red Cross – http://www.icrcr.org
International Federation of Red Cross and Red Crescent Societies – http://www.ifrc.org
International Institute of Humanitarian Law – http://tdm.dmw.it/.iihl/profile.html
Office of the UN High Commissioner for Refugees –
http://www.unhcr.ch/refworld/legal/refcas/refcas.htm

chapter 9

Section Two

Tracking the system

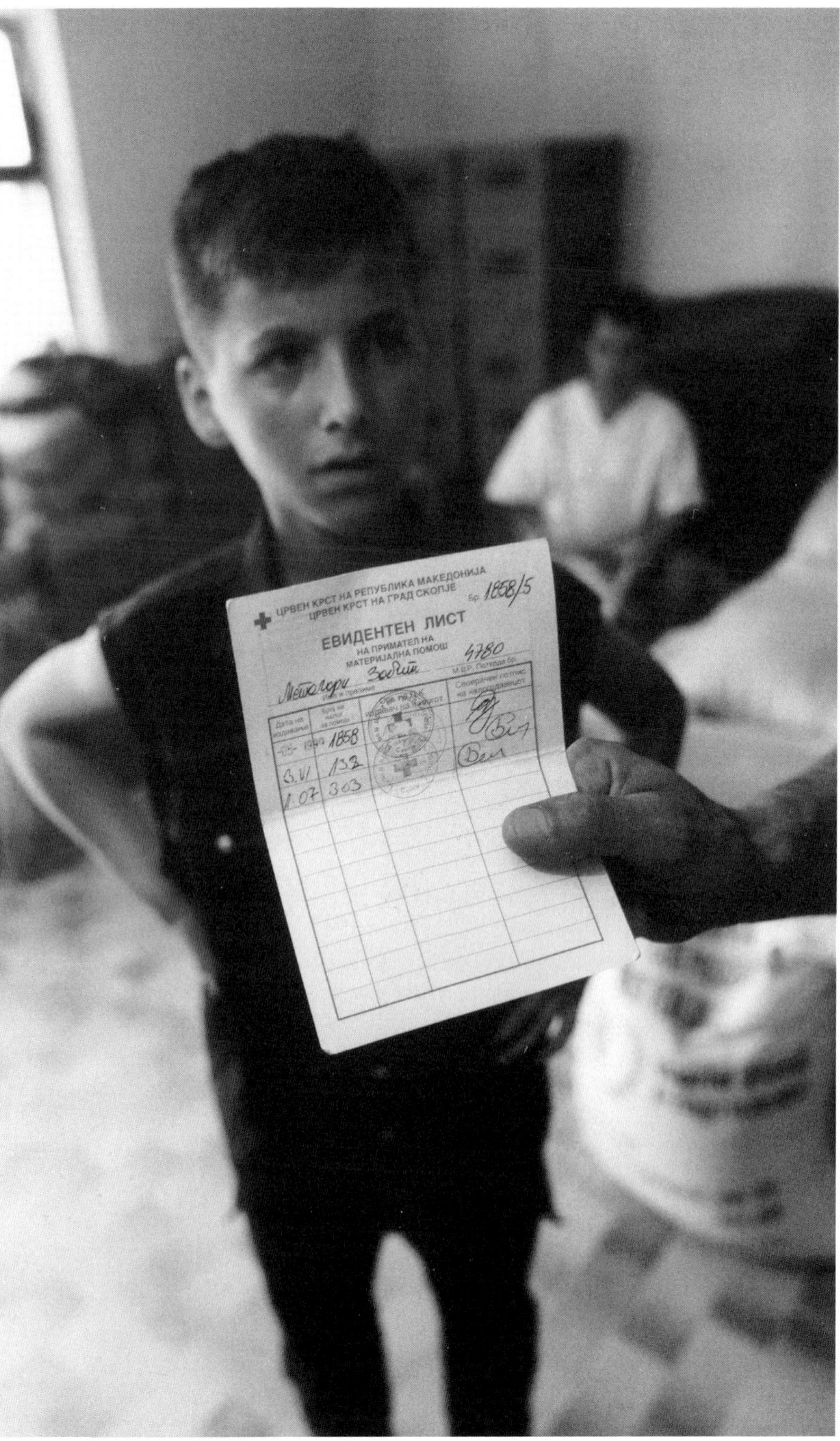

Disaster data: key to improved response

Data on disaster occurrence, its effect upon people and its cost to countries remain, at best, patchy. Despite a considerable increase in the funds being invested in disaster response, particularly international response, the international humanitarian community has been slow to recognize the need for consistent, and authoritative, objective data on disaster occurrence. More importantly, it has not been willing to invest the capital and authority necessary to allow any one institution to take on the role of prime providers of verified data. It is for this reason that the *World Disasters Report* draws upon four main sources of information for the data presented here: the Centre for Research on the Epidemiology of Disasters (CRED); the US Committee for Refugees (USCR); the Organisation for Economic Co-operation and Development's (OECD) Development Assistance Committee (DAC); and INTERFAIS, a World Food Programme (WFP) information system. Each organization is described in more detail below.

One of the key problems today with disaster data collection is the lack of standard, accepted definitions. Problems exist over such loose categories as 'internally displaced' people or even people 'affected' by disaster.

Much of the data in this chapter, except that on government humanitarian spending, is culled from a variety of public sources: newspapers, insurance reports, aid agencies, etc. The original information is not specifically gathered for statistical purposes and so, inevitably, even where the compiling organization applies strict definitions for disaster events and parameters, the original suppliers of the information may not.

The figures therefore should be regarded as indicative. Relative changes and trends are more useful to look at than absolute, isolated figures.

CRED

The Centre for Research on the Epidemiology of Disasters (CRED), established in 1973 as a non-profit institution, is located at the School of Public Health of the Louvain Catholic University (*Université Catholique de Louvain* (UCL)), in Brussels, Belgium. CRED became a World Health Organization (WHO) Collaborating Centre in 1980.

Although CRED's main focus is on safeguards, public health and the sanitary aspects of disasters, the centre also studies the socio-economic and long-term effects of these large-scale disasters. Increasingly preparedness, principally at the level of human resource development and problems linked to the management of crises, has gained a higher profile within CRED's activities.

Since 1988, the centre has maintained an Emergency Events Database – EM-DAT – sponsored by the International Federation of Red Cross and Red Crescent Societies, WHO, the United Nations Office for the Coordination of Humanitarian Affairs (OCHA) and the

Photo opposite page:
A young Kosovar refugee presents his registration card to receive a monthly food ration at the Macedonian Red Cross branch in Skopje. Accurate tracking of humanitarian needs and collation of data is essential to maximize aid efficiency.

Photo: Mikkel Oestergaard/ International Federation, Macedonia 1999.

European Community Humanitarian Office (ECHO). USAID's Office of Foreign Disaster Assistance (OFDA) also collaborated in getting the database started, and a recent OFDA/CRED initiative has made a specialized, validated disaster database available on CRED's website (http://www.cred.be). The database's main objective is to assist humanitarian action at both national and international levels and aims at rationalizing decision-making for disaster preparedness, as well as providing an objective base for vulnerability assessment and priority setting.

Tables 1 to 16 in this chapter have been drawn from EM-DAT, which contains essential core data on the occurrence and effects of over 12,000 mass disasters in the world from 1900 to the present. The database is compiled from various sources, including UN agencies, non-governmental organizations (NGOs), insurance companies, research institutes and press agencies. The entries are constantly reviewed for redundancies, inconsistencies and the completion of missing data.

A disaster is entered into the database if at least one of the following criteria is fulfilled:

- ten people are reported killed;
- 100 people are reported affected;
- an appeal for international assistance is issued; and/or
- a state of emergency is declared.

CRED consolidates and updates data on a daily basis; a further check is made at three-monthly intervals; and revisions are made annually at the end of the calendar year.

Priority is given to data from UN agencies, followed by OFDA, and then governments and the International Federation. This priority is not a reflection on the quality or value of the data, but the recognition that most reporting sources do not cover all disasters or have political limitations that may affect the figures.

USCR

The US Committee for Refugees (USCR), which supplied the data for tables 17 to 18, is the public information and advocacy arm of Immigration and Refugee Services of America, an NGO. USCR's activities are twofold: it reports on issues affecting refugees, asylum seekers and internally displaced people; and it encourages the public, policy-makers and the international community to respond appropriately and effectively to the needs of uprooted populations.

USCR travels to the scene of refugee emergencies to gather testimony from uprooted people, to assess their needs, and to gauge governmental and international response. The committee conducts public briefings to present its findings and recommendations, testifies before the US Congress, communicates concerns directly to governments, and provides first hand assessments to the media. USCR publishes the annual *World Refugee Survey,* the monthly *Refugee Reports,* and issue papers.

DAC/OECD

The data in table 19 have been supplied by the OECD's Development Assistance Committee, which is the principal body through which OECD deals with issues related to cooperation with developing countries. The committee is concerned with support for efforts in developing countries to strengthen local capacities to pursue integrated development strategies, and studies the financial aspects of development assistance, statistical problems, aid evaluation, and women in development.

INTERFAIS/WFP

The source of information for table 20 is INTERFAIS (the International Food Aid Information System), a system funded by WFP. It is a dynamic system, which involves the interaction of all users, represented by donor governments, international organizations, NGOs, recipient countries and WFP country offices. All information is cross-checked before being disseminated. Its comprehensive and integrated database allows the monitoring of food aid allocations and shipments for the purpose of improving food aid management, coordination and statistical analysis. The database is updated on a continuing basis, and data can therefore change as allocation plans and delivery schedules are subject to modifications. Data is available from 1988.

Disaster data

Information systems have improved vastly in the last 25 years and statistical data as a result are much more easily available. An increase in the number of disaster victims, for example, does not necessarily mean that disasters, or their impact, are increasing, but may simply be a reflection of better reporting.

However, the lack of systematic and standardized data collection from disasters, technological or natural, in the past is now revealing itself as a major weakness for any developmental planning. Despite efforts to verify, cross-check and review data, the quality of disaster databases can only be as good as the reporting system. Cost-benefit analyses, impact analyses of disasters or rationalization of preventive actions are severely compromised by unavailability and inaccuracy of data or even field methods for collection. Fortunately, as a result of increased pressures for accountability from various sources, many donor and development agencies have started placing priority on data collection and its methodologies, but this has yet to result in any recognized and acceptable international system for disaster data gathering, verification and storage.

Changes in national boundaries also cause ambiguities in the data, most notably the break-up of the Soviet Union and Yugoslavia, and the unification of Germany. In such cases, no attempt has been made to retrospectively desegregate or combine data. Statistics are presented for the country as it existed at the time the data were recorded.

The rationale behind data gathering may also impact upon statistics reported. Reinsurance companies, for instance, systematically gather data on disaster occurrence in order to assess insurance risk, but they do so mainly in areas of the world where disaster insurance is a regular occurrence, and thus often miss out whole regions where disasters affect some of the poorest for whom disaster insurance is an impossibility.

Data on the numbers of people affected by a disaster are some of the most potentially useful figures, for planing both disaster preparedness and response, yet these are also some of the most loosely reported figures. The definition of 'affected' is open to a great deal of interpretation, political or otherwise. In conflict, each party will wish to maximize sympathy for its cause and will thus maximize the number of people under its control who are said to be suffering. Even if political manipulation is absent, data is often derived by extrapolation from old census data, with assumptions being made about what percentage of an area's population is affected. Compounding errors in the original census, its extrapolation to present-day figures and the percentage of the population thought to be affected can sometimes render the final figure almost meaningless.

Part of the solution to this data problem lies in retrospective analysis. Data is most often publicly quoted and reported during a disaster event, but it is only long after the event, after the relief operation is over, that estimates of damage and death can be verified. Some data gatherers do this, and this accounts for retrospective annual disaster figures changing one, two and sometimes even three years after the event.

The bottom line, though, is that our data, at the aggregated international level, is still relative and indicative, rather than absolute. We can use it to identify potential trends and to understand the relative scale of things: which types of disasters affect most people, for instance, but we cannot use it to predict necessary investment in disaster preparedness or future needs for disaster response.

Tables 1 to 16

CRED's data have appeared in each edition of the *World Disasters Report* since the pilot issue in 1993. This year, the data are based on the following disaster types: avalanches and landslides, droughts, earthquakes, epidemics, extreme temperatures, floods, forest/scrub fires, volcanoes, wind storms and other natural disasters (which includes wave/surges and insect infestations) as well as non-natural disasters (i.e., industrial, miscellaneous and transport accidents). Famines, however, are no longer included in the report. In 1999, CRED carefully rechecked its data on famines and came to the conclusion that they were not reliable enough for publication in the report.

The number of disasters, the number of people reported killed or affected, and the estimated damage are successively presented by year, by continent and by type of phenomenon. Every table (except table 9) also includes a total figure for the whole ten-year period. The number of people affected includes those who were affected to a greater or lesser extent by disaster, injured and homeless people.

Estimates of damage need to be treated with caution. Inflation and currency fluctuation are not taken into account when calculating disaster-related damage. It is not always clear whether estimations are based on the cost of replacement or on the original value. Insurance figures, while using standard methodology, include only those assets that have been insured which, in most developing countries, represent a minor proportion of the losses.

- Tables 1, 2, 3 and 4 present the total numbers of reported disasters, people reported killed or affected, and the total amount of estimated damage, from 1990 to 1999, by continent.

- Tables 5, 6, 7 and 8 show the total numbers of reported disasters, people reported killed or affected, and the total amount of estimated damage, from 1990 to 1999, by type of phenomenon. Data on natural and man-made disasters, which include industrial, transport and miscellaneous accidents, are reported in these tables.

- Table 9 presents the total number of people reported killed or affected per country. Data are divided into two sets: the total number between 1990 and 1998; and the total for 1999. When a disaster strikes more than one country in a given region, data may only be given as a total of people reported killed or affected in the region as a whole. It was therefore decided to present such data in table 9 thus: NA-[region/continent].

- Tables 10, 11, 12 and 13 show the total number of reported disasters, people reported killed or affected, and the total amount of estimated damage, per continent and type of phenomenon, between 1990 and 1999. The tables also include a total figure for each continent and for each type of disaster.

- Tables 14, 15 and 16 present the total numbers of epidemics, people reported killed or affected by epidemics, from 1990 to 1999, by continent.

Tables 17 and 18

The data in these tables were provided by the USCR, and concern three categories of uprooted people: refugees; asylum seekers; and internally displaced people. Data concerning these populations are often controversial, for they involve judgements about why people have left their home areas. Differing definitions of the groups in question often promote confusion about the meaning of reported estimates.

USCR itself does not conduct censuses of these populations, although it does conduct first-hand site visits to assess refugee conditions. The committee evaluates population estimates circulated by governments, UN agencies and humanitarian assistance organizations, attempting to discern which of the various estimates appear to be most reliable. The estimates reproduced in these tables are USCR's preliminary year-end figures for 1999.
The quality of the data in these tables is affected by the less-than-ideal conditions often associated with flight. Unsettled conditions, the biases of governments and opposition groups, and the need to use population estimates to plan for providing humanitarian assistance can each contribute to inaccurate estimates.

Table 17 concerns refugees and asylum seekers and lists the two groups by host country. Refugees are people who are outside their home country and are unable or unwilling to return to that country because they fear persecution or armed conflict. Asylum seekers are people who claim to be refugees; many are awaiting a determination of their refugee status. While not all asylum seekers are refugees, they are nonetheless entitled to certain protections under international refugee law, at least until they are determined not to be refugees. Different standards for refugee status exist in different countries or regions. Recognition of refugee status, however, does not *make* someone a refugee, but rather *declares* her or him to be one. "He does not become a refugee because of recognition, but is recognized because he is a refugee," the Office of the UN High Commissioner for Refugees (UNHCR) has noted. Not all refugees are recognized as such by governments.

USCR includes in table 17 people who have been admitted as refugees or granted asylum during the year, but thereafter regards them as having been granted permanent protection, even if they have not yet officially become citizens of their adopted country. This method of record-keeping differs from that employed by UNHCR, which continues counting refugees until they gain citizenship.

Table 18 concerns 'internally displaced people'. Like refugees and asylum seekers, internally displaced people have fled their homes; unlike refugees and asylum seekers, however, they remain within their home country. No universally accepted definition of an 'internally displaced person' exists. USCR generally considers people who are uprooted within their country because of armed conflict or persecution – and thus would be refugees if they were to cross an international border – to be internally displaced. Broader definitions are employed by some agencies, however, who sometimes include people who are uprooted by natural or human-made disasters or other causes not directly related to human rights.

Internally displaced people often live in war-torn areas and may be subject to ongoing human rights abuse, sometimes at the hands of their own government. Most internally displaced people are neither registered nor counted in any systematic way. Estimates of the size of internally displaced populations are frequently subject to great margins of error.

(In the following tables, some totals may not correspond due to rounding.)

Data sources

CRED

School of Public Health
Catholic University of Louvain
30.94 Clos Chapelle-aux-Champs
1200 Brussels
Belgium
Tel.: (32)(2) 764 3369
Fax: (32)(2) 764 3441
E-mail: Caroline.Michellier@epid.ucl.ac.be
Web site: http://www.md.ucl.ac.be/cred

US Committee for Refugees

1717 Massachusetts Avenue, NW
Suite 200
Washington, DC 20036
USA
Tel: (1)(202) 347 3507
Fax: (1)(202) 347 3418
E-mail: aspringer@irsa-uscr.org
Web site: www.refugees.org

OECD/DAC
2, rue André-Pascal
75775 Paris Cedex 16
France
Tel.: (33)(1) 4524 9017
Fax: (33)(1) 4524 1980
E-mail: dac.contact@oecd.org

Food Aid Information Group
World Food Programme
Via Cristoforo Colombo, 426
00145 Rome
Italy
Tel.: (39)(6) 5228 2796
Fax: (39(6) 513 2879
E-mail: george.simon@wfp.org

Box 9.1 Disaster data: use with caution

When the 'World Disasters Report' started life in 1993, one of its key goals was to make good data on disasters systematically available to disaster response professionals. The report still holds to this goal, and today, eight years on, data on disasters still suffers from many of the same problems it did nearly a decade ago.

Two underlying issues continue to frustrate efforts to systemize the data.

First, the problem of definitions. It is doubtful that one could ever have a universally applied and meaningful definition of a disaster and so the very events that count as a disaster in one country may not be even looked at in another. Similarly, there is no definition of 'people affected' and no single methodology used for collecting the data. Figures can be culled from newspaper reports, government statements, insurance company returns. The data therefore around disasters is essentially soft and noisy. In many instances, it is better to look at it for trends rather than precise figures.

Second, because there are neither precise definitions behind the data nor a single source of statistics, figures for the same parameters for the same event may vary greatly according to source. Take, for example, figures quoted in the initial stages of a famine on the number of people affected. What the host government says, what the donor community say and what the NGOs say are rarely the same.

In the 'World Disasters Report', we have tried to be consistent in our sourcing of data from year to year as far as the compiled tables in chapter 9 are concerned; however, data used in individual chapters which focus on particular themes or countries may often come from different sources. Thus, the figure for, say, numbers affected by disaster in a country may well vary between the chapter and the main database. Neither figure is wrong, nor right. Both represent educated estimates.

The bottom line, therefore, is to use disaster data with caution. It represents a collection of estimates and educated extrapolations.

Table 1 Total number of reported disasters* by continent and by year (1990 to 1999)

	AFRICA	AMERICAS	ASIA	EUROPE	OCEANIA	TOTAL
1990	51	106	215	138	36	546
1991	69	141	245	95	18	568
1992	60	105	194	70	17	446
1993	52	110	247	60	14	483
1994	47	66	135	59	15	322
1995	62	110	180	71	8	431
1996	79	100	187	56	17	439
1997	87	101	208	63	15	474
1998	109	126	229	50	18	532
1999	182	123	231	72	15	623
Total	**798**	**1,088**	**2,071**	**734**	**173**	**4,864**

Source: EM-DAT, CRED, University of Louvain, Belgium

Table 2 Total number of people reported killed by continent and by year (1990 to 1999)

	AFRICA	AMERICAS	ASIA	EUROPE	OCEANIA	TOTAL
1990	3,049	2,374	53,528	1,762	124	60,837
1991	15,368	13,534	169,370	2,872	315	201,459
1992	5,622	2,874	15,667	835	6	25,004
1993	2,230	4,690	26,279	926	120	34,245
1994	4,583	2,459	12,867	1,996	70	21,975
1995	6,155	2,708	22,166	3,333	24	34,386
1996	16,873	2,720	16,688	928	111	37,320
1997	13,288	2,810	17,687	1,032	398	35,215
1998	12,217	13,254	32,875	1,005	2,341	61,692
1999	6,166	33,635	39,072	1,426	105	80,404
Total	**85,551**	**81,058**	**406,199**	**16,115**	**3,614**	**592,537**

Source: EM-DAT, CRED, University of Louvain, Belgium
* excluding conflict and chronic public health disasters

As can be seen from table 1, from 1990 to 1999, Asia was the continent the most frequently hit by disasters, with more than 40 per cent of the total number recorded in EM-DAT.

Globally, the number of reported disasters has remained relatively stable except for 1994 and 1999. However, since the mid-1990s in Africa and Asia, there seems to have been a gradual increase in the number of disasters; despite preparedness programmes, both continents have been more and more affected by disasters. Setbacks in development programmes and conflict may have contributed to these increases.

Table 2 shows that the number of fatalities resulting from disasters has increased each year since 1994. Once again, Asia represents more than two-thirds of the total number of fatalities. The worst year for fatalities was 1991, when a cyclone devastated Bangladesh, leading to some 139,000 deaths, and several cholera epidemics in Africa killed about 19,000 people. The Americas saw its worst year in 1999, when official estimates set the number of dead from the Venezuelan floods at 30,000. In Europe, deaths totalled less than 2,000 a year, except for 1991 (a flood in Soviet Union killed 1,700 people), 1994 (more than 1,800 died when the ferry 'Estonia' sank) and 1995 (an earthquake in Russia killed 1,989 people).

Table 3 Total number of people reported affected by continent and by year (1990 to 1999)

	AFRICA	AMERICAS	ASIA	EUROPE	OCEANIA	TOTAL
1990	14,880,561	3,355,949	93,509,065	527,829	211,897	112,485,301
1991	15,662,874	854,527	323,653,306	71,657	93,713	340,336,077
1992	21,409,805	2,532,078	52,003,996	46,756	1,848,802	77,841,437
1993	1,207,407	5,792,964	175,572,442	1,384,499	5,177,079	189,134,391
1994	15,294,614	3,295,780	169,811,321	593,883	6,139,042	195,134,640
1995	9,365,619	1,348,351	242,368,376	6,478,674	2,681,939	262,242,959
1996	7,463,691	1,494,614	163,649,742	3,529,364	652,127	176,789,538
1997	6,222,444	2,023,219	22,253,747	660,735	1,224,060	32,384,205
1998	6,650,746	22,502,581	330,031,355	522,869	328,059	360,035,610
1999	6,294,514	13,494,780	187,617,273	4,986,835	151,245	212,544,647
Total	**104,452,275**	**56,694,843**	**1,760,470,623**	**18,803,101**	**18,507,963**	**1,958,928,805**

Source: EM-DAT, CRED, University of Louvain, Belgium

Table 4 Total amount of estimated damage by continent and by year (1990 to 1999) in US$ thousands

	AFRICA	AMERICAS	ASIA	EUROPE	OCEANIA	TOTAL
1990	740,600	4,891,950	27,955,900	15,958,500	1,010,400	50,557,350
1991	21,200	13,425,695	34,182,422	66,182,700	1,315,520	115,127,537
1992	232,200	35,706,949	14,134,542	3,766,300	2,054,113	55,894,104
1993	23,875	21,587,877	14,110,181	2,581,960	1,419,600	39,723,493
1994	440,564	25,338,568	27,654,199	18,451,700	1,689,600	73,574,631
1995	123,339	22,848,939	156,313,591	11,337,189	1,278,700	191,901,758
1996	111,000	13,042,400	29,549,992	1,488,100	989,033	45,180,525
1997	89,500	8,055,887	25,446,600	9,799,500	206,700	43,598,187
1998	240,780	21,549,567	29,844,037	1,465,200	178,000	53,277,584
1999	516,744	11,782,450	41,887,927	17,158,331	852,762	72,198,214
Total	**2,539,802**	**178,230,282**	**401,079,391**	**148,189,480**	**10,994,428**	**741,033,383**

Source: EM-DAT, CRED, University of Louvain, Belgium

Globally, almost 2 billion people have been affected by disasters during the 1990s, of whom some 90 per cent live in Asia as can be seen from table 3. The decade's two El Niño years (1991 and 1998) show the highest numbers of affected, but floods in China account for some 60 per cent of the disaster-affected during these two years (210,232,227 in May 1991, and 238,973,000 in August 1998). Population density in disaster-prone countries obviously has a direct effect on the number of people affected.

In table 4, Asia again tops the list with more than 50 per cent of the total amount of estimated damage recorded during the 1990s. However, this percentage is essentially the consequence of the 1995 Kobe earthquake (US$ 131.5 million). In 1991, floods in Russia caused damage estimated at US$ 60 million. The financial value attached to infrastructure in the more developed nations is several magnitudes higher than that attached to equivalent structures in developing countries. Moreover, damage to infrastructure will always result in higher damage estimate than suffering of individuals, which cannot be calculated in economic terms.

Table 5 Total number of reported disasters by type of phenomenon and by year (1990 to 1999)

	Avalanches/ landslides	Droughts	Earth-quakes	Epidemics*	Extreme temperatures	Floods	Forest/ scrub fires	Volcanoes	Wind storms	Other natural disasters**	Non-natural disasters***	Total
1990	6	11	57	18	15	66	5	2	147		219	546
1991	11	14	29	45	10	87	9	11	70	2	280	568
1992	17	23	26	26	10	60	8	5	89		182	446
1993	25	10	18	4	5	88	2	6	106	2	217	483
1994	5	8	20	8	9	78	12	8	58		116	322
1995	15	12	24	22	14	93	7	4	58	4	178	431
1996	24	6	11	34	6	73	4	5	66	2	208	439
1997	13	11	14	49	13	80	15	4	69	3	203	474
1998	23	22	17	64	13	94	16	4	73	2	204	532
1999	14	26	33	70	7	110	22	5	85	2	249	623
Total	**153**	**143**	**249**	**340**	**102**	**829**	**100**	**54**	**821**	**17**	**2,056**	**4,864**

* Does not include chronic public health disasters, such as the AIDS pandemic
** Insect infestations, waves/surges
*** Industrial, transport and miscellaneous accidents
Source: EM-DAT, CRED, University of Louvain, Belgium

Table 5 shows the total number of reported disasters from 1990 to 1999. During this period, EM-DAT recorded more natural than man-made disasters (respectively, 57 and 43 per cent). Floods and wind storms represent more than 58 per cent of the total of natural disasters and about 34 per cent of the total number of recorded disasters. However, no link could be identified between the occurrence of a specific type of phenomenon and the El Niño years (1991 and 1998), although more people were affected in those years.

Table 6 Total number of people reported killed by type of phenomenon and by year (1990 to 1999)

	Avalanches/ landslides	Droughts	Earth-quakes	Epidemics*	Extreme temperatures	Floods	Forest/ scrub fires	Volcanoes	Wind storms	Other natural disasters**	Non-natural disasters***	Total
1990	200		38,068	2,864	996	3,662	1	33	5,689		9,324	60,837
1991	821	2,000	4,809	28,540	800	8,455	102	715	146,061	10	9,146	201,459
1992	1,106		3,554	5,533	390	4,942	122	2	2,223		7,132	25,004
1993	1,618		9,819	859	106	8,977	3	149	3,143	59	9,512	34,245
1994	158		1,336	2,240	380	7,398	62	124	4,371		5,906	21,975
1995	1,449		8,257	4,069	1,708	8,497	29		3,244		7,133	34,386
1996	1,129		582	9,948	300	7,131	45	4	5,232	32	8,961	37,320
1997	806	530	2,960	13,092	431	6,866	32	53	5,133	400	8,056	35,215
1998	1,044	260	7,423	11,224	3,225	13,644	109		14,804	2,182	7,777	61,692
1999	327		21,870	4,866	719	34,298	70		11,890	3	6,361	80,404
Total	**8,658**	**2,790**	**98,678**	**84,047**	**9,055**	**103,870**	**575**	**1,080**	**201,790**	**2,686**	**79,308**	**592,537**

* Does not include chronic public health disasters, such as the AIDS pandemic
** Insect infestations, waves/surges
*** Industrial, transport and miscellaneous accidents
Source: EM-DAT, CRED, University of Louvain, Belgium

Table 6 shows that, in the 1990s, wind storms were the biggest killers: approximately one-third of all reported deaths were due to wind storms. Fatalities were particularly high in 1991, largely due to the cyclone in Bangladesh (see table 2 comments). Floods, earthquakes and epidemics also killed about 1 million people each. The number of people reported killed by floods in 1999 is more than double the total of other years in the 1990s. This was due to the floods in Venezuela (see table 2 comments). The number of people killed by earthquakes was particularly high in 1990 (Iranian quake on 6 June 1990: 36,000 people reported killed) and in 1999 (Turkish quake on 17 August 1999: 17,127 people reported killed).

Table 7 Total number of people reported affected by type of phenomenon and by year (1990 to 1999)

	Avalanches/ landslides	Droughts	Earth-quakes	Epidemics*	Extreme temperatures	Floods	Forest/ scrub fires	Volcanoes	Wind storms	Other natural disasters**	Non-natural disasters***	Total
1990	5,115	15,753,160	2,107,674	44,015	1,000,260	67,391,247		46,851	26,098,695		38,284	112,485,301
1991	35,971	22,816,282	1,107,914	1,942,895	450	285,564,130	2,519	865,002	27,845,250	2,000	153,664	340,336,077
1992	57,735	37,047,103	775,897	680,420	16,240	21,842,835	52,025	361,075	16,934,932		73,175	77,841,437
1993	23,832	9,621,507	242,678	417,164	3,005,760	155,285,875	130	173,753	20,307,335		56,357	189,134,391
1994	162,366	11,615,000	618,737	6,564,353	1,608,184	130,411,797	3,292,413	291,869	40,545,837		24,084	195,134,640
1995	1,117,223	26,922,904	1,361,146	441,592	515,278	219,617,488	11,754	16,876	12,196,340	200	42,158	262,242,959
1996	8,686	5,910,000	1,908,498	643,470	60,200	151,952,638	5,811	6,572	16,259,513	24	34,126	176,789,538
1997	11,736	4,830,100	542,452	322,267	614,580	13,326,790	53,159	7,200	12,527,424	10,000	138,497	32,384,205
1998	230,131	20,329,335	1,827,021	915,180	36,286	306,928,966	166,432	7,808	29,488,992	9,867	95,592	360,035,610
1999	15,291	30,227,145	3,893,465	466,852	725,246	147,253,658	17,930	34,055	29,891,154	1,300	18,551	212,544,647
Total	**1,668,086**	**185,072,536**	**14,385,482**	**12,438,208**	**7,582,484**	**1,499,575,424**	**3,602,173**	**1,811,061**	**232,095,472**	**23,391**	**674,488**	**1,958,928,805**

* Does not include chronic public health disasters, such as the AIDS pandemic
** Insect infestations, waves/surges
*** Industrial, transport and miscellaneous accidents
Source: EM-DAT, CRED, University of Louvain, Belgium

During the last decade, floods have affected about 1.5 billion people, i.e., more than 75 per cent of the total of people reported affected by disasters worldwide. Floods in China, with 1,026,700,000 people affected over the last decade (i.e., almost 70 per cent of the floods' total), are the principal cause. The raw numbers of flood-affected people do not reflect a particular trend, but the worst numbers were recorded in the El Niño years, 1991 and 1998. Wind storms and droughts have also affected many people (respectively 11.8 and 9.4 per cent of the total of people reported affected). Non-natural disasters recorded have affected very few people (less than 0.035 per cent of the total); this, however, could be a reporting artefact.

Table 8 Total amount of estimated damage by type of phenomenon and by year (1990 to 1999) in US$ thousands

	Avalanches/ landslides	Droughts	Earth-quakes	Epidemics*	Extreme temperatures	Floods	Forest/ scrub fires	Volcanoes	Wind storms	Other natural disasters**	Non-natural disasters***	Total
1990		1,036,000	8,221,150		360,250	6,156,600	991,000	8,000	30,497,735		3,286,615	50,557,350
1991	15,400	2,073,000	2,287,088		972,000	73,658,693	14,780,000	239,200	11,753,183		9,348,973	115,127,537
1992	32,249	2,488,600	653,850		2,950,000	5,436,345	421,200		41,125,723		2,786,137	55,894,104
1993	710,790	1,105,200	1,929,000			23,275,328	1,000,000	488	8,046,158		3,656,529	39,723,493
1994	38,300	1,223,755	31,781,004		2,230,000	27,106,724	152,000	400,440	8,478,408		2,164,000	73,574,631
1995	10,289	5,776,539	132,977,000		1,134,300	26,459,042	134,500		23,644,689	104,000	1,661,399	191,901,758
1996		1,200,000	528,400		12,000	24,227,042	1,712,800	16,500	13,355,683		4,128,100	45,180,525
1997	116,300	2,000	4,792,000		3,004,000	11,148,287	17,009,200	8,000	7,127,900	3,500	387,000	43,598,187
1998	5,700	359,970	378,100		3,700,000	33,051,080	564,100		14,594,493	1,700	622,441	53,277,584
1999		6,676,000	31,475,619			13,042,759	210,636		20,767,721	267	25,212	72,198,214
Total	**929,028**	**21,941,064**	**215,023,211**		**14,362,550**	**243,561,900**	**36,975,436**	**672,628**	**179,391,693**	**109,467**	**28,066,406**	**741,033,383**

* Does not include chronic public health disasters, such as the AIDS pandemic
** Insect infestations, waves/surges
*** Industrial, transport and miscellaneous accidents
Source: EM-DAT, CRED, University of Louvain, Belgium

Damage estimations are notoriously unreliable. Methodologies are not standard, and coverage is not complete. Depending on where the disaster occurred and who is reporting, estimates will vary from none to billions of US dollars. Floods, earthquakes and wind storms were the most costly types of phenomenon in the 1990s. No direct damage is ever reported after epidemics. Estimates of life years lost or cost in terms of productivity losses, however, could be undertaken.

Table 9 Annual average (1990-1998) and total (1999) number of people reported killed and affected by country

	Annual average killed (1990–1998)	Annual average affected (1990–1998)	Killed (1999)	Affected (1999)
AFRICA	**8,821**	**10,906,418**	**6,166**	**6,294,514**
Algeria	46	9,793	46	33,433
Angola	89	110,138	216	726
Benin	26	81,184	12	57,710
Botswana	2	11,722		
Burkina Faso	714	294,271	6	1,560
Burundi	24	3,230	66	228,810
Cameroon	317	2,019	67	4,115
Cape Verde Is.	9	1,034	18	
Central African Rep.	7	3,448	14	45,991
Chad	159	39,303	0	173,506
Comoros	27	22	16	172
Congo, DR (ex-Zaire)	303	8,201	89	78,013
Congo, Rep. of	68	2,267	17	42,099
Côte d'Ivoire	16	45	53	71
Djibouti	24	27,116	0	100,000
Egypt	316	22,831	210	242
Eritrea	14	2,448		
Ethiopia	79	1,386,209	85	788,357
Gabon	16	6		
Gambia	27	752	53	32,000
Ghana	190	79,713	76	325,798
Guinea	87	3,563	32	148
Guinea-Bissau	136	4,431	158	1,149
Kenya	436	1,414,291	677	308,347
Lesotho	2	55,750		
Liberia	9	111,889	39	
Libyan Arab Jamah.	20			
Madagascar	89	326,919	301	5,633
Malawi	134	1,663,266	0	2,000
Mali	196	36,713	2	2,200
Mauritania	22	52,091	1	23,977
Mauritius	1	1,000	0	1,000
Morocco	76	10,356	102	162
Mozambique	339	816,787	23	70,000
Namibia	2	45,911	0	25,000
Niger	633	199,563	63	25,136
Nigeria	1,753	87,581	1,190	120,917
Reunion	7			
Rwanda	10	346	111	895,164
Senegal	26	35,928	659	98,784
Seychelles	1	28		
Sierra Leone	98	23,089	17	384
Somalia	404	119,965	193	4,476
South Africa	154	37,297	235	23,158
Sudan	481	1,160,236	777	2,004,201
Swaziland	12	58,581		
Tanzania	542	873,314	201	629
Togo	83	20,395	0	65,000
Tunisia	9	5,343		
Uganda	78	49,641	187	702,205
Zambia	290	477,550	87	1,779
Zimbabwe	217	1,128,842	67	462
AMERICAS	**5,269**	**4,800,008**	**33,635**	**13,494,780**
Anguilla			0	150
Antigua & Barbuda	0	7,859	1	5,957
Argentina	42	515,117	94	43
Bahamas	0	189	1	1,500
Belize	2	6,667		
Bolivia	80	71,067	44	7,916
Brazil	202	1,193,659	46	502,038
Canada	59	63,499	12	5,870
Chile	62	32,443	0	100
Colombia	204	32,498	1,284	1,360,763
Costa Rica	24	63,321	9	9,993
Cuba	77	256,091	4	254,990
Dominica	1	333	0	715
Dominican Rep.	82	506,313	16	
Ecuador	197	43,857	0	24,200
El Salvador	172	16,252	53	5,450
French Guiana		7,778		
Grenada		111	0	210
Guadeloupe			4	899
Guatemala	118	16,560	68	6,377
Guyana		88,578		
Haiti	446	178,269	26	50
Honduras	686	277,924	34	503,001
Jamaica	1	27,611		

	Annual average killed (1990–1998)	Annual average affected (1990–1998)	Killed (1999)	Affected (1999)
Martinique	1	501	0	600
Mexico	440	242,339	903	730,299
Montserrat	4	1,556		
Netherlands Antilles	0	4,444		
Nicaragua	301	211,937	55	113,300
Panama	23	5,379	1	895
Paraguay	6	65,962	0	100,000
Peru	1,402	527,215	150	250,579
Puerto Rico	8	11,832		
St Kitts & Nevis	1	1,311	0	1,180
St Lucia		103	0	200
St Vincent & Grenadines	0	22	0	100
Trinidad & Tobago	1	179		
United States	537	305,706	792	9,062,855
Uruguay	11	1,949	14	1,047
Venezuela	81	12,464	30,021	543,503
Virgin Is. (UK)		1		
Virgin Is. (US)	1	1,111	3	
ASIA	**40,792**	**174,761,483**	**39,072**	**187,617,273**
Afghanistan	1,363	42,756	393	149,018
Armenia[1]	12	868		
Azerbaijan[1]	55	286,815	1	15,265
Bahrain	1			
Bangladesh	16,954	14,570,974	158	558,730
Bhutan	4	7,286	0	
Cambodia	91	263,840	104	661,633
China	3,694	117,362,503	2,367	127,445,924
Cyprus	6	94	0	
Georgia[1]	49	29,691	38	
Hong Kong (China)	45	223,119	5	704
India	5,536	27,499,647	12,074	39,389,775
Indonesia	1,039	693,049	510	34,851
Iran	4,516	173,701	297	32,721
Iraq	10	32		
Israel	18	187	0	
Japan	747	150,872	98	51,317
Jordan	3	2,028	0	180,000
Kazakhstan[1]	24	71,848		
Korea, DPR	97	1,003,629	42	42,135
Korea, Rep.	209	80,826	145	30,797
Kuwait	0	27		

	Annual average killed (1990–1998)	Annual average affected (1990–1998)	Killed (1999)	Affected (1999)
Kyrgyzstan[1]	26	31,548		
Lao, PDR	92	95,370	0	20,000
Lebanon	8	6,008		
Macau		443		
Malaysia	76	5,233	100	2,157
Maldives		2,650	10	
Mongolia	35	11,685		
Myanmar	87	515,074	22	50,000
Nepal	785	160,108	409	23,048
Pakistan	936	2,692,530	531	668,297
Palestine (West Bank)			14	20
Philippines	1,664	5,257,255	312	2,147,607
Saudi Arabia	256	422	74	127
Singapore	0	160		
Sri Lanka	75	335,262	9	604,485
Syrian Arab Rep.	4	1	62	329,079
Taiwan (China)	93	2,271	2,264	108,987
Tajikistan[1]	227	40,738	30	11,092
Thailand	309	1,753,499	57	6,283,854
Turkey	328	37,917	18,019	1,569,866
Turkmenistan[1]	4	47		
United Arab Emirates	9	11	12	
Uzbekistan[1]	15	7,983	12	2,688
Viet Nam	1,077	1,288,960	893	7,183,314
Yemen	105	52,516	10	19,782
NA-Asia	57			
NA-South Asia	49			
EUROPE	**1,632**	**1,535,141**	**1,426**	**4,986,835**
Albania	7	5,179		
Austria	4	25	68	10,032
Azores	4	135	35	
Belarus[1]	2	4,581	56	2,078
Belgium	8	235	0	905
Bosnia and Herzegovina[2]	1		0	1,090
Bulgaria	3	638	0	850
Croatia[2]	5	231		
Czech Republic[3]	5	11,350		
Czechoslovakia[3]	5			
Denmark	35	16	7	
Estonia[1]	101	16		
Finland	2	4		

	Annual average killed (1990–1998)	Annual average affected (1990–1998)	Killed (1999)	Affected (1999)
France	62	36,104	209	3,701,405
Germany	32	16,210	20	100,000
Germany, Fed. Rep.[4]	3	8		
Greece	26	3,259	154	172,000
Hungary	1	27	48	133,495
Iceland	4	9		
Ireland	5	389	0	700
Italy	86	22,458	67	10
Lithuania[1]	2	86,667		
Luxembourg		10		
Macedonia, FYR[2]	22	2		
Malta	1			
Moldova[1]	5	2,778	0	3,360
Netherlands	14	29,349	18	213
Norway	46	444	16	
Poland	30	25,090	134	
Portugal	12	157		
Romania	51	73,653	34	14,106
Russian Fed.[1]	545	40,410	356	738,609
Serbia Montenegro[2]	6	674	35	71,008
Slovakia[3]	7	1,396	2	36,148
Soviet Union[1]	264	7,078		
Spain	53	674,265	33	45
Sweden	31	21		
Switzerland	6	599	46	6
Ukraine[1]	59	48,939	49	
United Kingdom	35	442,721	39	775
Yugoslavia[2]	18	13		
NA-European Union	10			
NA-Europe	12			

	Annual average killed (1990–1998)	Annual average affected (1990–1998)	Killed (1999)	Affected (1999)
OCEANIA	**390**	**2,039,635**	**105**	**151,245**
American Samoa	3			
Australia	32	1,762,211	8	12,726
Cook Is.	2	100		
Fiji	5	48,194	29	1,772
French Polynesia	1	57		
Guam	25	1,337		
Micronesia		3,200		
New Zealand	0	335	0	350
Niue		22	1	297
Palau	0	1,333		
Papua New Guinea	313	176,501	23	38,000
Samoa	2	31,444		
Solomon Is.	4	11,989		
Tokelau		11		
Tonga	0	1,075		
Tuvalu		94		
Vanuatu	1	1,730	44	14,100
Wallis & Futuna Is.	1	1		
Grand total	**56,904**	**194,042,685**	**80,404**	**212,544,647**

Source: EM-DAT, CRED, University of Louvain, Belgium

1 Prior to 1991, the Soviet Union is considered one country; after this date as separate countries. Belarus, Estonia, Latvia, Lithuania, Moldova, Russian Federation and Ukraine are included in Europe. Armenia, Azerbaijan, Georgia, Kazakhstan, Kyrgyzstan, Tajikistan, Turkmenistan and Uzbekistan are included in Asia.

2 Prior to 1992, Yugoslavia is considered one country; after this date as separate countries: Bosnia and Herzegovina, Croatia, FRY Macedonia, Serbia Montenegro, Slovenia and Yugoslavia.

3 Prior to 1993, Czechoslovakia is considered one country; after this date as separate countries (Czech and Slovak Republics).

4 Prior to October 1990, Germany was divided into the Federal Republic of Germany and the German Democratic Republic; after this date is considered as one country.

Globally and compared to the annual average established for 1990 to 1998, 1999 reported more disaster victims. Two specific disaster events account for this: the Venezuelan flood (30,000 people reported killed) and hurricane Floyd in the United States (9,000,000 people reported affected). The devastating effects of last year's winter storm can also be seen with France reporting a larger number of affected people than usual. In Asia, the total number of people reported affected and killed are close to the average, despite the fact that wide differences can be found in some countries: Turkish earthquakes, centennial floods in Viet Nam and drought in Thailand may be highlighted in this regard.

Table 10 Total number of reported disasters by continent and type of phenomenon (1990 to 1999)

	AFRICA	AMERICAS	ASIA	EUROPE	OCEANIA	TOTAL
Avalanches/landslides	7	39	83	18	6	153
Droughts	65	24	31	11	12	143
Earthquakes	13	56	126	38	16	249
Epidemics*	183	51	88	16	2	340
Extreme temperatures	5	23	39	30	5	102
Floods	149	206	351	97	26	829
Forest/scrub fires	6	43	20	23	8	100
Wind storms	39	269	332	115	66	821
Volcanoes	3	24	20	2	5	54
Other natural disasters**	3	4	9		1	17
Non-natural disasters***	325	349	972	384	26	2,056
Total	**798**	**1,088**	**2,071**	**734**	**173**	**4,864**

Source: EM-DAT, CRED, University of Louvain, Belgium

Table 11 Total number of people reported killed by continent and by type of phenomenon (1990 to 1999)

	AFRICA	AMERICAS	ASIA	EUROPE	OCEANIA	TOTAL
Avalanches/landslides	225	2,010	5,500	644	279	8,658
Droughts	12		2,680		98	2,790
Earthquakes	816	3,519	91,878	2,395	70	98,678
Epidemics*	57,082	12,123	14,316	411	115	84,047
Extreme temperatures	102	1,998	5,974	954	27	9,055
Floods	9,487	35,598	55,916	2,839	30	103,870
Forest/scrub fires	79	101	260	127	8	575
Wind storms	1,612	13,264	185,739	913	262	201,790
Volcanoes		77	994		9	1,080
Other natural disasters**		15	489		2,182	2,686
Non-natural disasters***	16,136	12,353	42,453	7,832	534	79,308
Total	**85,551**	**81,058**	**406,199**	**16,115**	**3,614**	**592,537**

* Does not include chronic public health disasters, such as the AIDS pandemic

** Insect infestation, waves/surges

*** Industrial, transport and miscellaneous accidents

Source: EM-DAT, CRED, University of Louvain, Belgium

In Africa, between 1990 and 1999, epidemics and floods caused the largest number of disasters, whereas the biggest disaster killer was epidemics which caused over 70 per cent of deaths. In the Americas and Asia, floods and wind storms were the most common disasters and killed the highest numbers of people. In Europe, non-natural disasters represent more than 52 per cent of the total (of which half are transport accidents), but it is the only continent where deaths caused by non-natural disasters equal those of natural disasters. In Oceania, wind storms were the most frequent types of disasters, while waves/surges were responsible for more than 60 per cent of total disaster deaths.

Table 12 Total number of people reported affected by continent and by type of phenomenon (1990 to 1999)

	AFRICA	AMERICAS	ASIA	EUROPE	OCEANIA	TOTAL
Avalanches/ landslides	2,875	178,995	1,467,552	13,044	5,620	1,668,086
Droughts	76,436,356	16,458,160	77,595,385	6,000,000	8,582,635	185,072,536
Earthquakes	150,993	1,990,885	11,788,179	416,017	39,408	14,385,482
Epidemics*	8,291,889	1,144,188	2,831,558	170,276	297	12,438,208
Extreme temperatures	1,000,000	32,400	706,130	1,243,170	4,600,784	7,582,484
Floods	13,016,814	8,475,133	1,475,640,966	2,206,325	236,186	1,499,575,424
Forest/scrub fires	4,505	89,616	3,105,109	121,782	281,161	3,602,173
Wind storms	5,407,540	27,675,256	185,873,049	8,555,803	4,583,824	232,095,472
Volcanoes	9,516	510,611	1,130,033	7,000	153,901	1,811,061
Other natural disasters**		3,124	10,400		9,867	23,391
Non-natural disasters***	131,787	136,475	322,262	69,684	14,280	674,488
Total	**104,452,275**	**56,694,843**	**1,760,470,623**	**18,803,101**	**18,507,963**	**1,958,928,805**

Table 13 Total amount of estimated damage by continent and by type of phenomenon (1990-1999) in US$ thousands

	AFRICA	AMERICAS	ASIA	EUROPE	OCEANIA	TOTAL
Avalanches/ landslides		515,549	388,790	24,689		929,028
Droughts	116,939	4,440,000	2,819,525	9,888,600	4,676,000	21,941,064
Earthquakes	282,129	23,810,360	183,782,218	6,893,504	255,000	215,023,211
Extreme temperatures	47,000	8,251,250	3,968,000	2,096,300		14,362,550
Floods	576,269	35,975,752	112,575,329	93,638,450	796,100	243,561,900
Forest/scrub fires		3,498,100	32,299,300	1,021,336	156,700	36,975,436
Wind storms	1,149,565	86,941,171	60,640,928	26,114,101	4,545,928	179,391,693
Volcanoes		33,000	223,128	16,500	400,000	672,628
Other natural disasters**	5,200	104,000	267			109,467
Non-natural disasters***	362,700	14,661,100	4,381,906	8,496,000	164,700	28,066,406
Total	**2,539,802**	**178,230,282**	**401,079,391**	**148,189,480**	**10,994,428**	**741,033,383**

* Does not include chronic public health disasters, such as the AIDS pandemic
** Insect infestation, waves/surges
*** Industrial, transport and miscellaneous accidents
Source: EM-DAT, CRED, University of Louvain, Belgium

In the 1990s, floods were responsible for more than half the total number of people reported affected worldwide. In Asia, they affected more than 83 per cent of the total, but earthquakes caused the most economic damage. Droughts affected African populations the most in the 1990s, but the most economic damage was due to wind storms. In the Americas, wind storms accounted for almost half the number of people reported affected and half the total economic damage. In Europe, more than 63 per cent of the total estimated damage was registered as a consequence of floods, but wind storms affected the greatest number of people. In Oceania, wind storms also caused more than 41 per cent of economic losses.

Table 14 Total number of reported epidemics,* by continent and by year (1990 to 1999)

	AFRICA	AMERICAS	ASIA	EUROPE	OCEANIA	TOTAL
1990	8	4	6			18
1991	17	14	13	1		45
1992	10	9	6	1		26
1993	2	1	1			4
1994	5		2	1		8
1995	4	12	3	3		22
1996	20	1	11	2		34
1997	33	2	11	3		49
1998	36	7	20		1	64
1999	48	1	15	5	1	70
Total	**183**	**51**	**88**	**16**	**2**	**340**

Source: EM-DAT, CRED, University of Louvain, Belgium

Table 15 Total number of people reported killed by epidemics,* by continent and by year (1990 to 1999)

	AFRICA	AMERICAS	ASIA	EUROPE	OCEANIA	TOTAL
1990	1,910	277	677			2,864
1991	11,992	10,319	6,229	0		28,540
1992	3,188	1,222	1,103	20		5,533
1993	721	100	38			859
1994	1,616		553	71		2,240
1995	3,339	79	434	217		4,069
1996	13,335	62	455	52		13,904
1997	9,335	12	601	0		9,948
1998	7,824	36	3,250		114	11,224
1999	3,822	16	976	51	1	4,866
Total	**57,082**	**12,123**	**14,316**	**411**	**115**	**84,047**

* Does not include chronic public health disasters, such as the AIDS pandemic
Source: EM-DAT, CRED, University of Louvain, Belgium

It should be noted that epidemics are in general badly reported, so figures are probably underestimated. Africa represents more than 50 per cent of the decade's total number of epidemics, mostly due to diarrhoeal/enteric epidemics. Two-thirds of the total numbers of people reported killed by epidemics were registered in Africa. The worst year of the 1990s was 1991, when 8,000 people died due to a diarrhoeal/enteric disease in Peru, and cholera caused 7,289 deaths in Nigeria. Most deaths are due to cholera or enteric diseases, which remain the most important causes for children mortality at any time. High mortality is usually a sign of weak health infrastructure.

Table 16 Total number of people reported affected by epidemics,* by continent and by year (1990 to 1999)

	AFRICA	AMERICAS	ASIA	EUROPE	OCEANIA	TOTAL
1990	12,159	9,856	22,000			44,015
1991	59,493	252,925	1,630,377	100		1,942,895
1992	249,470	550	430,400			680,420
1993	8,504	403,000	5,660			417,164
1994	6,549,870		13,150	1,333		6,564,353
1995	66,847	197,647	21,480	155,618		441,592
1996	607,378	3,000	32,480	612		643,470
1997	254,929	28,900	33,193	5,245		322,267
1998	131,058	248,310	535,812			915,180
1999	352,181		107,006	7,368	297	466,852
Total	**8,291,889**	**1,144,188**	**2,831,558**	**170,276**	**297**	**12,438,208**

* Does not include chronic public health disasters, such as the AIDS pandemic

Source: EM-DAT, CRED, University of Louvain, Belgium

Africa represents three-quarters of the total number of people affected by epidemics, in particular in 1994, when a malaria epidemic affected 6,500,000 people in Kenya. Malaria is a disease of increasing importance. Resistance of the vector to insecticide and of the parasite to drugs is making a greater number of people susceptible to the disease.

Table 17 Refugees and asylum seekers by host country (1993 to 1999)

	1993	1994	1995	1996	1997	1998	1999
Africa	**5,824,700**	**5,879,700**	**5,222,300**	**3,682,700**	**2,944,000**	**2,924,000**	**3,118,000**
Algeria	121,000	130,000	120,000	114,000	104,000	84,000	85,000
Angola	11,000	11,000	10,900	9,300	9,000	10,000	12,000
Benin	120,000	50,000	25,000	11,000	3,000	3,000	3,000
Botswana	500	–	–	–	–	–	1,000
Burkina Faso	6,000	30,000	21,000	26,000	2,000	–	–
Burundi	110,000	165,000	140,000	12,000	12,000	5,000	5,000
Cameroon	2,500	2,000	2,000	1,000	1,000	3,000	10,000
Central African Republic	41,000	42,000	34,000	36,400	38,000	47,000	55,000
Chad	–	–	–	–	–	10,000	20,000
Congo, DR of *	452,000	1,527,000	1,332,000	455,000	255,000	220,000	200,000
Congo, PR of	13,000	16,000	15,000	16,000	21,000	20,000	40,000
Côte d'Ivoire	250,000	320,000	290,000	320,000	202,000	128,000	135,000
Djibouti	60,000	60,000	25,000	22,000	22,000	23,000	23,000
Egypt	11,000	10,700	10,400	46,000	46,000	46,000	45,000
Eritrea	–	–	–	–	3,000	3,000	2,000
Ethiopia	156,000	250,000	308,000	328,000	313,000	251,000	245,000
Gabon	200	–	1,000	1,000	1,000	1,000	15,000
Gambia	2,000	1,000	5,000	5,000	8,000	13,000	25,000
Ghana	133,000	110,000	85,000	35,000	20,000	15,000	12,000
Guinea	570,000	580,000	640,000	650,000	430,000	514,000	450,000
Guinea-Bissau	16,000	16,000	15,000	15,000	4,000	5,000	5,000
Kenya	332,000	257,000	225,000	186,000	196,000	192,000	255,000
Lesotho	100	–	–	–	–	–	–
Liberia	110,000	100,000	120,000	100,000	100,000	120,000	90,000
Libya	–	–	28,100	27,200	27,000	28,000	3,000
Malawi	700,000	70,000	2,000	–	–	–	–
Mali	13,000	15,000	15,000	15,000	17,000	5,000	7,000
Mauritania	46,000	55,000	35,000	15,000	5,000	20,000	25,000
Namibia	5,000	1,000	1,000	1,000	1,000	2,000	8,000
Niger	3,000	3,000	17,000	27,000	7,000	3,000	3,000
Nigeria	4,400	5,000	8,000	8,000	9,000	5,000	6,000
Rwanda	370,000	–	–	20,000	28,000	36,000	30,000
Senegal	66,000	60,000	68,000	51,000	41,000	30,000	40,000
Sierra Leone	15,000	20,000	15,000	15,000	15,000	10,000	8,000
South Africa	300,000	200,000	90,000	22,500	28,000	29,000	55,000
Sudan	633,000	550,000	450,000	395,000	365,000	360,000	360,000
Swaziland	57,000	–	–	–	–	–	–
Tanzania	479,500	752,000	703,000	335,000	295,000	329,000	400,000
Togo	–	5,000	10,000	10,000	12,000	11,000	10,000
Tunisia	–	–	500	300	–	–	–
Uganda	257,000	323,000	230,000	225,000	185,000	185,000	200,000
Zambia	158,500	123,000	125,400	126,000	118,000	157,000	230,000

Source: US Committee for Refugees

	1993	1994	1995	1996	1997	1998	1999
Zimbabwe	200,000	20,000	–	1,000	1,000	1,000	–
East Asia and Pacific	**467,600**	**444,100**	**452,850**	**449,600**	**535,100**	**559,200**	**650,700**
Australia	2,950	5,300	7,500	7,400	18,000	15,000	16,000
Cambodia	–	–	–	–	–	200	–
China##	296,900	297,100	294,100	294,100	281,800	281,800	281,000
Hong Kong##	3,550	1,900	1,900	1,300	n.a.	n.a.	n.a
Indonesia	2,400	250	–	–	100	100	140,000
Japan	950	7,350	9,900	300	300	500	400
Malaysia**	8,150	6,100	5,300	5,200	5,200	50,600	50,000
Papua New Guinea	7,700	9,700	9,500	10,000	8,200	8,000	8,200
Philippines	1,700	250	450	50	100	300	100
Solomon Islands	–	3,000	1,000	1,000	800	n.a.	–
Thailand	108,300	83,050	98,200	95,850	205,600	187,700	140,000
Viet Nam	35,000	30,100	25,000	34,400	15,000	15,000	15,000
Europe	**2,542,100**	**2,421,500**	**2,520,700**	**2,479,100**	**2,020,300**	**1,728,400**	**1,774,500**
Albania	–	–	–	–	–	25,000	5,000
Armenia	290,000	295,800	304,000	150,000	219,150	229,000	240,000
Austria	77,700	59,000	55,900	80,000	11,400	16,500	24,000
Azerbaijan	251,000	279,000	238,000	249,150	244,100	235,300	222,000
Belarus	10,400	18,800	7,000	10,800	33,500	16,500	3,400
Belgium	32,900	19,400	16,400	18,200	14,100	25,800	42,000
Bosnia and Herzegovina	–	–	–	–	40,000	40,000	60,000
Bulgaria	–	900	500	550	2,400	2,800	2,700
Croatia	280,000	188,000	189,500	167,000	50,000	27,300	24,000
Cyprus	–	–	–	–	–	200	200
Czech Republic	6,300	4,700	2,400	2,900	700	2,400	1,800
Denmark	23,300	24,750	9,600	24,600	13,000	6,100	8,300
Estonia	–	100	–	–	–	–	–
Finland	3,700	850	750	1,700	1,600	2,300	3,300
France	30,900	32,600	30,000	29,200	16,000	17,400	30,000
Georgia	–	–	–	–	100	300	5,200
Germany	529,100	430,000	442,700	436,400	277,000	198,000	166,000
Greece	800	1,300	1,300	5,600	2,100	2,800	1,300
Hungary	10,000	11,200	9,100	5,400	3,400	3,200	6,000
Iceland	–	–	–	–	–	–	100
Ireland	–	–	–	1,800	4,300	6,900	8,500
Italy	33,550	31,800	60,700	10,600	20,000	6,800	7,700
Latvia	–	150	150	–	–	–	–
Lithuania	–	–	400	–	100	100	100
Macedonia	12,100	8,200	7,000	5,100	3,500	7,300	17,000
Netherlands	35,400	52,600	39,300	46,200	64,200	47,000	40,000
Norway	14,200	11,600	11,200	12,700	3,100	2,500	6,000
Poland	600	500	800	3,200	1,200	1,300	1,000

Source: US Committee for Refugees

	1993	1994	1995	1996	1997	1998	1999
Portugal	2,250	600	350	200	150	1,400	200
Romania	1,000	600	1,300	600	2,000	900	900
Russian Federation	347,500	451,000	500,000	484,000	324,000	161,900	140,000
Slovak Republic	1,900	2,000	1,600	2,000	100	300	400
Slovenia	38,000	29,000	24,000	10,300	5,300	7,300	5,000
Spain	14,000	14,500	4,300	7,200	3,300	2,500	4,500
Sweden	58,800	61,000	12,300	60,500	8,400	16,700	21,000
Switzerland	27,000	23,900	29,000	41,700	34,100	40,000	69,000
Turkey	24,600	30,650	21,150	13,000	5,000	12,000	9,600
Ukraine	–	5,000	6,000	8,000	4,900	8,600	6,300
United Kingdom	28,100	32,000	44,000	40,500	58,100	74,000	112,000
Yugoslavia #	357,000	300,000	450,000	550,000	550,000	480,000	480,000
Americas and the Caribbean	**272,450**	**297,300**	**256,400**	**232,800**	**616,000**	**739,950**	**616,200**
Argentina	–	–	–	400	10,700	1,100	3,300
Bahamas	–	–	200	–	50	100	100
Belize	8,900	8,800	8,650	8,700	4,000	3,500	2,900
Bolivia	600	600	600	550	300	350	50
Brazil	1,000	2,000	2,000	2,200	2,300	2,400	2,300
Canada	20,500	22,000	24,900	26,100	48,800	46,000	49,800
Chile	100	200	300	200	300	100	300
Colombia	400	400	400	200	200	200	200
Costa Rica	24,800	24,600	20,500	23,150	23,100	23,100	19,800
Cuba	–	–	1,800	1,650	1,500	1,100	1,500
Dominican Republic	1,300	1,350	900	600	600	600	650
Ecuador	100	100	100	200	200	250	350
El Salvador	150	150	150	150	100	100	–
Guatemala	4,700	4,700	2,500	1,200	1,300	800	750
Honduras	100	100	50	–	–	100	–
Jamaica	–	–	–	–	–	50	–
Mexico	52,000	47,700	38,500	34,450	30,000	7,500	23,800
Nicaragua	4,750	300	450	900	700	150	500
Panama	950	900	800	650	300	1,300	2,100
Peru	400	700	700	300	–	–	700
United States	150,400	181,700	152,200	129,600	491,000	651,000	505,000
Uruguay	–	–	–	–	–	–	100
Venezuela	1,300	1,000	700	1,600	300	150	2,000
Middle East	**4,923,800**	**5,447,750**	**5,499,100**	**5,840,550**	**5,708,000**	**5,814,100**	**5,969,100**
Gaza Strip	603,000	644,000	683,600	716,900	746,000	773,000	798,000
Iran	1,995,000	2,220,000	2,075,500	2,020,000	1,900,000	1,931,000	1,980,000
Iraq	39,500	120,500	115,200	114,400	110,000	104,000	104,700
Israel	–	–	–	–	–	–	400
Jordan	1,073,600	1,232,150	1,294,800	1,362,500	1,413,800	1,463,800	1,518,000
Kuwait	–	25,000	55,000	42,000	90,000	52,000	52,000

Source: US Committee for Refugees

	1993	1994	1995	1996	1997	1998	1999
Lebanon	329,000	338,200	348,300	355,100	362,300	368,300	378,000
Saudi Arabia	25,000	17,000	13,200	257,850	116,750	128,300	128,100
Syria	319,200	332,900	342,300	384,400	361,000	369,800	379,200
United Arab Emirates	–	150	400	400	500	200	700
West Bank	479,000	504,000	517,400	532,400	543,000	555,000	570,000
Yemen	60,500	13,850	53,400	54,600	64,900	68,700	60,000
South and central Asia	**2,151,400**	**1,776,450**	**1,386,300**	**1,794,800**	**1,743,000**	**1,708,700**	**1,621,500**
Afghanistan	35,000	20,000	18,400	18,900	–	–	–
Bangladesh	199,000	116,200	55,000	40,000	40,100	53,100	53,000
India	325,600	327,850	319,200	352,200	323,500	292,100	290,000
Kazakhstan	6,500	300	6,500	14,000	14,000	4,100	15,000
Kyrgyzstan	3,500	350	7,600	17,000	15,500	15,000	11,000
Nepal	99,100	104,600	106,600	109,800	116,000	118,000	120,000
Pakistan	1,482,300	1,202,650	867,500	1,215,700	215,650	1,217,400	1,125,000
Tajikistan	400	2,500	2,500	2,200	3,800	5,500	5,000
Turkmenistan	–	–	–	22,000	13,000	500	1,500
Uzbekistan	–	2,000	3,000	3,000	1,250	3,000	1,000
World total	**16,182,050**	**16,266,800**	**15,337,650**	**14,479,550**	**13,566,400**	**13,474,350**	**13,750,000**

Source: US Committee for Refugees

The total number of refugees and asylum seekers increased by about 300,000 in 1999, reversing a decade-long downward trend. That downward trend was due to many factors, including refugee repatriations to several countries and to the unwillingness of many states, especially those in the developed world, to accept new refugees and asylum seekers. The number of refugees and asylum seekers increased in Africa, east Asia and Europe during 1999, largely because of ongoing or renewed conflicts. The overwhelming majority of the world's refugees and asylum seekers continued to seek protection in the countries of the developing world. More than half of the world's refugees and asylum seekers were found in just six countries or territories: Iran; Jordan; the Gaza Strip and the West Bank; Pakistan; Yugoslavia; and Guinea.

Notes: – indicates zero or near zero; n.a. not available, or reported estimates unreliable; # for 1993, refugees from Croatia and Bosnia included in Yugoslavia total, for 1994-95 Yugoslavia total includes only refugees from Serbia and Montenegro; ## as of 1997, figures for Hong Kong are included in total for China; * formerly Zaire; ** USCR reclassified as refugees 45,000 Filipino Muslims from the island of Mindanao previously regarded as "refugee-like". Malaysia regards them as refugees and permits them to reside legally, but temporarily, in Sabah. Another 450,000 are living in refugee-like conditions in Malaysia.

Table 18 Significant populations of internally displaced people (1993 to 1999)

	1993	1994	1995	1996	1997	1998	1999
Africa	**16,890,000**	**15,730,000**	**10,185,000**	**8,805,000**	**7,590,000**	**8,958,000**	**10,005,000**
Algeria	–	–	–	10,000	n.a.	200,000	100,000
Angola	2,000,000	2,000,000	1,500,000	1,200,000	1,200,000	1,500,000	1,500,000
Burundi	500,000	400,000	300,000	400,000	500,000	500,000	600,000
Congo, DR of*	700,000	550,000	225,000	400,000	100,000	300,000	800,000
Congo, PR of	–	–	–	–	–	250,000	500,000
Djibouti	140,000	50,000	–	25,000	5,000	–	–
Eritrea	200,000	–	–	–	–	100,000	250,000
Ethiopia	500,000	400,000	–	–	–	150,000	300,000
Ghana	–	20,000	150,000	20,000	20,000	20,000	–
Guinea-Bissau	–	–	–	–	–	200,000	50,000
Kenya	300,000	210,000	210,000	100,000	150,000	200,000	100,000
Liberia	1,000,000	1,100,000	1,000,000	1,000,000	500,000	75,000	50,000
Mozambique	2,000,000	500,000	500,000	–	–	–	–
Nigeria	–	–	–	30,000	50,000	3,000	50,000
Rwanda	300,000	1,200,000	500,000	–	50,000	500,000	600,000
Senegal	–	–	–	–	10,000	10,000	5,000
Sierra Leone	400,000	700,000	1,000,000	800,000	500,000	300,000	300,000
Somalia	700,000	500,000	300,000	250,000	200,000	250,000	350,000
South Africa	4,000,000	4,000,000	500,000	500,000	5,000	–	–
Sudan	4,000,000	4,000,000	4,000,000	4,000,000	4,000,000	4,000,000	4,000,000
Togo	150,000	100,000	–	–	–	–	–
Uganda	–	–	–	70,000	300,000	400,000	450,000
Americas and Caribbean	**1,400,000**	**1,400,000**	**1,280,000**	**1,220,000**	**1,624,000**	**1,755,000**	**1,886,000**
Colombia	300,000	600,000	600,000	600,000	1,000,000	1,400,000	1,800,000
Guatemala	200,000	200,000	200,000	200,000	250,000	–	–
Haiti	300,000	–	–	–	–	–	–
Mexico	–	–	–	–	14,000	15,000	18,000
Peru	600,000	600,000	480,000	420,000	360,000	340,000	68,000
South and central Asia	**880,000**	**1,775,000**	**1,600,000**	**2,400,000**	**2,253,500**	**2,130,000**	**1,630,000**
Afghanistan	n.a.	1,000,000	500,000	1,200,000	1,250,000	1,000,000	750,000
Bangladesh	–	–	–	–	–	50,000	80,000
India	250,000	250,000	250,000	250,000	200,000	520,000	500,000
Sri Lanka	600,000	525,000	850,000	900,000	800,000	560,000	550,000
Tajikistan	30,000	–	–	50,000	3,500	–	–
Europe	**2,765,000**	**5,195,000**	**5,080,000**	**4,735,000**	**3,695,000**	**3,685,000**	**4,135,000**
Armenia	–	–	75,000	50,000	70,000	60,000	–
Azerbaijan	600,000	630,000	670,000	550,000	550,000	576,000	570,000
Bosnia and Herzegovina	1,300,000	1,300,000	1,300,000	1,000,000	800,000	836,000	830,000
Croatia	350,000	290,000	240,000	185,000	110,000	61,000	50,000

Source: US Committee for Refugees

	1993	1994	1995	1996	1997	1998	1999
Cyprus	265,000	265,000	265,000	265,000	265,000	265,000	265,000
Georgia	250,000	260,000	280,000	285,000	275,000	280,000	280,000
Russian Federation	n.a.	450,000	250,000	400,000	375,000	350,000	1,000,000
Turkey	n.a.	2,000,000	2,000,000	2,000,000	1,250,000	1,000,000	600,000
Yugoslavia#	–	–	–	–	–	257,000	640,000
Middle East	**1,960,000**	**1,710,000**	**1,700,000**	**1,475,000**	**1,475,000**	**1,575,000**	**1,700,000**
Iran	260,000	–	–	–	–	–	–
Iraq	1,000,000	1,000,000	1,000,000	900,000	900,000	1,000,000	900,000
Lebanon	700,000	600,000	400,000	450,000	450,000	450,000	350,000
Syria**	–	–	–	125,000	125,000	125,000	450,000
Yemen	–	110,000	300,000	–	–	–	–
East Asia and Pacific	**595,000**	**613,000**	**555,000**	**1,070,000**	**800,000**	**1,150,000**	**1,260,000**
Cambodia	95,000	113,000	55,000	32,000	30,000	22,000	–
Myanmar	500,000	500,000	500,000	1,000,000	750,000	1,000,000	600,000
Indonesia	–	–	–	–	–	–	500,000
Papua New Guinea	–	–	–	70,000	20,000	6,000	5,000
Philippines	–	–	–	–	–	122,000	120,000
Solomon Islands	–	–	–	–	–	–	35,000
World total	**24,490,000**	**26,423,000**	**20,400,000**	**19,705,000**	**17,437,500**	**19,253,000**	**20,931,000**

Source: US Committee for Refugees

Large internally displaced populations remained in Sudan, Angola, Iraq, Bosnia and Herzegovina, Afghanistan, Myanmar and Rwanda in 1999. Significant new displacement occurred in Colombia, Democratic Republic of the Congo, Eritrea, Ethiopia, Indonesia, the Russian Federation, Sierra Leone, Somalia, Uganda and Yugoslavia, while some internally displaced persons were able to return home in Liberia and the People's Republic of Congo. About half of the world's internally displaced people were in Africa. Colombia's displaced population became the second largest in the world, growing from 1 million in 1997 to 1.8 million by the end of 1999, the result of political violence, which continued unabated.

Notes: – indicates zero or near zero; n.a. not available, or reported estimates unreliable; # for 1993, refugees from Croatia and Bosnia included in Yugoslavia total, for 1994-95 Yugoslavia total includes only refugees from Serbia and Montenegro; * formerly Zaire; ** includes about 125,000 IDPs originally displaced from the Golan Heights in 1967 and their progeny.

Table 19 Non-food emergency and distress relief, grant disbursements in US$ millions (1990 to 1998)

	1990	1991	1992	1993	1994	1995	1996	1997	1998
Australia	12.23	13.23	29.56	26.56	25.49	35.80	32.44	31.91	66.41
Austria	43.96	93.87	145.83	123.45	127.04	114.72	92.17	37.15	34.14
Belgium	4.59	5.71	13.18	19.05	14.02	15.75	23.99	37.15	19.73
Canada	45.76	85.§4	78.86	273.96	228.45	164.72	174.38	159.15	105.50
Denmark	108.27	52.83	104.85	77.14	78.62	71.38	54.15	94.56	91.78
Finland	70.54	102.24	61.55	21.61	27.48	22.64	38.85	28.61	26.07
France	0.00	0.00	25.88	125.08	122.23	138.43	96.38	70.04	88.95
Germany	45.21	415.31	680.32	549.52	392.53	438.71	294.20	204.86	173.24
Ireland	2.09	2.89	2.10	5.15	8.53	8.34	16.34	11.20	10.10
Italy	104.06	456.33	137.39	341.69	105.40	87.89	96.68	50.25	21.52
Japan	26.46	20.48	14.93	40.37	31.08	60.08	71.94	73.66	123.97
Luxembourg	3.80	10.30	7.21	8.49	5.09	7.03	9.05	8.13	10.39
Netherlands	63.58	109.74	197.45	303.29	302.37	350.42	340.88	278.89	297.15
New Zealand	3.85	1.51	5.12	4.96	2.68	1.84	3.86	5.98	4.56
Norway	88.62	77.60	86.48	113.21	180.75	183.78	198.76	192.08	212.60
Portugal	0.00	0.11	0.11	8.35	3.70	3.52	5.56	0.43	0.66
Spain	5.00	8.42	6.43	7.74	5.04	19.53	12.91	17.97	26.65
Sweden	124.49	181.65	342.56	277.28	334.17	269.75	268.61	233.81	211.69
Switzerland	46.75	67.78	68.61	66.85	80.98	97.20	81.34	122.18	131.30
United Kingdom	37.95	116.48	56.83	187.27	260.52	181.76	194.73	164.32	186.79
United States	221.00	596.00	521.00	669.00	1,132.00	789.00	585.00	340.00	897.78
Total	**1,058.21**	**2,417.62**	**2,586.25**	**3,250.02**	**3,468.17**	**3,062.29**	**2,692.23**	**2,163.03**	**2,785.98**
Proportion for refugees	**348.21**	**1,052.41**	**1,713.30**	**1,976.28**	**1,976.28**	**1,799.49**	**1,489.06**	**832.62**	**1,260.83**

Source: OECD/DAC

The funding of emergency assistance rose in 1998, but still represents well under 1 per cent of official development assistance. The waxing and waning of the figures over the years graphically demonstrate how dependent funding is upon the political climate.

Table 20 Breakdown of food aid deliveries by category per year (1991 to 1999) in thousand tonnes – cereals in grain equivalent

	1991	1992	1993	1994	1995	1996	1997	1998	1999*
Emergency	3,540	4,991	4,202	4,208	3,451	2,351	3,363	2,983	4,690
Programme	6,650	7,663	10,170	5,730	4,046	2,846	1,599	2,726	7,392
Project	2,980	2,578	2,498	2,779	2,408	1,683	2,328	2,570	2,419
Total	**13,170**	**15,232**	**16,870**	**12,717**	**9,905**	**6,880**	**7,290**	**8,279**	**14,501**

* Figures for 1999 are provisional

Source: WFP/INTERFAIS

In response to the increase of major disasters in 1999, food aid deliveries are once again climbing to the levels of the 1980s: both food aid for emergency relief and that allocated to longer-term planning.

chapter 10

Section Two

Tracking the system

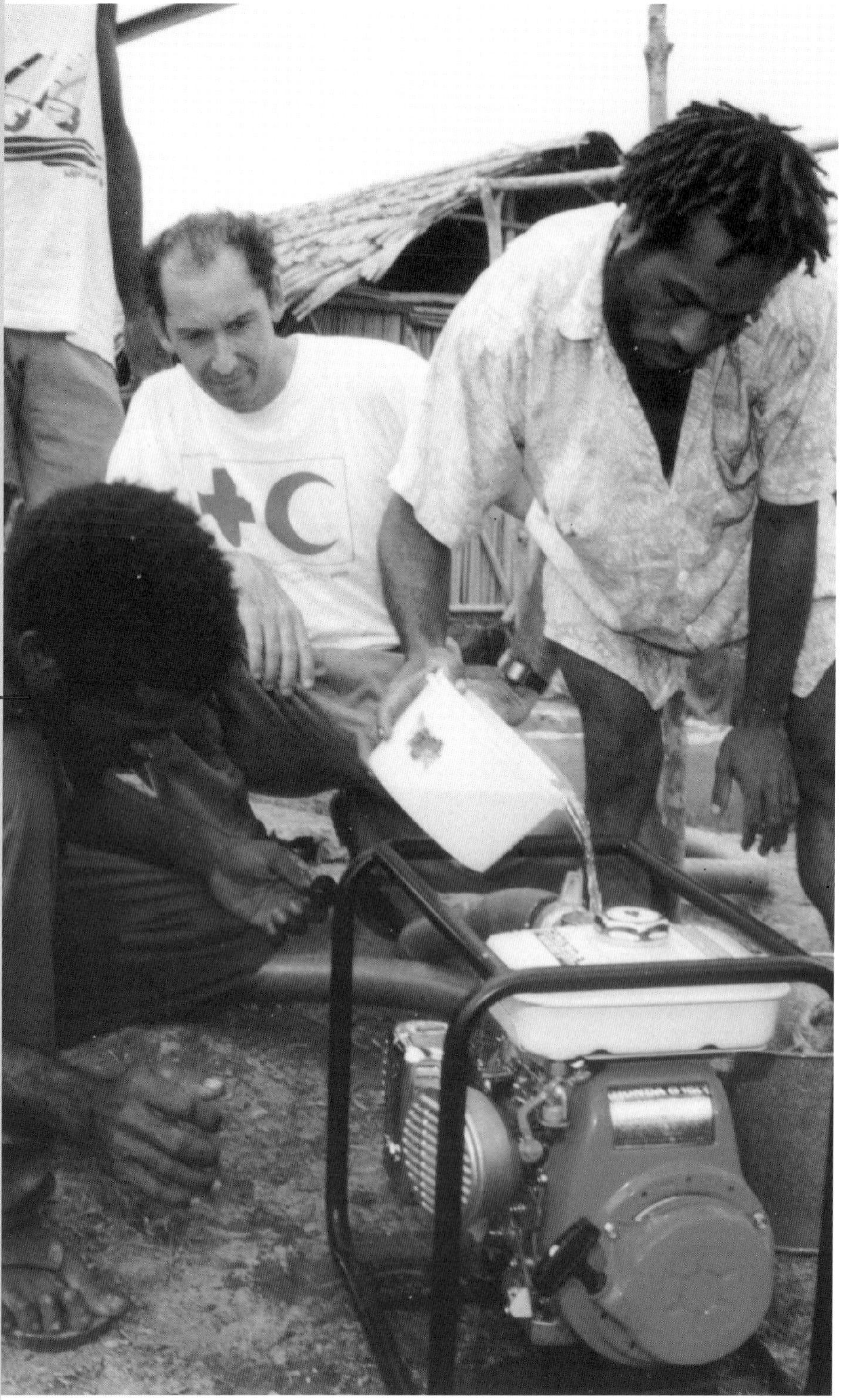

International Federation: humanitarian operations worldwide since 1919.

Photo: Jerry Galea/ International Federation, Papua New Guinea 1999.

Years of response to disasters

Since it was founded in 1919, the International Federation of Red Cross and Red Crescent Societies has sought to assist the victims of natural, technological, economic and social disasters. The International Federation works through its network of 176 national Red Cross and Red Crescent societies to bring relief to people whose lives and livelihoods have been shattered by such events and helps the world's poorest countries – which are also often the most disaster-prone – whose economic growth and development may be set back for years after a disaster.

The year 1999 was no exception – disasters once again took a heavy toll on lives and livelihoods as earthquakes and heavy flooding struck Asia, Europe and Latin America. And the crisis in Kosovo, with its mass population movements, led to the largest-ever joint appeal between the International Federation and the International Committee of the Red Cross (see Chapter 6).

The figures in this chapter give an idea of International Federation operations over the years, and looks at two initiatives to improve its response: ARCHI 2010 and the ProVention Consortium. The chapter also lists the organizations that have agreed to support the *Code of Conduct for the International Red Cross and Red Crescent Movement and NGOs in Disaster Response* by incorporating its principles into their work.

From 1919 to 1999

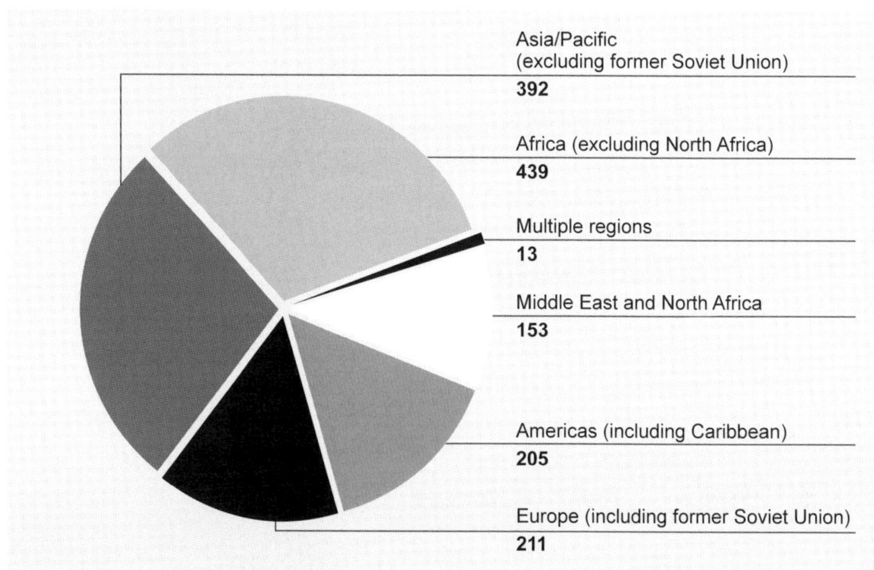

Figure 10.1 International Federation/League operations by region from 1919 to 1999

Source: International Federation

Figure 10.2
The most frequent disasters (in terms of programmes and operations to receive international support) from 1919 to 1999

Source: International Federation

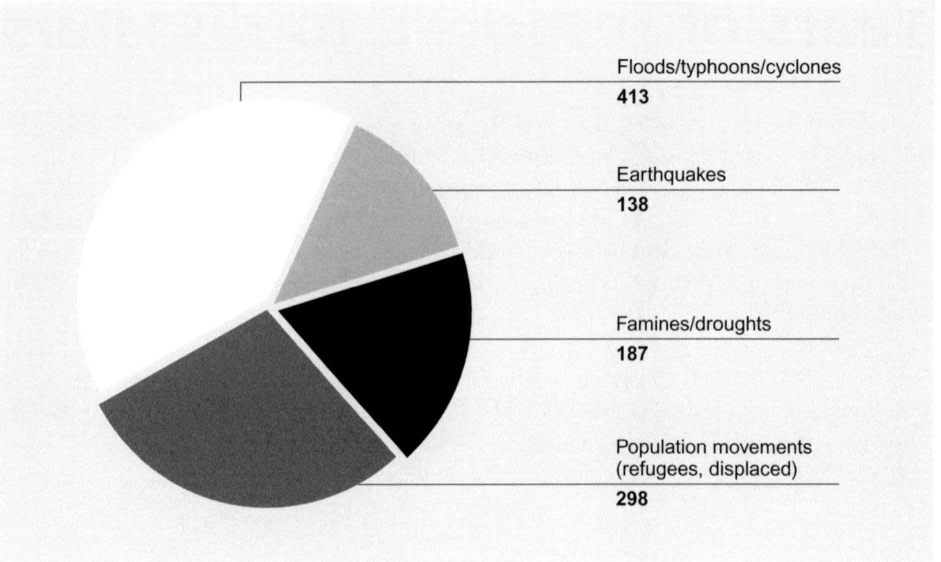

Figure 10.3
Top ten countries – relief appeals and main relief operations

Source: International Federation

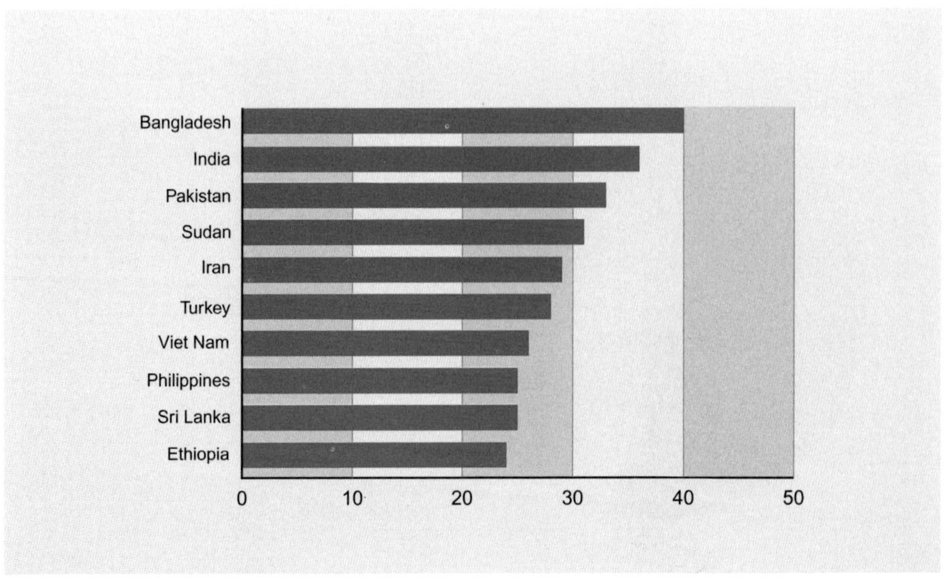

1992 to 1999

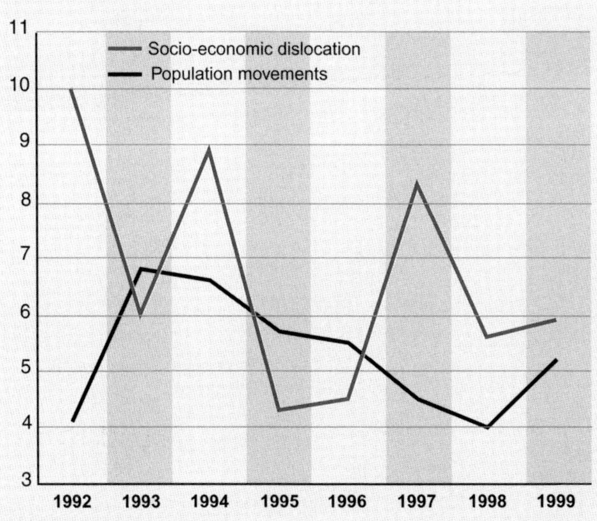

Figure 10.4
Number of beneficiaries (in millions) per year from 1992 to 1999 in operations responding to socio-economic dislocation and population movements

Source: International Federation

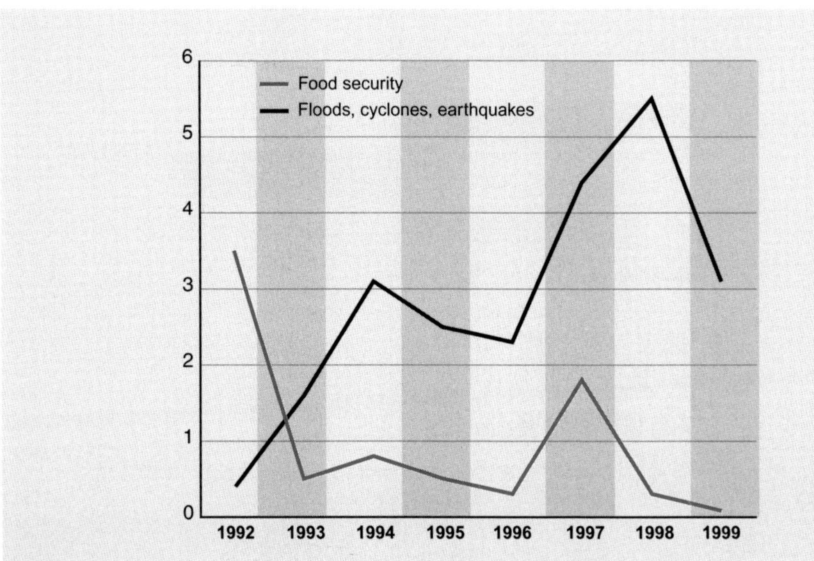

Figure 10.5
Number of beneficiaries (in millions) per year from 1992 to 1999 in operations responding to food security and floods, cyclones and earthquakes

Source: International Federation

1999

Figure 10.6 Relief appeals by type in 1999 (percentage)

Source: International Federation

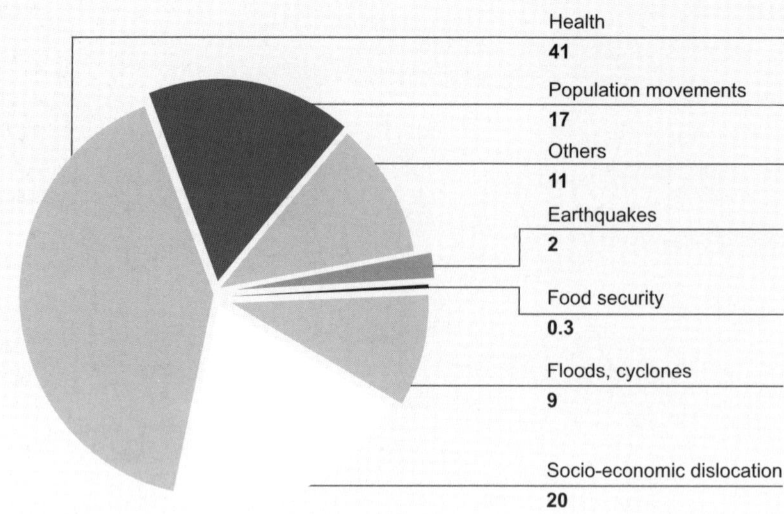

Figure 10.7 Number of beneficiaries by type of disaster in 1999

Source: International Federation

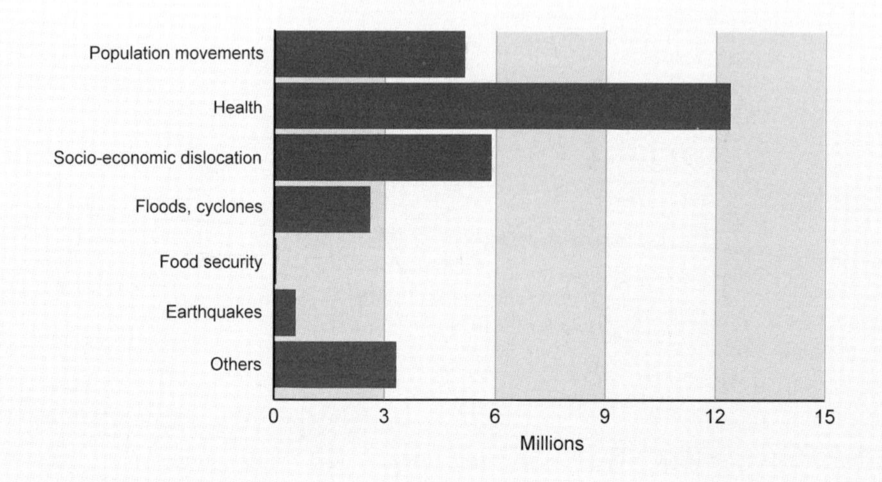

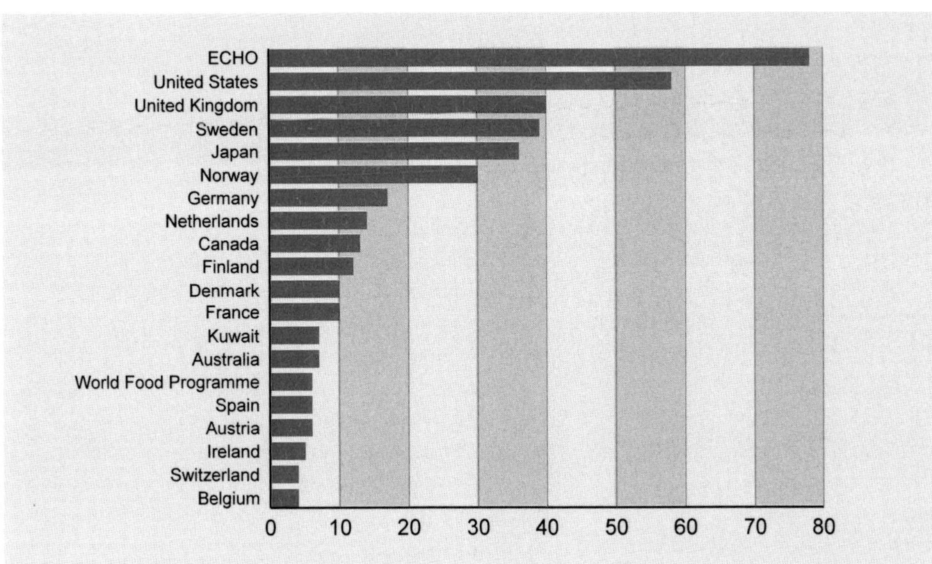

Figure 10.8
Twenty largest donors to 1999 International Federation appeals in millions of Swiss francs (contributions in cash, kind and services)

Source: International Federation

Box 10.1 ARCHI 2010: investing in health

Millions of Africans die each year from preventable or curable diseases. The HIV/AIDS pandemic has devastated life expectancy. A baby born today in Zambia can expect to live just 37 years – 30 years less than the global average. In Zimbabwe, under-fives' mortality has rocketed 144 per cent because of AIDS. Malnutrition and stunted children are on the increase in Africa. Inadequate resources devoted to public health coupled with increased health-care costs have created a tremendous gap between needs and services – with catastrophic consequences for the continent's poorest.

Over the last century, numerous vaccines, cures and treatments for many common infectious diseases have been produced. Health education has increased people's acceptance of vaccinations and their practical knowledge of how to prevent illnesses. Despite this progress, infectious diseases, malnutrition and poor maternal and child health account for one-third of the entire disease burden in the world – rising to 50 per cent in poorer countries.

In Africa today, access to quality public health services remains disappointingly low, especially when compared to developments elsewhere in the world. Vaccination coverage has deteriorated. Displaced populations and conflicts have disrupted already fragile systems of basic health care. Continued poverty has severely limited access to essential drugs. Meanwhile, ever-increasing populations (a 70 per cent increase is predicted in Africa by 2020) stretch existing systems beyond breaking point. As a result, too many people today die too young from diseases that are either preventable or curable.

The International Federation of Red Cross and Red Crescent Societies has embarked on a ten-year effort to work towards reversing these negative trends in African health. For many decades, national Red Cross and Red Crescent (RC/RC) societies in Africa have provided health services to the most vulnerable populations. Of the estimated 2 million RC/RC volunteers and staff in Africa, scores have been trained to implement health programmes in every country. But in the face of increasing challenges, new health strategies need to be identified.

The African Red Cross/Red Crescent Health Initiative 2010 (ARCHI 2010), aims to "improve the impact of RC/RC basic health support on the most vulnerable by focusing on selected priority public-health problems in partnerships with ministries of health and other health partners by taking advantage of a reinvigorated RC/RC network of community volunteers throughout Africa."

More high-tech interventions and referral hospitals are not what is urgently needed. Changes in behaviour and in living environments at the family and community levels can have a far more immediate impact on major public health problems in Africa. ARCHI 2010 proposes massive and long-term support to:

- the promotion of healthy behaviour at the family and community level; and
- community-based health interventions to improve the immediate living environments of the most vulnerable.

Community education will focus on understanding the main causes of public health problems and on promoting basic preventive behaviour. Research in the US suggests that while investing in improved lifestyles (behaviour) and environments can reduce mortality by over 60 per cent, governments typically allocate larger proportions of their national budgets to health infrastructure (hospitals, equipment, etc.), which have far less impact on cutting mortality rates (see Chapter 1, Figure 1.1).

More than half the deaths in African children could be prevented through lifestyle changes, such as promoting breastfeeding of infants, full and complete immunizations, clean water and sanitation. With its unique advantage of a presence in all communities in Africa, the RC/RC

.../

.../

networks of volunteers are particularly well placed to fill this gap in community education and health promotion.

The strategy developed by ARCHI 2010 is identifying the main fields and priorities for RC/RC public health interventions in Africa – in turn enabling National Societies to prioritize activities within their health programmes, based on their capacities, their actual needs and existing interventions of ministries of health and other health actors. The strategy will guide bilateral and International Federation support to these health programmes and lead to a consistent and coordinated approach for all RC/RC interventions in each country. More emphasis on targeting selected public health priorities will lead to a greater impact at the community level.

The ARCHI 2010 process has developed as follows:

- **From data to decisions.** During 1998-1999, an in-depth study of existing literature identified Africa's major public health problems and current recommendations for their prevention and control. These findings were enhanced by questionnaires from African National Societies in 1998, which provided additional information on current RC/RC activities and country-specific problems. Data from these questionnaires were validated during 13 in-depth country assessments conducted by African RC/RC staff.
- **From decisions to priorities.** In mid-1999, five subregional workshops were held in Africa to discuss findings emanating from the literature search, questionnaires and field assessments. Fifty National Societies, more than 20 ministries of health and representatives from the World Health Organization, UNICEF, UNAIDS and the United Nations Population Fund participated. These workshops field-tested a decision-tree methodology to identify selected priority public health interventions out of a multitude of African health problems. By applying a series of RC/RC-specific criteria, National Societies narrowed down 140 identified problems to around 40 possible options. These options were later refined down to eight pan-African public health priorities for RC/RC engagement in the next decade. These included: HIV/AIDS, malaria, vaccine-preventable diseases, acute respiratory illnesses, diarrhoea, malnutrition, maternal health, and accidents and injuries. Two other priorities, substance abuse and poverty were also identified as important issues for which there were no simple public health solutions. In late 1999, a committee of experts representing African National Societies, public health authorities and institutions reviewed the results of the subregional workshops.
- **From priorities to action.** In late 1999, the conclusions of the subregional workshops and the committee of experts were presented and approved at a special session bringing together all 53 African National Societies. The International Federation was then charged with presenting a draft Red Cross/Red Crescent health strategy at the Pan African 2000 Conference in Burkina Faso in September 2000. Discussions at the Pan African conference will aim to enlist strong commitment from RC/RC societies to implement more focused large-scale public health interventions through more effective use of community volunteers and partnerships.

  To assist National Societies implement the health strategy, the International Federation is developing simple and appropriate tools that will address both the management and the technical components of implementing selected priority interventions. The International Federation will also aim to strengthen National Society infrastructures, to enable better recruitment, motivation, training and retention of volunteer networks in the community.
- **From action to impact.** Four National Societies (Central African Republic, Malawi, Sudan and Togo) are participating in pilot

.../

.../

studies in early 2000 to examine their roles in maintaining nationwide networks of community volunteers for social mobilization and for emergency response. These pilots will test the proposed ARCHI 2010 strategy in order to present concrete results at the Pan African conference.

Clear objectives and indicators are being established for each of the ARCHI 2010 priority public health interventions for use by all National Societies. These will be included in the technical and management tools under development. As more National Societies incorporate these standard objectives and indicators into their health programmes, it will be possible through regular reporting and monitoring to measure progress towards outcomes and the impact at community, national and regional levels.

Figure 10.9 Public health under threat in sub-Saharan Africa

Country	Life expectancy without AIDS	Life expectancy with AIDS	Under-five mortality without AIDS	Under-five mortality with AIDS
Botswana	61.5	40.0	57.4	121.1
Kenya	65.6	47.6	64.9	107.0
Namibia	65.3	41.5	125.7	181.2
Zambia	56.2	37.1	125.7	181.2
Zimbabwe	64.9	39.0	50.5	123.4

Source: USAID/US Department of Commerce, HIV/AIDS in the Developing World, May 1999.

Box 10.2 ProVention consortium on natural and technological catastrophes

"Already, 96 per cent of all deaths from natural disasters occur in developing countries. One billion people are living in the world's unplanned shanty towns and 40 of the 50 fastest growing cities are located in earthquake zones. Another 10 million people live under constant threat of floods."

'World Disasters Report 1999'

Over the last two decades, the number and scale of natural and technological disasters have increased greatly. In 1998, natural disasters claimed more than 50,000 human lives and resulted in economic losses of more than US$ 65 billion. These losses are difficult for any economy to absorb, but the impact upon developing countries – which are disproportionately affected by disasters – is often devastating.

Developing countries are less likely to have the resources and agility necessary to respond effectively to disasters. And they often lack the latest technical and scientific expertise to prevent or mitigate future catastrophes. The economic cost of natural disasters can be 20 times higher in terms of gross domestic product for developing countries than for industrialized nations – but the economic impact pales in comparison to the devastation of lives and institutions.

"In light of the experience gained from natural phenomena such as El Niño and hurricane Mitch, the [World] Bank and the international community must make room in their agendas for initiatives dealing with emergencies arising from natural disasters," said Angel Gurría, Mexico's minister of finance, in April 1999. Calling for a "culture of prevention" to be added to the development agenda, Gurría added: "Dealing with such damage absorbs resources which could otherwise be used to promote development."

In February 2000, a new international partnership to minimize the impact of disasters on developing countries was launched by the Disaster Management Facility of the World Bank. Known as the ProVention Consortium, this global partnership brings together governments, international organizations, academic institutions, private sector and civil society. Its aim is to reduce risk from natural and technological disasters in developing countries and to make disaster prevention and mitigation an integral part of development efforts. To achieve its goals, the following priority activities are envisaged:

- Strengthen donor coordination and promote policy aimed at reducing disaster risk.
- Promote a culture of safety through education, training and dissemination of good practices for reducing vulnerability to disasters.
- Develop institutional capacity for disaster prevention and effective response at every level of government.
- Promote linkages between public and private sectors, and between scientific communities and policy-makers, for disaster risk reduction.
- Support pilot projects that may help demonstrate risk reduction or risk transfer strategies.

Three key areas on which the consortium will focus, in order to help prevent and mitigate the social and economic impacts of disasters on the environment, communities and individuals, include:

- **Poverty and vulnerability.**
  Poverty is inextricably linked to disaster vulnerability. These links will be analysed and strategies will be developed to reduce disaster vulnerability of the poor.
- **Environmental services that reduce disasters.**
  Mechanisms will be promoted to protect natural ecosystems such as forests, coastal mangrove and coral reefs that buffer the impact of disasters on human settlements.
- **Risk sharing/transfer mechanisms in the formal and informal sectors.**
  Emphasis will be placed on improving access of low-income groups to risk reduction strategies, insurance mechanisms or safety nets.

Disaster risk management is integral to the social and economic development of many of the world's nations. Through the ProVention Consortium, developing countries will be able to approach these problems in a new light and move their economies and their peoples into a new era of increased stability and economic growth.

Box10.3 Sponsors and signatories of the Code of Conduct

The agencies sponsoring the 'Code of Conduct for the International Red Cross and Red Crescent Movement and NGOs in Disaster Response' are:

International Federation of Red Cross and Red Crescent Societies
International Committee of the Red Cross
Caritas International
Catholic Relief Services
International Save the Children Alliance
Lutheran World Federation
Oxfam
World Council of Churches

As at March 2000, the following humanitarian organizations support the Code of Conduct and are endeavouring to incorporate its principles into their work:

Albania
CAFOD
Nature Protectionists Association

Argentina
Fundación Evangélica "El Buen Pastor"

Australia
AUSTCARE (Australian's Caring for Refugees)
Care
Pax Christi Australia, NSW Section
RedR Australia Ltd
Tulara Pty. Ltd

Austria
Association for Afro-Asian Affairs
Austrian Relief Programme, ARP

Bangladesh
Youth Approach for Development and Cooperation, (YADC)

Belgium
Agora – Vitrine du Monde
Care International
Centre International de Formation des Cadres du Développement C.I.F.C.D.
Handicap International
Médecins sans Frontières
OXFAM

Benin
Conseil des Activités Educatives du Bénin

Canada
ADRA
Canadian Feed the Children
Family to Family
OXFAM

Congo, Dem. Rep. of
Humanitas, Corps de Sauvetage
OXFAM

Côte d'Ivoire
ADRA

Croatia
ADEH International, Trogir
Pax Christi (Germany)

Denmark
ADRA
Dan Church Aid
Danish Refugee Council
Mission East
Save the Children

Djibouti
Caritas – Djibouti

Dominica
Brisin Agencies, Ltd.
Dominica Christian Council
Society of St Vincent de Paul

Ethiopia
Selam Children's Village

Finland
Save the Children

France
ADRA – France Adventist Development and Relief Agency
Benoit Frankel Estate
Enfants du Monde, Marseille
Enfants Réfugiés du Monde
Handicap International
Médecins du Monde
Pharmaciens sans Frontières

Germany
ADRA
Care Deutschland e.V.

Deutsche Arztegemeinschaft fur medizinische Zusammenarbeit e.V. (DAZ)
Deutsche Medikamenten-Hilfswerk action medeor e.V.
Deutsche Welthungerhilfe
HELP – Hilfe zur Selbsthife e.V.
Johanniter-Unfall-Hilfe e.V.
TERRA TECH

Greece
Institute of International Social Affairs

Guinea
Commission Africaine des Promoteurs de la Santé et des Droits de l'Homme

Haiti
Star of Hope International

Hong Kong
OXFAM

India
ADRA
Ambiha Charitable Trust
ASHA (Action for Social & Human Acme)
Centre for Research on Ecology, Environmental Education, Training and Education (CREATE)
Federation of Interfaith Orphanage and Allied Educational Relief Technical Training Institutions
Global Forum for NGOs for Disaster Reduction
Institute for Youth and Disaster Preparedness
Joint Assistance Centre
Mahila Udyamita Vikas Kalya Evan Siksha Sansthah
Tear Fund India Committee on Relief and Rehabilitation Service (TFICORRS)

Ireland
Concern Worldwide
Express Aid International
GOAL
OXFAM
Trocaire

Italy
Associazione Amici dei Bambini
CISP – MOVIMONDO – Comitato Internazionale per lo Sviluppo dei Popoli
Comitato Collaborazione Medica, CCM
Comitato di Coordinamento delle Organizzazioni per il Servizio Volontario – COSV
Cooperazione Internazionale – COOPI
CUAMM – International College for Health Cooperation in Developing Countries
Movimondo, Roma
Reggio Terzo Mondo, R.T.M.
Volontari Italiani Solidarietà Paesi Emergenti V.I.S.P.E.

Japan
AMDA, Association of Medical Doctors of Asia
Association to Aid Refugees (AAR)
Sotoshu Volunteer Association (SVA)

Laos
ADRA

Lebanon
Disaster Control Centre

Luxembourg
Amicale Rwanda-Luxembourg

Myanmar
ADRA

Netherlands
Caritas Nederland
ZOA Refugee Care
Disaster Relief Agency
Dorcas Aid International, Andijk
Dutch Interchurch Aid
Foundation "Call for Homes"
Hope for Albania
Memisa Medicus Mundi
NOVIB, Netherlands Organisation for International Cooperation
Quick Home Systems
Stichting Agriterra,
Stichting Vluchteling
Terre des Hommes, Den Haag
The Tear Fund Holland
Transcultural Psychological Organisation

New Zealand
OXFAM
Tear Fund

Norway
- Norwegian Organisation for Asylum Seekers
- Norwegian Refugee Council

Pakistan
- Caritas Pakistan

Philippines
- ADRA
- Star of Hope Philippines, Inc.

Portugal
- Instituto Portugues de Medicina Preventiva, I.P.M.P.

Russian Federation
- ADRA, Euro-Asia Division

Sierra Leone
- Association for International Development and Services – AID-SL

Somalia
- Caritas

Spain
- Intermón
- Radioaficionados Sin Fronteras

Sri Lanka
- ADRA
- Consortium of Humanitarian Agencies
- The Family Rehabilitation Centre

Swaziland
- Save the Children Fund

Sweden
- African Medical Association in Scandinavia (AMAS)
- BAFUK
- International Aid
- The Mission Convenant Church of Sweden – Svenska Missionsförbundet
- PMU Interlife
- Qandil Project
- SAMS – Scandinavian African Mission Sweden
- Sangha Societas Work of Charity
- Star of Hope International
- Swedish Fellowship of Reconciliation (SWEFOR)/Kristna Fredsrörelsen
- The Swedish Organisation for Individual Relief – SOIR, Lund

Switzerland
- ASEM; Association for the Children of Mozambique
- Commission Internationale Catholique pour les Migrations
- Food for the Hungry International
- Foundation Amurt
- Interaid International
- MEDAIR
- RedR International
- World Vision International, Geneva

Thailand
- ADRA

United Kingdom
- Ace Aviation
- Action Against Hunger
- Actionaid
- ADRA Trans-Europe
- CAFOD
- Children in Crisis
- Children's Aid Direct
- Christian Aid
- Christian Children's Fund of Great Britain
- Christian Outreach
- Community Aid Abroad
- Containers of Hope
- European Mental Health Trust
- Feed the Children
- FOCUS Humanitarian Assistance Europe Foundation
- Helpage International
- Help the Aged
- Hope and Homes for Children
- Human Appeal International
- International Care and Relief (ICR)
- International Extension College
- Islamic Relief
- ITACoR International Association for Conflict Resolution
- Marie Stopes International
- Medical Emergency Relief International (MERLIN)

The Ockenden Venture
Partnership for Growth
Post-War Reconstruction and Development Unit (PRDU)
RedR
The Salvation Army
Save the Children Fund
Tear Fund
United Kingdom Foundation for the Peoples of the South Pacific
War on Want
World Association of Girl Guides and Girl Scouts

United States

American Refugee Committee
International Medical Corps
International Rescue Committee
Life for Relief and Development
Lutheran World Relief
MAP International
Mercy International – U.S.A., Inc.
Operation USA Los Angeles
OXFAM America
Truck Aid International, Baltimore
Women's Commission for Refugee Women and Children
Worldwide Servers' International Org.

Yugoslavia

Institute for Mental Health and Recovery

Zambia

PIMMPRO International NGO for Relief and Development

chapter 11

Section Two

Tracking the system

Teaching public health in Sudan.

Photo: Jenny Matthews/ International Federation, Sudan 1999.

chapter 11

The global reach

Contact details for the members of the International Red Cross and Red Crescent Movement

THE INTERNATIONAL RED CROSS AND RED CRESCENT MOVEMENT

THE INTERNATIONAL FEDERATION OF RED CROSS AND RED CRESCENT SOCIETIES

P.O. Box 372
1211 Geneva 19
SWITZERLAND
Tel. (41)(22) 730 42 22
Fax (41)(22) 733 03 95
Tlx (045) 412 133 FRC CH
Tlg. LICROSS GENEVA
E-mail secretariat@ifrc.org
Web http://www.ifrc.org

THE INTERNATIONAL COMMITTEE OF THE RED CROSS

19 avenue de la Paix
1202 Geneva
SWITZERLAND
Tel. (41)(22) 734 60 01
Fax (41)(22) 733 20 57
Tlx 414 226 CCR CH
Tlg. INTERCROIXROUGE GENEVE
E-mail icrc.gva@gwn.icrc.org
Web http://www.icrc.org

NATIONAL RED CROSS AND RED CRESCENT SOCIETIES

National Red Cross and Red Crescent Societies are listed alphabetically by International Organization for Standardization Codes for the Representation of Names of Countries, English spelling. Details correct as of 1 March 2000. Please forward any corrections to the International Federation's Information Resource Centre in Geneva (e-mail: irc@ifrc.org).

Afghan Red Crescent Society

Pul Artel
Kabul
Postal address: P.O. Box 3066
Shar-e-Now
Kabul
AFGHANISTAN
Tel. (873) 32357 / 3305934288 / 32211

Albanian Red Cross

Rruga "Muhammet Gjollesha"
Sheshi "Karl Topia"
Tirana
Postal address: C.P. 1511
Tirana
ALBANIA
Tel. (355)(42) 25855 / 22037
Fax (355)(42) 25855 / 22037
Tlg. ALBCROSS TIRANA

Algerian Red Crescent

15 bis, Boulevard Mohammed V
Alger 16000
ALGERIA
Tel. (213) (2) 725407 / 725408
Fax (213) (2) 725405
Tlx 56056 HILAL ALGER
Tlg. HILALAHMAR ALGER

Andorra Red Cross

Prat de la Creu 22
Andorra la Vella
ANDORRA
Tel. (376) 825225
Fax (376) 828630
E-mail creuroja@creuroja.ad
Web http://www.creuroja.ad

Angola Red Cross

Rua 1° Congresso no 21
Caixa Postal 927
Luanda
ANGOLA
Tel. (244)(2) 336543 / 333991
Fax (244)(2) 345065
Tlx 3394 CRUZVER AN

Antigua and Barbuda Red Cross Society

Red Cross Headquarters
Old Parham Road
P.O. Box 727
St. Johns, Antigua W.I.
ANTIGUA AND BARBUDA
Tel. (1)(268) 4620800 / 4609599
Fax (1)(268) 4609595
Tlx 2195 DISPREP "For Red Cross"
E-mail redcross@candw.ag

Argentine Red Cross
Hipólito Yrigoyen 2068
1089 Buenos Aires
ARGENTINA
Tel. (54)(114) 9511391 / 9511854
Fax (54)(114) 9527715
Tlx 21061 CROJA AR
Tlg. ARGENCROSS BUENOS AIRES

Armenian Red Cross Society
21 Paronian Street
375015 Yerevan
Armenia
Tel. (374)(2) 538064
Fax (374)(2) 151129
Tlx 243345 ODER SU, Country code 64

Australian Red Cross
National Office
155 Pelham Street
P.O. Box 196
Carlton South VIC 3053
AUSTRALIA
Tel. (61)(3) 93451800
Fax (61)(3) 93482513
E-mail redcross@nat.redcross.org.au
Web http://www.redcross.org.au

Austrian Red Cross
Wiedner Hauptstrasse 32
Postfach 39
1041 Wien 4
AUSTRIA
Tel. (43)(1) 58900-0
Fax (43)(1) 58900-199
Tlx oerk a 133111
Tlg. AUSTROREDCROOS WIEN
E-mail oerk@redcross.or.at
Web http://www.redcross.or.at

Red Crescent Society of Azerbaijan
Prospekt Azerbaidjan 19
Baku
AZERBAIJAN
Tel. (994)(12) 931912
Fax (994)(12) 931578

The Bahamas Red Cross Society
John F. Kennedy Drive
P.O. Box N-8331
Nassau
BAHAMAS
Tel. (1)(242) 3237370 / 3237371
Fax (1)(242) 3237404
Tlx 20657 BAHREDCROSS
Tlg. BAHREDCROSS NASSAU
E-mail info@bahamsredcross.org
Web http://www.bahamasrc.com

Bahrain Red Crescent Society
P.O. Box 882
Manama
BAHRAIN
Tel. (973) 293171
Fax (973) 291797
Tlg. HILAHAMAR MANAMA
E-mail hilal@baletco.com.bh

Bangladesh Red Crescent Society
684-686 Bara Maghbazar
G.P.O. Box 579
Dhaka - 1217
BANGLADESH
Tel. (880)(2) 9330188 / 9330189
Fax (880)(2) 831908
Tlx 632232 BDRC BJ
Tlg. RED CRESCENT DHAKA
E-mail bdrcs@bdonline.com

The Barbados Red Cross Society
Red Cross House
Jemmotts Lane
Bridgetown
BARBADOS
Tel. (1)(246) 4262052 / 4300646
Fax (1)(246) 4262052 "For Red Cross"
Tlx 2201 P.U.B. T.L.X. W.B.
Tlg. REDCROSS BARBADOS
E-mail bdosredcross@caribsurf.com

Belarusian Red Cross
35, Karl Marx Str.
220030 Minsk
BELARUS
Tel. (375)(17) 2272620
Fax (375)(17) 2272620
Tlx 252290 KREST SU
E-mail redcross@un.minsk.by/ brc@home.by

Belgian Red Cross
Ch. de Vleurgat 98
1050 Bruxelles
BELGIUM
Tel. (32)(2) 6454411
Fax (32)(2) 6460439 (French); 6460441 (Flemish)
Tlx 24266 BELCRO B
Tlg. CROIXROUGE BELGIQUE BRUXELLES
E-mail info@redcross-fr.be (French) documentatie@redcross-fl.be (Flemish)
Web http://www.redcross.be

Belize Red Cross Society
1 Gabourel Lane
P.O. Box 413
Belize City
BELIZE
Tel. (501)(2) 73319
Fax (501)(2) 30998
Tlx BTL BOOTH 211 Bze attn. Red Cross
E-mail bzercshq@btl.net

Red Cross of Benin
B.P. No. 1
Porto-Novo
BENIN
Tel. (229) 212886
Fax (229) 214927
Tlx 1131 CRBEN

Bolivian Red Cross
Avenida Simón Bolívar N° 1515
Casilla No. 741
La Paz
BOLIVIA
Tel. (591)(2) 340948 / 326568
Fax (591)(2) 359102
Tlx 2220 BOLCRUZ
Tlg. CRUZROJA - LA PAZ

Botswana Red Cross Society
135 Independance Avenue
P.O. Box 485
Gaborone
BOTSWANA
Tel. (267) 352465 / 312353
Fax (267) 312352
Tlg. THUSA GABORONE
E-mail brcs@info.bw

Brazilian Red Cross
Praça Cruz Vermelha No. 10
20230-130 Rio de Janeiro RJ
BRAZIL
Tel. (55)(21) 5075543 / 5075544
Fax (55)(21) 5071538 / 5071594
Tlx (38) 2130532 CVBR BR
Tlg. BRAZCROSS RIO DE JANEIRO
Web http://www.interlize.com/brazil/cruz-vermelha

Brunei Darussalam Red Crescent Society
P.O. Box 3065
Bandar Seri Begawan BS 8675
BRUNEI DARUSSALAM
Tel. (673)(2) 339774 / 421948
Fax (673)(2) 339572

Bulgarian Red Cross
76, James Boucher Boulevard
1407 Sofia
BULGARIA
Tel. (359)(2) 650595
Fax (359)(2) 656937
Tlx 23248 B CH K BG
Tlg. BULGAREDCROSS SOFIA
E-mail redcross@mail.bol.bg
Web http://www.usd.edu/dmhi/brc/brc/brcindex.html

Burkinabe Red Cross Society
01 B.P. 4404
Ouagadougou 01
BURKINA FASO
Tel. (226) 361340
Fax (226) 363121
Tlx LSCR 5438 BF OUAGADOUGOU

Burundi Red Cross
18, Av. de la Croix-Rouge
B.P. 324
Bujumbura
BURUNDI
Tel. (257) 216246 / 218871
Fax (257) 211101
Tlx 5081 CAB PUB BDI

Cambodian Red Cross Society
17, Vithei de la Croix-Rouge Cambodgienne
Phnom-Penh
CAMBODIA
Tel. (855)(23) 362140 / 362876
Fax (855)(23) 362140 / 362876
E-mail crc@forum.igc.apc.org

Cameroon Red Cross Society
Rue Henri Dunant
B.P. 631
Yaoundé
CAMEROON
Tel. (237) 224177
Fax (237) 224177
Tlx (0970) 8884 KN

The Canadian Red Cross Society
1430 Blair Place
Gloucester
Ontario KIJ 9N2
CANADA
Tel. (1)(613) 7401900
Fax (1)(613) 7401911
Tlx CANCROSS 05-33784
Tlg. CANCROSS OTTAWA
E-mail cancross@redcross.ca
Web http://www.redcross.ca

Red Cross of Cape Verde
Rua Andrade Corvo
Caixa Postal 119
Praia
CAPE VERDE
Tel. (238) 611701 / 614169
Fax (238) 614174 / 613909
Tlx 6004 CV CV

Central African Red Cross Society
Avenue Koudoukou Km, 5
B.P. 1428
Bangui
CENTRAL AFRICAN REPUBLIC
Tel. (236) 612223 / 502130
Fax (236) 613561
Tlx DIPLOMA 5213
"Pour Croix-Rouge"

Red Cross of Chad
B.P. 449
N'Djamena
CHAD
Tel. (235) 523434
Fax (235) 525218
Tlg. CROIXROUGE N'DJAMENA
E-mail croix-rouge@intnet.td

Chilean Red Cross
Avenida Santa María No. 150
Providencia
Correo 21, Casilla 246 V
Santiago de Chile
CHILE
Tel. (56)(2) 7771448
Fax (56)(2) 7370270
Tlx 340260 PBVTR CK
Tlg. "CHILECRUZ"
E-mail cruzroja@rdc.cl

Red Cross Society of China
53 Ganmian Hutong
100010 Beijing
CHINA
Tel. (86)(10) 65124447 / 65135838
Fax (86)(10) 65124169
Tlx 210244 CHNRC CN
Tlg. HONGHUI BEIJING
E-mail
hq@chineseredcross.org.ac.cn
xiaox9@hns.cjfh.ac.cn
Web http://www.chineseredcross.org.cn

Colombian Red Cross Society
Avenida 68 N° 66-31
Apartado Aéreo 11-10
Santafé de Bogotá D.C.
COLOMBIA
Tel. (57)(1) 4280520 / 4289423
Fax (57)(1) 4281725 / 4285163
Tlx 45433 CRC CO
Tlg. CRUZ ROJA BOGOTA
E-mail crsecret@gaitana.interred.net.co
Web http://www.crcol.org.co/

Congolese Red Cross
Place de la Paix
B.P. 4145
Brazzaville
CONGO
Tel. (242) 824410
Fax (242) 828825
Tlx UNISANTE 5364
Pour "Croix-Rouge"

Red Cross of the Democratic Republic of the Congo
41, Avenue de la Justice
Zone de la Gombe
B.P. 1712
Kinshasa I
CONGO, D.R. OF THE
Tel. (243)(12) 34897
Fax (243) 8804151
E-mail: secretariat@crrdc.aton.cd

Costa Rican Red Cross
Calle 14, Avenida 8
Apartado 1025
San José 1000
COSTA RICA
Tel. (506) 2337033 / 2553761
Fax (506) 2237628
Tlx 2547 COSTACRUZ SAN JOSÉ
Tlg. COSTACRUZ SAN JOSÉ
E-mail bcrcsn@sol.racsa.co.cr

Red Cross Society of Côte d'Ivoire
P.O. Box 1244
Abidjan 01
COTE D'IVOIRE
Tel. (225) 22321335
Fax (225) 22225355
Tlx 24122 SICOGI CI

Croatian Red Cross
Ulica Crvenog kriza 14
10000 Zagreb
CROATIA
Tel. (385)(1) 4655814
Fax (385)(1) 4550072
E-mail redcross@hck.hr
Web http://www.hck.hr/

Cuban Red Cross
Calle Calzada No. 51 Esquina a 13
Vedado
C.P. 10400
CUBA
Tel. (53)(7) 552555 /552556
Fax (53)(7) 662057
Tlx 511149 MSP CU para Cruz Roja
Tlg. CRUROCU HABANA
E-mail crsn@infomed.sld.cu

Czech Red Cross
Thunovska 18
CZ-118 04 Praha 1
CZECH REPUBLIC
Tel. (420)(2) 57320196 / 57320207
Fax (420)(2) 57320207
Tlx 122 400 csrc c
Tlg. CROIX PRAHA

Danish Red Cross

Blegdamsvej 27
P.O. Box 2600
DK-2100 Köbenhavn Ö
DENMARK
Tel. (45) 35259200
Fax (45) 35259292
Tlx 15726 DANCRO DK
Tlg. DANCROIX KÖBENHAVN
E-mail drc@redcross.dk
Web http://www.redcross.dk

Red Crescent Society of Djibouti

B.P. 8
Djibouti
DJIBOUTI
Tel. (253) 352451
Fax (253) 355049
Tlx 5871 PRESIDENCE DJ

Dominica Red Cross Society

Federation Drive
Goodwill
DOMINICA
Tel. (1)(767) 4488280
Fax (1)(767) 4487708
Tlx 8625 TELAGY DO -
for Dominica RC
Tlg. DOMCROSS
E-mail redcross@cwdom.dm

Dominican Red Cross

Calle Juan E. Dunant No. 51
Ens. Miraflores
Apartado Postal 1293
Santo Domingo, D.N.
DOMINICAN REPUBLIC
Tel. (1)(809) 6823793 / 6897344
Fax (1)(809) 6822837
Tlx rca sdg 4112 "PARA CRUZ ROJA DOM."
Tlg. CRUZ ROJA DOMINICANA, SANTO DOMINGO
E-mail cruz.roja@codetel.net.do

Ecuadorian Red Cross

Antonio Elizalde E 4-31 y Av.
Colombia (esq.)
Casilla 1701 2119
Quito
ECUADOR
Tel. (593)(2) 582481 / 582480
Fax (593)(2) 570424
E-mail crequi@attglobal.net

Egyptian Red Crescent Society

29, El Galaa Street
Cairo
EGYPT
Tel. (20)(2) 5750558 / 5750397
Fax (20)(2) 5740450
Tlx 93249 ERCS UN
Tlg. 124 HELALHAMER
E-mail erc@brainyl.ie-eg.com

Salvadorean Red Cross Society

17 C. Pte. y Av. Henri Dunant
Apartado Postal 2672
San Salvador
EL SALVADOR
Tel. (503) 2227743 / 2227749
Fax (503) 2227758
Tlx 20550 cruzalva
Tlg. CRUZALVA SAN SALVADOR
E-mail crsalvador@vianet.com.sv

Red Cross of Equatorial Guinea

Alcalde Albilio Balboa 92
Apartado postal 460
Malabo
EQUATORIAL GUINEA
Tel. (240)(9) 3701
Fax (240)(9) 3701
Tlx 099/1111 EG.PUB MBO
"Favor Transmetien Cruz Roja Tel. 2393"

Estonia Red Cross

Lai Street 17
EE0001 Tallinn
ESTONIA
Tel. (372) 6411643
Fax (372) 6411641
Tlx 173491
E-mail didi@online.ee

Ethiopian Red Cross Society

Ras Desta Damtew Avenue
P.O. Box 195
Addis Ababa
ETHIOPIA
Tel. (251)(1) 519364 / 159074
Fax (251)(1) 512643
Tlx 21338 ERCS ET
Tlg. ETHIOCROSS ADDISABABA
E-mail ercs@padis.gn.apc.org

Fiji Red Cross Society

22 Gorrie Street
GPO Box 569
Suva
FIJI
Tel. (679) 314133 / 314138
Fax (679) 303818
Tlx 2279 Red Cross (Public facility)
Tlg. REDCROSS SUVA

Finnish Red Cross

Tehtaankatu 1 a
P.O. Box 168
FIN-00141 Helsinki
FINLAND
Tel. (358)(9) 12931
Fax (358)(9) 1293326
Tlx 121331 FINCR FI
Tlg. FINCROSS HELSINKI
E-mail forename.surname@redcross.fi
Web http://www.redcross.fi

French Red Cross

1, Place Henry-Dunant
F-75384 Paris Cedex 08
FRANCE
Tel. (33)(1) 44431100
Fax (33)(1) 44431101
Tlx CR PARIS 642760 F CRPAR
Tlg. CROIROUGE PARIS 086
E-mail cr@croix-rouge.fr
Web http://www.croix-rouge.fr

Gabonese Red Cross Society

Boîte Postale 2274
Libreville
GABON
Tel. (241) 766160 / 766159
Fax (241) 766160
E-mail gab.cross@internetgabon.com

The Gambia Red Cross Society

Kanifing Industrial Area - Banjul
P.O. Box 472
Banjul
GAMBIA
Tel. (220) 392405 / 393179
Fax (220) 394921
Tlg. GAMREDCROSS BANJUL
E-mail redcrossgam@delphi.com

Red Cross Society of Georgia

15, Krilov St.
38002 Tbilisi
GEORGIA
Tel. (995)(32) 954282 / 951386
Fax (995)(32) 953304
E-mail grc@caucasus.net

German Red Cross

Friedrich-Ebert-Allee 71
Postal address: Postfach 1460
D-53004 Bonn
GERMANY
Tel. (49)(228) 5410
Fax (49)(228) 5411290
Tlx 886619 DKRB D
Tlg. DEUTSCHROTKREUZ BONN
E-mail drk@drk.de
Web http://www.rotkreuz.de

Ghana Red Cross Society

Ministries Annex Block A3
Off Liberia Road Extension
P.O. Box 835
Accra
GHANA
Tel. (233)(21) 662298
Fax (233)(21) 667226
Tlx 2655 GRCS GH
Tlg. GHANACROSS ACCRA
E-mail ifrcsrc@ghana.com

Hellenic Red Cross

Rue Lycavittou 1
Athens 106 72
GREECE
Tel. (30)(1) 3621681 / 3615606
Fax (30)(1) 3615606
Tlx 225156 EES GR
Tlg. HELLECROIX ATHENES
E-mail hrc@nermode.ntua.gr
Web http://www.redcross.gr

Grenada Red Cross Society

Upper Lucas Street
P.O. Box 551
St. George's
GRENADA
Tel. (1)(473) 4401483
Fax (1)(473) 4401829
E-mail grercs@caribsurf.com

Guatemalan Red Cross

3a Calle 8 - 40, Zona 1
Guatemala, C.A.
GUATEMALA
Tel. (502)(2) 322026 / 532027
Fax (502)(2) 324649
E-mail crg@guate.net

Red Cross Society of Guinea

B.P. 376
Conakry
GUINEA
Tel. (224) 443825
Fax (224) 414255
Tlx 22101

Red Cross Society of Guinea-Bissau

Avenida Unidade Africana, No. 12
Caixa postal 514-1036 BIX, Codex Bissau
GUINEA-BISSAU
Tel. (245) 202408
Tlx 251 PCE BI

The Guyana Red Cross Society

Eve Leary
P.O. Box 10524
Georgetown
GUYANA
Tel. (592)(2) 65174
Fax (592)(2) 77099 / 67852
Tlx 2226 FERNA GY "For Guyana Red Cross"
Tlg. GUYCROSS GEORGETOWN
E-mail redcross@solutions2000.net
Web http://www.sdnp.org.gy/redcross/

Haitian National Red Cross Society
1, rue Eden
Bicentenaire
CRH, B.P. 1337
Port-Au-Prince
HAITI
Tel. (509) 2231035
Fax (509) 2231054
Tlg. HAITICROSS PORT AU PRINCE
E-mail croroha@haitiworld.net

Honduran Red Cross
7a Calle
entre 1a. y 2a. Avenidas
Comayagüela D.C.
HONDURAS
Tel. (504) 2378876 / 2374628
Fax (504) 2380185 / 2374558
Tlx 1437 CRUZ R HO
Tlg. HONDUCRUZ COMAYAGUELA
E-mail honducruz@datum.hn

Hungarian Red Cross
Arany János utca 31
Magyar Vöröskereszt
1367 Budapest 5, Pf. 121
HUNGARY
Tel. (36)(1) 3313950 / 3317711
Fax (36)(1) 1533988
Tlg. REDCROSS BUDAPEST
E-mail intdept@hrc.hu

Icelandic Red Cross
Efstaleiti 9
103 Reykjavik
ICELAND
Tel. (354) 5704000
Fax (354) 5704010
E-mail central@redcross.is
Web http://www.redcross.is/

Indian Red Cross Society
Red Cross Building
1 Red Cross Road
New Delhi 110001
INDIA
Tel. (91)(11) 3716441 / 3716442
Fax (91)(11) 3717454
Tlx 3166115 IRCS IN
Tlg. INDCROSS NEW DELHI
E-mail indcross@nde.vsnl.net.in

Indonesian Red Cross Society
Jl. Jenderal Datot Subroto Kav. 96
P.O. Box 2009
Jakarta 12790
INDONESIA
Tel. (62)(21) 7992325
Fax (62)(21) 7995188
Tlx 66170 MB PMI IA
Tlg. INDONCROSS JKT

Red Crescent Society of the Islamic Republic of Iran
Ostad Nejatolahi Ave.
Tehran
IRAN, ISLAMIC REPUBLIC OF
Tel. (98)(21) 8849077 / 8808164
Fax (98)(21) 8849079
Tlx 224259 RCIA-IR
Tlg. CROISSANT-ROUGE TEHERAN
E-mail helal@www.dci.co.ir

Iraqi Red Crescent Society
Al-Mansour
P.O. Box 6143
Baghdad
IRAQ
Tel. (964)(1) 8862191 / 5343922
Fax (964)(1) 8840872
Tlx 213331 HELAL IK
Tlg. REDCRESCENT BAGHDAD

Irish Red Cross Society
16, Merrion Square
Dublin 2
IRELAND
Tel. (353)(1) 6765135 / 6765136
Fax (353)(1) 6614461
Tlx 32746 IRCS EI
E-mail redcross@iol.ie
Web http://foolscap.com/irishredcross/

Italian Red Cross
Via Toscana 12
I - 00187 Roma - RM
ITALY
Tel. (39)(06) 47591
Fax (39)(6) 44244534
Tlx 613421 CRIROM I
Tlg. CRIROM 00187
Web http://www.cri.it/

Jamaica Red Cross
Central Village
Spanish Town, St. Catherine
76 Arnold Road
Kingston 5
JAMAICA WEST INDIES
Tel. (1)(876) 98478602
Fax (1)(876) 9848272
Tlx COLYB JA 2397 "For Red Cross"
Tlg. JAMCROSS KINGSTON
E-mail jrcs@infochan.com
Web http://www.infochan.com/ja-red-cross/

Japanese Red Cross Society
1-3 Shiba Daimon, 1-Chome,
Minato-ku
Tokyo-105-8521
JAPAN
Tel. (81)(3) 34381311
Fax (81)(3) 34358509
Tlx JARCROSS J 22420
Tlg. JAPANCROSS TOKYO
E-mail rcjpn@ppp.bekkoame.or.jp
Web http://www.sphere.ad.jp/redcross/

Jordan National Red Crescent Society
Madaba Street
P.O. Box 10001
Amman 11151
JORDAN
Tel. (962)(64) 773141 / 773142
Fax (962)(64) 750815
Tlx 22500 HILAL JO
Tlg. HALURDON AMMAN
E-mail jrc@index.com.jo

Kenya Red Cross Society
Nairobi South "C"
(Belle Vue), off Mombasa Road
P.O. Box 40712
Nairobi
KENYA
Tel. (254)(2) 503781 / 503789
Fax (254)(2) 503845
Tlx 25436 IFRC KE
Tlg. KENREDCROSS NAIROBI
E-mail kenyarc@africaonline.co.ke

Kiribati Red Cross Society
P.O. Box 213
Bikenibeu
Tarawa
KIRIBATI
Tel. (686) 28128
Fax (686) 28128

Red Cross Society of the Democratic People's Republic of Korea
Ryonwa 1, Central District
Pyongyang
KOREA, DEMOCRATIC PEOPLE'S REPUBLIC OF
Tel. (850)(2) 18111 / 18222
Fax (850)(2) 3814644 / 3814410
Tlx 5355 DAEMUN KP
Tlg. KOREACROSS PYONGYANG

The Republic of Korea National Red Cross
32 - 3ka, Namsan-dong
Choong-Ku
Seoul 100 - 043
KOREA, REPUBLIC OF
Tel. (82)(2) 37053705 / 37053661
Fax (82)(2) 37053667
Tlx ROKNRC K28585
Tlg. KORCROSS SEOUL
E-mail knrc@redcross.or.kr
Web http://www.redcross.or.kr

Kuwait Red Crescent Society
Al-Jahra St.
Shuweek
P.O. Box 1359
13014 Safat
KUWAIT
Tel. (965) 4839114 / 4815478
Fax (965) 4839114
Tlx 22729

Red Crescent Society of Kyrgyzstan
10, prospekt Erkindik
720040 Bishkek
KYRGYZSTAN
Tel. (996)(312) 222414 / 222411
Fax (996)(312) 662181
E-mail redcross@imfiko.bishkek.su

Lao Red Cross
Avenue Sethathirath
B.P. 650
Vientiane
LAO PEOPLE'S DEMOCRATIC REPUBLIC
Tel. (856)(21) 222398 / 216610
Fax (856)(21) 212128
Tlx 4491 TE via PTT LAOS
Tlg. CROIXLAO VIENTIANE

Latvian Red Cross
1, Skolas Street
RIGA, LV-1010
LATVIA
Tel. (371)(7) 310902 / 2275635
Fax (371)(7) 310902 / 2275635

Lebanese Red Cross
Rue Spears
Beyrouth
LEBANON
Tel. (961)(1) 372802 / 372803
Fax (961)(1) 378207 / 371391
Tlx CROLIB 20593 LE
Tlg. LIBACROSS BEYROUTH
E-mail lrc-comm@dm.net.lb
Web http://www.dm.net.lb/redcross/

Lesotho Red Cross Society
23 Mabile Road
P.O. Box 366
Maseru 100
LESOTHO
Tel. (266) 313911
Fax (266) 310166
Tlx 4515 LECROS LO
Tlg. LESCROSS MASERU
E-mail lesred@lessoft.co.za

Liberian Red Cross Society
107 Lynch Street
P.O. Box 20-5081
1000 Monrovia 20
LIBERIA
Tel. (231) 225172 / 227521
Fax (231) 226231 / 227521
Tlx 44210 / 44211

Libyan Red Crescent

P.O. Box 541
Benghazi
LIBYAN ARAB JAMAHIRIYA
Tel. (218)(61) 9095202 / 9095152
Fax (218)(61) 9095829
Tlx 40341 HILAL PY
Tlg. LIBHILAL BENGHAZI

Liechtenstein Red Cross

Heiligkreuz 25
FL-9490 Vaduz
LIECHTENSTEIN
Tel. (41)(75) 2322294
Fax (41)(75) 2322240
Tlg. ROTESKREUZ VADUZ

Lithuanian Red Cross Society

Gedimino ave. 3a
2600 Vilnius
LITHUANIA
Tel. (370)(2) 628037
Fax (370)(2) 619923
E-mail redcross@tdd.lt
Web http://www.tdd.lt/lrk.redcross.lt/

Luxembourg Red Cross

Parc de la Ville
B.P. 404
L - 2014 LUXEMBOURG
Tel. (352) 450202 / 450201
Fax (352) 45726
Web http://www.croix-rouge.lu/

The Red Cross of The Former Yugoslav Republic of Macedonia

No. 13
Bul. Koco Racin
91000 Skopje
MACEDONIA, THE FORMER YUGOSLAV REPUBLIC OF
Tel. (389)(91) 114355
Fax (389)(91) 230542

Malagasy Red Cross Society

1, rue Patrice Lumumba Tsavalalana
B.P. 1168
Antananarivo
MADAGASCAR
Tel. (261)(20) 2222111
Fax (261)(20) 2235457
E-mail crm@dts.mg

Malawi Red Cross Society

Red Cross House
(along Presidential Way)
P.O. Box 30096
Capital City
Lilongwe 3
MALAWI
Tel. (265) 732877 / 732878
Fax (265) 730210
E-mail mrcs@unima.wn.apc.org

Malaysian Red Crescent Society

JKR 32, Jalan Nipah
Off Jalan Ampang
55000 Kuala Lumpur
MALAYSIA
Tel. (60)(3) 4578122 / 4578236
Fax (60)(3) 4533191
Tlx MACRES MA 30166
Tlg. MALREDCRES KUALA LUMPUR
E-mail mrcs@po.jaring.my
Web http://www.redcrescent.org.my/

Mali Red Cross

Route Koulikoro
B.P. 280
Bamako
MALI
Tel. (223) 224569
Fax (223) 240414
Tlx 2611 MJ

Malta Red Cross Society

104 St Ursula Street
Valletta VLT 05
MALTA
Tel. (356) 222645 / 226010
Fax (356) 243664
E-mail redcross@waldonet.net.mt
Web http://www.redcross.org.mt/

Mauritanian Red Crescent

Avenue Gamal Abdel Nasser
B.P. 344
Nouakchott
MAURITANIA
Tel. (222)(2) 51249
Fax (222)(2) 54784
Tlx 5830 CRM

Mauritius Red Cross Society

Ste. Thérèse Street
Curepipe
MAURITIUS
Tel. (230) 6763604
Fax (230) 6748855
Tlx YBRAT IW* 4258
"For Mauritius Red Cross"
Tlg. MAUREDCROSS CUREPIPE

Mexican Red Cross

Calle Luis Vives 200
Colonia Polanco
México, D.F. 11510
MEXICO
Tel. (52)(5) 3950606 / 5575270
Fax (52)(5) 3951598 / 3950044
Tlx 01777617 CRMEME
Tlg. CRUZROJA MEXICO
E-mail cruzroja@mexporta.com
Web http://www.cruz-roja.org.mx/

Red Cross of Monaco

27, Boulevard de Suisse
Monte Carlo
MONACO
Tel. (377)(97) 976800
Fax (377)(93) 159047
Tlg. CROIXROUGE MONTECARLO
E-mail redcross@monaco.mc
Web http://www.croixrouge.mc/

Mongolian Red Cross Society

Central Post Office
Post Box 537
Ulaanbaatar
MONGOLIA
Tel. (976)(1) 312578 / 312684
Fax (976)(1) 320934
Tlx 79358 MUIW
Tlg. MONRECRO
E-mail redcross@magicnet.mn

Moroccan Red Crescent

Palais Mokri
Takaddoum
B.P. 189
Rabat
MOROCCO
Tel. (212)(7) 650898 / 651495
Fax (212)(7) 759395
Tlx ALHILAL 319-40 M RABAT
Tlg. ALHILAL RABAT

Mozambique Red Cross Society

Avenida Agostinhoaero 284
Caixa Postal 2488
Maputo
MOZAMBIQUE
Tel. (258)(1) 490943 / 497721
Fax (258)(1) 497725
Tlx 6-169 CV MO
E-mail cvm@mail.tropical.co.mz

Myanmar Red Cross Society

Red Cross Building
42 Strand Road
Yangon
MYANMAR
Tel. (95)(1) 296552 / 295238
Fax (95)(1) 296551
Tlx 21218 BRCROS BM
Tlg. MYANMARCROSS YANGON

Namibia Red Cross

Red Cross House
Erf 2128, Independence Avenue
Katutura
P.O. Box 346
Windhoek
NAMIBIA
Tel. (264)(61) 235216 / 235226
Fax (264)(61) 228949
E-mail namcross@iafrica.com.na
Web http://members.xoom.com/namcross/

Nepal Red Cross Society

Red Cross Marg
Kalimati
P.O. Box 217
Kathmandu
NEPAL
Tel. (977)(1) 270650 / 270167
Fax (977)(1) 271915
Tlx 2569 NRCS NP
Tlg. REDCROSS KATHMANDU
E-mail nrcs@nhqs.wlink.com.np

The Netherlands Red Cross

Leeghwaterplein 27
P.O. Box 28120
2502 KC The Hague
NETHERLANDS
Tel. (31)(70) 4455666 / 4455755
Fax (31)(70) 4455777
Tlx 32375 NRCS NL
Tlg. ROODKRUIS THE HAGUE
E-mail hq@redcross.nl
Web http://www.redcross.nl/

New Zealand Red Cross

69 Molesworth Street
P.O. Box 12-140
Thorndon
Wellington 6038
NEW ZEALAND
Tel. (64)(4) 4723750
Fax (64)(4) 4730315
E-mail sej@redcross.org.nz
Web http://www.redcross.org.nz/

Nicaraguan Red Cross

Reparto Belmonte
Carretera Sur, Km 7
Apartado 3279
Managua
NICARAGUA
Tel. (505)(2) 651307 / 651517
Fax (505)(2) 651643
Tlx 2363 NICACRUZ
Tlg. NICACRUZ-MANAGUA
E-mail nicacruz@ibw.com.ni

Red Cross Society of Niger

B.P. 11386
Niamey
NIGER
Tel. (227) 733037
Fax (227) 732461
Tlx CRN GAP NI 5371

Nigerian Red Cross Society

11, Eko Akete Close
off St. Gregory's Road
South West Ikoyi
P.O. Box 764
Lagos
NIGERIA
Tel. (234)(1) 2695188 / 2695189
Fax (234)(1) 2691599
Tlx 21470 NCROSS NG
Tlg. NIGERCROSS LAGOS

Norwegian Red Cross

Hausmannsgate 7
Postbox 1. Gronland
0133 Oslo
NORWAY
Tel. (47) 22054000
Fax (47) 22054040
Tlx 76011 NORCR N
Tlg. NORCROSS OSLO
E-mail documentation.
center@redcross.no
Web http://www.redcross.no/

Pakistan Red Crescent Society

Sector H-8
Islamabad
PAKISTAN
Tel. (92)(51) 435831 / 435832
Fax (92)(51) 435830
Tlg. HILALAHMAR
ISLAMABAD
E-mail hilal@isb.comsats.net.pk

Palau Red Cross Society

P.O. Box 6043
Koror
REPUBLIC OF PALAU 96940
Tel. (680) 4885780 / 4885781
Fax (680) 4884540
E-mail palredcross@palaunet.com

Red Cross Society of Panama

Albrook, Areas Revertidas
Calle Principal
Edificio # 453
Apartado 668
Zona 1 Panamá
PANAMA
Tel. (507) 2325589 / 2325559
Fax (507) 2327450
Tlx 2661 STORTEXPA
Tlg. PANACRUZ PANAMA
E-mail cruzroja@pan.gbm.net

Papua New Guinea Red Cross Society

Taurama Road
Port Moresby
P.O. Box 6545
Boroko
PAPUA NEW GUINEA
Tel. (675) 3258577 / 3258759
Fax (675) 3259714

Paraguayan Red Cross

Brasil 216 esq. José Berges
Asunción
PARAGUAY
Tel. (595)(21) 222797 / 208199
Fax (595)(21) 211560
Tlg. CRUZ ROJA PARAGUAYA
E-mail cruzroja@pla.net.py

Peruvian Red Cross

Av. Arequipa No 1285
Lima
PERU
Tel. (51)(1) 2658784 / 2658785
Fax (51)(1) 2658788
Tlg. CRUZROJA PERUANA
LIMA
E-mail scrperu@mail.iaxis.com.pe

The Philippine National Red Cross

Bonifacio Drive
Port Area
P.O. Box 280
Manila 2803
PHILIPPINES
Tel. (63)(2) 5270866 / 5270856
Fax (63)(2)5270857
Tlx 27846 PNRC PH
Tlg. PHILCROSS MANILA
E-mail pnrcnhq@redcross.org.ph

Polish Red Cross

Mokotowska 14
P.O. Box 47
00-950 Warsaw
POLAND
Tel. (48)(22) 6285201 / 6285202
Fax (48)(22) 6284168
Tlx 813561 PCK PL
Tlg. PECEKA WARSZAWA
E-mail pck@atomnet.pl
Web http://www.pck.org.pl/

Portuguese Red Cross

Jardim 9 de Abril, 1 a 5
1293 Lisboa Codex
PORTUGAL
Tel. (351)(1) 3905571 / 3905650
Fax (351)(1) 3951045
Tlg. CRUZVERMELHA
E-mail cvp.sede@mail.telepac.pt

Qatar Red Crescent Society

P.O. Box 5449
Doha
QATAR
Tel. (974) 435111
Fax (974) 439950
Tlg. hilal doha

Romanian Red Cross

Strada Biserica Amzei, 29
Sector 1
Bucarest
ROMANIA
Tel. (40)(1) 6593385 / 6506233
Fax (40)(1) 3128452
Tlx 10531 romcr r
Tlg. ROMCROIXROUGE
BUCAREST

The Russian Red Cross Society
Tcheryomushkinski Proezd 5
117036 Moscow
RUSSIAN FEDERATION
Tel. (7)(095) 1265731
Fax (7)(095) 3107048
Tlx 411400 IKPOL SU
Tlg. IKRESTPOL MOSKWA

Rwandan Red Cross
B.P. 425
Kigali
RWANDA
Tel. (250) 74402
Fax (250) 73233
Tlx 22663 CRR RW

Saint Kitts and Nevis Red Cross Society
Red Cross House
Horsford Road
P.O. Box 62
Basseterre
SAINT KITTS AND NEVIS
Tel. (1)(869) 4652584
Fax (1)(869) 4668129
E-mail skbredcr@caribsurf.com

Saint Lucia Red Cross
Vigie
P.O. Box 271
Castries St Lucia, W.I.
SAINT LUCIA
Tel. (1)(758) 4525582
Fax (1)(758) 4537811
Tlx 6256 MCNAMARA LC
Attn. Mrs Boland
E-mail sluredcross@candw.lc

Saint Vincent and the Grenadines Red Cross
Halifax Street
Ministry of Education compound
Kingstown
P.O. Box 431
SAINT VINCENT AND
THE GRENADINES
Tel. (1)(784) 4561888
Fax (1)(784) 4856210
E-mail svgredcross@caribsurf.com

Samoa Red Cross Society
P.O. Box 1616
Apia
SAMOA
Tel. (685) 23686
Fax (685) 22676
Tlx 779 224 MORISHED SX
(Attention Red Cross)

Red Cross Republic of San Marino
Via Scialoja, Cailungo
REPUBLIC OF SAN MARINO
47031
Tel. (37)(8) 994360
Fax (37)(8) 994360
Tlg. CROCE ROSSA
REPUBBLICA DI SAN MARINO
Web http://www.tradecenter.sm/crs/

Sao Tome and Principe Red Cross
Avenida 12 de Julho No.11
B.P. 96
Sao Tome
SAO TOME AND PRINCIPE
Tel. (239)(12) 22305 / 22469
Fax (239)(12) 22305
Tlx 213 PUBLICO ST
pour "Croix-Rouge"
E-mail cvstp@sol.stome.telepac.net

Saudi Arabian Red Crescent Society
General Headquarters
Riyadh 11129
SAUDI ARABIA
Tel. (966)(1) 4740027
Fax (966)(1) 4740430
Tlx 400096 HILAL SJ
E-mail redcrescent@zajil.net

Senegalese Red Cross Society
Boulevard F. Roosevelt
B.P. 299
Dakar
SENEGAL
Tel. (221) 8233992
Fax (221) 8225369

Seychelles Red Cross Society
Place de la République
B.P. 53
Victoria
Mahé
SEYCHELLES
Tel. (248) 324646
Fax (248) 321663
E-mail redcross@seychelles.net
Web http://www.seychelles.net/redcross/

Sierra Leone Red Cross Society
6 Liverpool Street
P.O. Box 427
Freetown
SIERRA LEONE
Tel. (232)(22) 229082 / 229854
Fax (232)(22) 229083
Tlx 3692 SLRCS
Tlg. SIERRA RED CROSS
E-mail slrcs@sierratel.sl

Singapore Red Cross Society

Red Cross House
15 Penang Lane
SINGAPORE 238486
Tel. (65) 3360269
Fax (65) 3374360
E-mail tplsrcs@singnet.com.sg
Web http://www.redcross.org.sg/

Slovak Red Cross

Grösslingova 24
814 46 Bratislava
SLOVAKIA
Tel. (421)(7) 52925305 / 52923576
Fax (421)(7) 52923279

Slovenian Red Cross

Mirje 19
P.O. Box 236SI-
61111 Ljubljana
SLOVENIA
Tel. (386)(61) 1261200
Fax (386)(61) 1252142
E-mail rdeci.kriz-slo@guest.arnes.si

The Solomon Islands Red Cross

P.O. Box 187
Honiara
SOLOMON ISLANDS
Tel. (677) 22682
Fax (677) 25299
Tlx 66347 WING HQ
E-mail sirc@solomon.com.sb

Somali Red Crescent Society

c/o ICRC Box 73226
Nairobi
KENYA
Tel. (871 or 873) 131 2646 (Mogadishu) / (254)(2) 723963 (Nairobi)
Fax 1312647 (Mogadishu) / 715598 (Nairobi)
Tlx 25645 ICRC KE

The South African Red Cross Society

Red Cross House
21 Broad Road
Private Bag x26
Wynberg 7824
SOUTH AFRICA
Tel. (27)(21) 7975360
Fax (27)(21) 7974711
Tlg. REDCROSS JOHANNESBURG

Spanish Red Cross

Rafael Villa, s/n (Vuelta Ginés Navarro)
28023 El Plantio
Madrid
SPAIN
Tel. (34)(91) 3354444 / 3354545
Fax (34)(91) 3354455
Tlx 23853 OCCRE E
Tlg. CRUZ ROJA ESPANOLA MADRID
E-mail informa@cruzroja.es
Web http://www.cruzroja.es/

The Sri Lanka Red Cross Society

307, T.B. Jaya Road
P.O. Box 375
Colombo 10
SRI LANKA
Tel. (94)(1) 699935
Fax (94)(1) 695434
Tlx 23312 SLRCS CE
Tlg. RED CROSS COLOMBO
E-mail slrc@sri.lanka.net

The Sudanese Red Crescent

P.O. Box 235
Khartoum
SUDAN
Tel. (249)(11) 772011
Fax (249)(11) 772877
Tlx 23006 LRCS SD
Tlg. EL NADJA KHARTOUM
E-mail srcs@sudanmail.net

Suriname Red Cross

Gravenberchstraat 2
Postbus 2919
Paramaribo
SURINAME
Tel. (597) 498410
Fax (597) 464780
E-mail surcross@sr.net

Baphalali Swaziland Red Cross Society

104 Johnstone Street
P.O. Box 377
Mbabane
SWAZILAND
Tel. (268) 4042532
Fax (268) 4046108
Tlx 2260 WD
Tlg. BAPHALALI MBABANE
E-mail bsrcs@redcross.sz

Swedish Red Cross

Oesthammarsgatan 70
Box 27316
SE-102 54 Stockholm
SWEDEN
Tel. (46)(8) 6655600
Fax (46)(8) 6612701
Tlg. SWEDCROS STOCKHOLM
E-mail postmaster@redcross.se
Web http://www.redcross.se/

Swiss Red Cross

Rainmattstrasse 10
Postfach
3001 Bern
SWITZERLAND
Tel. (41)(31) 3877111
Fax (41)(31) 3877122
Tlx 911102 CRSB CH
Tlg. CROIXROUGE SUISSE BERNE
E-mail info@redcross.ch
Web http://www.redcross.ch/

Syrian Arab Red Crescent
Al Malek Aladel Street
Damascus
SYRIAN ARAB REPUBLIC
Tel. (963)(11) 4429662 / 4441366
Fax (963)(11) 4425677
Tlx 412857 HLAL
Tlg. CROISSANROUGE DAMAS
E-mail SARC@net.sy

Red Crescent Society of Tajikistan
120, Omari Khayom St.
734017, Dushanbe
TAJIKISTAN
Tel. (7)(3772) 240374
Fax (7)(3772) 245378
E-mail rcstj@rcstj.td.silk.org

Tanzania Red Cross National Society
Upanga Road
P.O. Box 1133
Dar es Salaam
TANZANIA, UNITED REPUBLIC OF
Tel. (255)(51) 116514 / 151236
Tlx TACROS 41878
E-mail redcross@unidar.gn.apc.org

The Thai Red Cross Society
Terdprakiat Building
Administration Office, 4th floor
1871, Henry Dunant Road
Bangkok 10330
THAILAND
Tel. (66)(2) 2564037 / 2564038
Fax (66)(2) 2527795
E-mail wmaster@redcross.or.th
Web http://www.redcross.or.th/

Togolese Red Cross
51, rue Boko Soga
Amoutivé
B.P. 655
Lome
TOGO
Tel. (228) 212110
Fax (228) 215228
Tlx UNDERVPRO 5261/5145 "pour Croix-Rouge"
Tlg. CROIX-ROUGE TOGOLAISE LOME
E-mail crtogol@syfed.tg.refer.org

Tonga Red Cross Society
P.O. Box 456
Nuku'Alofa
South West Pacific
TONGA
Tel. (676) 21360 / 21670
Fax (676) 24158
Tlx 66222 CW ADM TS
Attn. Redcross
Tlg. REDCROSS TONGA

The Trinidad and Tobago Red Cross Society
7A, Fitz Blackman Drive
Wrightson Road
P.O. Box 357
Port of Spain
TRINIDAD AND TOBAGO
Tel. (1)(868) 6278215 / 6278128
Fax (1)(868) 6278215
Tlx (294) 9003 for "Red Cross"
Tlg. TRINREDCROSS
E-mail ttrcs@carib-link.net

Tunisian Red Crescent
19, Rue d'Angleterre
Tunis 1000
TUNISIA
Tel. (216)(1) 320630 / 325572
Fax (216)(1) 320151
Tlx 12524 HILAL TN
Tlg. HILALAHMAR TUNIS

Turkish Red Crescent Society
Atac Sokak 1 No. 32
Yenisehir
Ankara
TURKEY
Tel. (90)(312) 4302300 / 4311158
Fax (90)(312) 4300175
Tlx 44593 KZLY TR
Tlg. KIZILAY ANKARA
Web http://www.kizilay.org.tr/

Red Crescent Society of Turkmenistan
48 A. Novoi str.
744000 Ashgabat
TURKMENISTAN
Tel. (993)(12) 395511
Fax (993)(12) 351750
E-mail nrcst@cat.glasnet.ru

The Uganda Red Cross Society
Plot 97, Buganda Road
P.O. Box 494
Kampala
UGANDA
Tel. (256)(41) 258701 / 258702
Fax (256)(41) 258184
Tlx (0988) 62118 redcrosug
Tlg. UGACROSS KAMPALA

Ukrainian Red Cross Society
30, Pushkinskaya St.
252004 Kiev
UKRAINE
Tel. (380)(44) 2250157 / 2293484
Fax (380)(44) 2251096
Tlx 131329 LICRO SU
E-mail redcross@ukrpack.net

Red Crescent Society of the United Arab Emirates

P.O. Box 3324
Abu Dhabi
UNITED ARAB EMIRATES
Tel. (9)(712) 219000
Fax (9)(712) 212727
Tlx 23582 RCS EM
Tlg. HILAL AHMAR ABU DHABI

British Red Cross

9 Grosvenor Crescent
London SW1X 7EJ
UNITED KINGDOM
Tel. (44)(171) 2355454
Fax (44)(171) 2456315
Tlx 918657 BRCS G
Tlg. REDCROS, LONDON, SW1
E-mail information@redcross.org.uk
Web http://www.redcross.org.uk

American Red Cross

1601 N. Kent Street, 2nd Floor
Arlington, Virginia 22209
UNITED STATES
Tel. (1)(703) 4654800 / 4654800
Fax (1)(703) 4654853
Tlx ARC TLX WSH 892636
Tlg. AMCROSS WASHINGTON DC
E-mail postmaster@usa.redcross.org
Web http://www.redcross.org/

Uruguayan Red Cross

Avenida 8 de Octubre, 2990
11600 Montevideo
URUGUAY
Tel. (598)(2) 4802112
Fax (598)(2) 4800714
Tlg. CRUZ ROJA URUGUAYA MONTEVIDEO
E-mail cruzroja@adinet.com.uy

Red Crescent Society of Uzbekistan

30, Yusuf Hos Hojib St.
700031 Tashkent
UZBEKISTAN
Tel. (988)(712) 563741
Fax (988)(712) 561801
E-mail rcuz@uzpak.uz
Web http://www.redcrescent.uz/

Vanuatu Red Cross Society

P.O. Box 618
Port Vila
VANUATU
Tel. (678) 27418
Fax (678) 22599
Tlx VANRED
Tlg. VANRED

Venezuelan Red Cross

Avenida Andrés Bello, 4
Apartado 3185
Caracas 1010
VENEZUELA
Tel. (58)(2) 5714380 / 5782829
Fax (58)(2) 5712143
Tlx 27237 CRURO VC
Tlg. CRUZ ROJA CARACAS
E-mail dirnacsoc@cantv.net

Red Cross of Viet Nam

82, Nguyen Du Street
Hanoï
VIET NAM
Tel. (844)(8) 225157 / 266283
Fax (844)(8) 266285
Tlx 411415 VNRC VT
Tlg. VIETNAMCROSS HANOI
E-mail vnrchq@netnam.org.vn

Yemen Red Crescent Society

Head Office, Building N° 10
26 September Street
P.O. Box 1257
Sanaa
YEMEN
Tel. (967)(1) 283132 / 283133
Fax (967)(1) 283131
Tlx 3124 HILAL YE
Tlg. SANAA HELAL AHMAR

Yugoslav Red Cross

Simina 19
11000 Belgrade
YUGOSLAVIA
Tel. (381)(11) 623564
Fax (381)(11) 622965
Tlx 11587 YU CROSS
Tlg. YUGOCROSS BELGRADE
E-mail jckbg@jck.org.yu

Zambia Red Cross Society

2837 Los Angeles Boulevard
Longacres
P.O. Box 50001 (Ridgeway 15101)
Lusaka
ZAMBIA
Tel. (260)(1) 250607 / 253661
Fax (260)(1) 252219
Tlx ZACROS ZA 45020
Tlg. REDRAID LUSAKA
E-mail zrcs@zamnet.zm

Zimbabwe Red Cross Society

Red Cross House
98 Cameron Street
P.O. Box 1406
Harare
ZIMBABWE
Tel. (263)(4) 775416 / 773912
Fax (263)(4) 751739
Tlx 24626 ZRCS ZW
Tlg. ZIMCROSS HARARE
E-mail zrcs@harare.iafrica.com

chapter 12

Section Two

Tracking the system

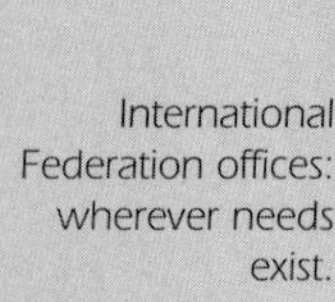

International Federation offices: wherever needs exist.

Photo: Mikkel Oestergaard/ International Federation, Albania 1999.

Wherever needs exist

Contact details for regional and country offices of the International Federation of Red Cross and Red Crescent Societies. Information correct as of 1 March 2000.

THE INTERNATIONAL FEDERATION OF RED CROSS AND RED CRESCENT SOCIETIES
P.O. Box 372
1211 Geneva 19
SWITZERLAND
Tel. (41)(22) 730 42 22
Fax (41)(22) 733 03 95
Tlx (045) 412 133 FRC CH
Tlg. LICROSS GENEVA
E-mail secretariat@ifrc.org
http://www.ifrc.org

Red Cross/EU Liaison Bureau
Rue J. Stallaert 1, bte 14
1050 - Brussels
BELGIUM
Tel. (32)(2) 3475750
Fax (32)(2) 3474365
E-mail rceulb.brux@inforboard.be

International Federation of Red Cross and Red Crescent Societies at the United Nations
630 Third Avenue
21st floor
Suite 2104
New York NY10017
UNITED STATES
Tel. (1)(212) 3380161
Fax (1)(212) 3389832

International Federation regional offices

Buenos Aires
Lucio V. Mansilla 2698 2o
1425 Buenos Aires
ARGENTINA
Tel. (54)(114) 9638659 / 9638660
Fax (54)(114) 9613320
E-mail ifrcar01@ifrc.org

Yaounde
Rue Mini-Prix (Bastos)
BP 11507
Yaounde
CAMEROON
Tel. (237) 217437 / 217438
Fax (237) 217439
E-mail ifrccm04@ifrc.org

Beijing
c/o Red Cross Society of China
53 Ganmian Hutong
100010 Beijing
CHINA
Tel. (8610) 65231704
Fax (8610) 65599553
E-mail redcross@candw.ag

Abidjan
rue C 43 CHU Cocody Nord
BP 2090
Abidjan 04
COTE D'IVOIRE
Tel. (225) 22486737 / 22486738
Fax (225) 22486740
E-mail fedecr-r@africaonline.co.ci

Santo Domingo
C/Juan E. Dunant, 51
Ensanche Miraflores
P.O. Box 5358
Santo Domingo
DOMINICAN REPUBLIC
Tel. (1)(809) 6869412
Fax (1)(809) 6869495
E-mail ifrcsd@codetel.net.do

Suva
P.O. Box 2507
Government Building
Suva
FIJI
Tel. (679) 311855 / 311665
Fax (679) 311406
E-mail ifrcrds@is.com.fj

Guatemala City

19 Calle 1-26, Zona 14
Av. de las América
Pl. Uruguay
Ciudad de Guatemala
GUATEMALA
Tel. (502) 3371686
Fax (502) 3631449
E-mail fedecruz@guate.net

Budapest

Zolyomi Lepcso Ut 22
1124 Budapest
HUNGARY
Tel. (36)(1) 3193423 / 3193052
Fax (36)(1) 3193424
E-mail ifrc@mail.datanet.hu

New Delhi

F-25A Hauz Khas Enclave
New Delhi 110 016
INDIA
Tel. (9111) 6858671 / 6858672
Fax (9111) 6857567
E-mail ifrcin01@ifrc.org

Amman

Al Shmeisani
Maroof Al Rasafi Street
Building No. 19
P.O. Box 830511 / Zahran
Amman
JORDAN
Tel. (962)(6) 5681060 / 5694911
Fax (962)(6) 5694556
E-mail ifrc@index.com.jo

Almaty

86, Kunaeva Street
480100 Almaty
KAZAKHSTAN
Tel. (7)(3272) 918838 / 914156
Fax (7)(3272) 9142 67
E-mail ifrckz01@ifrc.org

Nairobi

Chaka Road (off Argwings Kodhele)
P.O. Box 41275
Nairobi
KENYA
Tel. (254)(2) 714255 / 714313
Fax (254)(2) 718415
E-mail ifrcke01@ifrc.org

Kuala Lumpur

No. 32, Jalan Nipah
P.O. Box 13255
50804 Kuala Lumpur
MALAYSIA
Tel. (603) 4510723 / 4524046
Fax (603) 4519359
E-mail ifrcmy01@ifrc.org

Harare

9, Coxwell Road
Milton Park
Harare
ZIMBABWE
Tel. (263)(4) 720315 / 720316
Fax (263)(4) 708784
E-mail ifrczw01@ifrc.org

International Federation country offices

Afghanistan

43D S. Jamal-ud-Din Afghani Rd.
University Town
Peshawar
PAKISTAN
Tel. (873) 761241875
Fax (873) 761241877
E-mail ifrc@pes.comsat.net.pk

Albania

c/o Tirana Trade Centre
Rruga Durrësit Street
ish-Shkolla e Partise
Tirana
ALBANIA
Tel. (355) 4256704 / 4256705
Fax (355) 4256707
E-mail irfca102@ifrc.org

Angola

Caixa Postal 3324
Rua Emilio M'Bidi 51 - 51A
Bairro Alvalade
Luanda
ANGOLA
Tel. (244)(2) 322001 / 325211
Fax (244)(2) 320648
E-mail ifrcao01@ifrc.org

Armenia
Gevorg Chaush St. 50/1
Yerevan 375088
ARMENIA
Tel. (3742) 354649 / 341708
Fax (3742) 151072
E-mail kelemu@ifrc.org

Azerbaijan
Niazi Street 11
Baku 370000
AZERBAIJAN
Tel. (99)(412) 925792
Fax (99)(412) 971889
E-mail office@ifrc.azerin.com

Bangladesh
c/o Bangladesh Red Crescent Society
684-686 Bara Magh Bazar
Dhaka - 1217
BANGLADESH
Tel. (880)(2) 8315401 / 8315402
Fax (880)(2) 9341631
E-mail ifrcbd@citecho.net

Belarus
Ulitsa Mayakovkosgo 14
Minsk 220006
BELARUS
Tel. (375)(17) 2217273
Fax (375)(17) 2219060
E-mail ifrcby01@ifrc.org

Bosnia and Herzegovina
Titova 7
71000 Sarajevo
BOSNIA AND HERZEGOVINA
Tel. (387)(71) 660609 / 660612
Fax (387)(71) 666010
E-mail ifrc_sar@bih.net.ba

Burundi
Avenue des Etats-Unis 3674A
B.P. 324
Bujumbura
BURUNDI
Tel. (257) 229524 / 229525
Fax (257) 229408

Cambodia
53 Deo, Street Croix-Rouge
Central Post Office/P.O. Box 620
Phnom Penh
CAMBODIA
Tel. (855)(23) 210162 / 362690
Fax (855)(23) 210163
E-mail ifrckh01@ifrc.org

Congo, Democratic Republic of the
288 Avenue des Trois Z
Gombé
Kinshasa
DEMOCRATIC REPUBLIC OF THE CONGO
Tel. (243) 1221495

Congo, Republic of
60, Av. de la Libération de Paris
B.P. 88
Brazzaville
CONGO, REPUBLIC OF
Tel. (242) 511671

El Salvador
c/o Salvadorean Red Cross Society
17 Calle Pte. y Av. Henri Dunant
Apartado postal 2672
San Salvador
EL SALVADOR
Tel. (505)(2) 652082
Fax (505)(2) 651643
E-mail cruzrojasal@ejje.com

Eritrea
c/o Red Cross Society of Eritrea
Andnet Street
P.O. Box 575
Asmara
ERITREA
Tel. (291)(1) 150550
Fax (291)(1) 151859
E-mail ifrc@eol.com.er

Ethiopia
Ras Destra Damtew Avenue
P.O. Box 195
Addis Ababa
ETHIOPIA
Tel. (251)(1) 514571 / 514317
Fax (251)(1) 512888
E-mail ifrcet04@ifrc.org

Georgia
7, Anton Katalikosi Street
Tbilisi
GEORGIA
Tel. (995)(32) 950945
Fax (995)(32) 985976
E-mail ifrcge01@ifrc.org

Guinea
Immeuble Le Golfe, 6ème étage
Quartier Lanseboundji
B.P. No 376
Conakry
GUINEA
Tel. (224) 413825
Fax (224) 412310

Guinea-Bissau
Ave. Praca de Herois Naciones
Bissau
GUINEA-BISSAU
Tel. (245) 203659 (ICRC) / 202407 (Guinea-Bissau Red Cross)

Honduras
Colonia Florencia Norte segunda
calle casa No 1030
contigua al edificio Tovar Lopez
Tegucigalpa
HONDURAS
Tel. (504) 2320710 / 2357885
Fax (504) 2320718
E-mail cenasa@gbm.hn

Indonesia
c/o Indonesian Red Cross Society
P.O. Box 2009
Jakarta
INDONESIA
Tel. (6221) 79191841
Fax (6221) 79191841

Iran
c/o Red Crescent Society of
the Islamic Republic of Iran
Taleghani Avenue, Gharani Corner
Tehran
IRAN
Tel. (9821) 8890568 / 8844036
Fax (9821) 8849079
E-mail helai@www.dci.co.ir

Iraq
c/o Iraqi Red Crescent Society
PO Box 6143
Baghdad
IRAQ
Tel. (964)(1) 5434184 / 8844036
Fax (964)(1) 5434184

Korea, Democratic People's Republic of
c/o Red Cross Society of the DPR
Korea
Ryonwa 1, Central District
Pyongyang
KOREA, DEMOCRATIC
PEOPLE'S REPUBLIC OF
Tel. (850)(2) 3813490 / 3814350
Fax (850)(2) 3813490

Laos
c/o Lao Red Cross
P.O.Box 2948
Setthatirath Road, Xiengnhune
Vientiane
LAO PEOPLE'S DEMOCRATIC
REPUBLIC
Tel. (856) 21215762
Fax (856) 21215935

Latvia
c/o Latvian Red Cross
Skolas Street 1
Riga LV - 1010
LATVIA
Tel. (3717) 333058
Fax (3717) 333058

Lebanon
N. Dagher Building
Mar Tacla
Beirut
LEBANON
Tel. (9611) 424851
Fax (9615) 459658
E-mail ifrc@mail.palnet.com

Liberia
c/o Liberian Red Cross Society
107, Lynch Street
P.O. Box 5081
Monrovia
LIBERIA
Tel. (231) 227485 / 226231
Fax (231) 226263
E-mail ifrc.org.li@libnet.net

Macedonia
Bul. Koco Racin 13
Skopje 9100
MACEDONIA, FORMER
YUGOSLAV REPUBLIC OF
Tel. (38991) 114271 / 212818
Fax (38991) 115240
E-mail ifrcmk02@ifrc.org

Moldova
c/o Moldovan Red Cross
'67-A Uélitsa Asachi
Chisinau 277028
MOLDOVA
Fax (3732) 729700

Mozambique
Avenida Agostinho Neto, No 284
Caixa postal 2488
Maputo
MOZAMBIQUE
Tel. (258)(1) 492277
Fax (258)(1) 492278
E-mail ifrcmz01@ifrc.org

Myanmar
c/o Myanmar Red Cross Society
Red Cross Building
42 Strand Road
Yangon
MYANMAR
Tel. (95)(1) 297877
Fax (95)(1) 297877

Nicaragua
c/o Nicaraguan Red Cross
Reparto Belmonte, Carretera Sur
Apartado Postal 3279
Managua
NICARAGUA
Tel. (505) 2650192 / 2652082
Fax (505) 2650186
E-mail fabian@ibw.com.ni

Nigeria
c/o Nigerian Red Cross Society
11, Eko Akete Close
Off St. Gregory's Road
South West Ikoyi
P.O. Box 764
Lagos
NIGERIA
Tel. (234)(1) 2695228
Fax (234)(1) 2695229
E-mail fedcross@infoweb.abs.net

Pakistan
c/o Pakistan Red Crescent Society
National Headquarters
Sector H-8
Islamabad
PAKISTAN
Tel. (925)(1) 430832 / 820838
Fax (925)(1) 430745
E-mail ifrcaf01@ifrc.org

Palestine
c/o Palestine Red Crescent Society
P.O. Box 3637
Al Bireh / West Bank
PALESTINE
Tel. (9722) 2406515 / 2406516
Fax (9722) 2406518
E-mail ifrc@cyberia.net.lb

Papua New Guinea
c/o Papua New Guinea Red Cross Society
P.O. Box 6545
Boroko
PAPUA NEW GUINEA
Tel. (675) 3112277
Fax (675) 3230731
E-mail ifrcpg@ifrc.org

Russian Federation
c/o Russian Red Cross Society
Tcheryomushkinski Proezd 5
117036 Moscow
RUSSIAN FEDERATION
Tel. (7502) 9375267 / 9375268
Fax (7502) 9375263
E-mail moscow@ifrc.org

Rwanda
c/o Rwandan Red Cross
B.P. 425, Nyamiranbo
Kigali
RWANDA
Tel. (250) 73232 / 73874
Fax (250) 73233
E-mail ifrcrw01@ifrc.org

Sierra Leone
c/o Sierra Leone Red Cross Society
6, Liverpool Street
P.O. Box 427
Freetown
SIERRA LEONE
Tel. (23)(222) 227772
Fax (23)(222) 228180
E-mail ifrc@sierratel.sl

Somalia
Chaka Road
(off Argwings Kodhele)
P.O. Box 41275
Nairobi
KENYA
Tel. (254)(2) 712266 / 728194
Fax (254)(2) 729070

Sri Lanka
c/o F-25A Hauz Khas Enclave
New Delhi 110 016
INDIA
Tel. (941) 571275 / (9477) 7753355

Sudan
Al Mak Nimir Street/Gamhouria Street
Plot No 1, Block No. 4
P.O. Box 10697
East Khartoum
SUDAN
Tel. (249)(11) 771033
Fax (249)(11) 770484

Tajikistan
c/o Tajikistan Red Crescent Society
120, Omari Khayom St.
734017 Dushanbe
TAJIKISTAN
Tel. (992)(372) 244296 / 245981
Fax (992)(372) 9015006
E-mail ifrcdsb@ifrc.org

Tanzania
Ali Hassan Mwinyi
Plot No. 294/295
P.O. Box 1133
Dar es Salaam
TANZANIA, UNITED REPUBLIC OF
Tel. (255)(51) 116514 / 135526
Fax (255)(51) 117308
E-mail ifrctz01@ifrc.org

Tunisia
c/o Tunisian Red Crescent Society
19 rue d'Angleterre
Tunis 1000
TUNISIA
Tel. (2)(161) 325572
Fax (2)(161) 320151

Turkey
c/o Turkish Red Crescent Society
Nuzheitiye Caddesi Derya Dil Sokak
No. 1 Besiktas
Istanbul
TURKEY
Tel. (902)(12) 2367902 / 2367903
Fax (902)(12) 2367711

Turkmenistan
c/o Turkmenistan Red Crescent Society
48 A. Novoi St.
744000 Ashgabat
TURKMENISTAN
Tel. (993)(12) 394349
Fax (993)(12) 394349
E-mail ifrctm@cat.glasnet.ru

Uganda
c/o Uganda Red Cross Society
Plot 97, Buganda Road
P.O. Box 494
Kampala
UGANDA
Tel. (256)(41) 234968 / 343742
Fax (256)(41) 258184
E-mail ifrc@imul.com

Ukraine
c/o Red Cross Society of Ukraine
30 Ulitsa Pushkinskaya
Kyiv 252004
UKRAINE
Tel (38044) 2286110
Fax (38044) 2345082
E-mail ifrcua01@ifrc.org

Uzbekistan
30, Yusuf Hos Hojib St
700031 Tashkent
UZBEKISTAN
Tel. (998)(71) 554587
Fax (998)(71) 562904
E-mail ifrcuz01@ifrc.org

Venezuela
c/o Venezuela Red Cross
Avenida Andrés Bello 4
Apartado 3185
Caracas 1010
VENEZUELA
Tel. (582) 5782825 / 5781579
Fax (582) 5781876
E-mail ifrcven@telcel.net.ve

Viet Nam
19 Mai Hac De Street
Hanoï
VIET NAM
Tel. (84)(4) 8252250 / 8229283
Fax (84)(4) 8266177
E-mail ifrc@hn.vnn.vn

Yugoslavia
Simina Ulica Broj 21
11000 Belgrade
YUGOSLAVIA
Tel. (381)(11) 3282202 / 3281376
Fax (381)(11) 3281791
E-mail telecom@ifrc.org.yu

Zambia
c/o Zambia Red Cross
2837 Los Angeles Boulevard
P.O. Box 50001
Ridgeway 15101
Lusaka
ZAMBIA
Tel. (2601) 254074 / 251599
Fax (2601) 254074
E-mail ifrczm01@ifrc.org

The world of disasters in the World Disasters Report 1993 to 2000

The *World Disasters Report* is the only annual, interdisciplinary report focusing on disasters, from natural hazards to human-induced crises, and the millions of people affected by them. The report analyses cutting-edge issues, assesses practical methodologies, examines recent experience and collates a comprehensive disasters database.

It is backed by the expertise and resources of the International Federation of Red Cross and Red Crescent Societies, whose relief operations and National Societies in 176 countries make it the most extensive and experienced humanitarian network.

The *World Disasters Report 2000* studies public health in disasters, the legacy of Chernobyl, public health concerns in Kosovo and DPR Korea, AIDS in Africa, the case for an international disaster response law and the quantity of aid. Plus the comprehensive disasters database and Red Cross/Red Crescent listings. Fully illustrated with maps and index.

The *World Disasters Report 1999* looks at environmental trends, disasters and their implications; floods; Hurricane Mitch; institutional collapse in Russia; Afghan earthquakes; the effects of El Niño; the SPHERE project and falling aid budgets. Plus the comprehensive disasters database and Red Cross/Red Crescent listings. Fully illustrated with maps and index.

The *World Disasters Report 1998* examines cities and crisis: urban disasters; the toll of traffic accidents; shelter and reconstruction, psychological support, the 1997 Eastern European floods, sanctions in Iraq, rebuilding Bosnia, refugee camp 'cities' and urban Red Cross action in Colombia. The report includes new data and full Red Cross/Red Crescent listings. Fully illustrated, with maps and index.

The *World Disasters Report 1997* includes: the future of NGOs and the military-humanitarian relationship, information management, epidemiological data for disasters, aid trends and disaster-response standards, China's floods, Caribbean natural hazards, the challenge of Somalia, and the former Soviet Union's re-emerging diseases. Plus a comprehensive 25-year disasters database and the International Federation's global activities. Indexed and fully illustrated. Maps.

The *World Disasters Report 1996* includes: global population movements, causes and consequences; global food security; emergency food aid and nutrition; developmental relief; trends in aid; the Kobe earthquake; Rwanda; Oklahoma's trauma; DPR Korea's crisis; meeting the need for systematic data; *Code of Conduct* update; full listings of National Societies and delegations; 25-year disasters database. Indexed and fully illustrated.

The *World Disasters Report 1995* includes: UN sanctions and the humanitarian crisis; good disaster-relief practice; early warning monitoring; measuring the effects of evaluation; psychological support; surviving cyclones in Bangladesh; Ethiopia ten years on; success and failure in Rwanda; working in Somalia's grey zone. Fully illustrated.

The *World Disasters Report 1994* includes: drought success in southern Africa; Somalia; challenges within the former Yugoslavia; Brazil's vulnerability; India's earthquake myths; Caucasus collapse; secrecy's role in disasters; anti-personnel mines; Chernobyl; African peace mechanisms; human rights and disasters; indigenous knowledge and response; and the full text of the *Code of Conduct* for disaster-relief agencies.

The *World Disasters Report 1993* – the pilot issue – includes: humanitarian gap, preparedness versus relief, role of foreign medical teams and military forces, equity in impact, media in disasters, AIDS, famine, flood, high winds, refugees, epidemics, earthquakes, volcanoes. Case histories from: Uganda, Sudan, China, Bangladesh, Afghanistan, Peru, Zambia, Turkey, United States, Philippines. Fully illustrated.

And coming up... World Disasters Report 2001

The 2001 edition of the *World Disasters Report* will examine disasters, particularly repetitive disasters and those, like civil war, that devastate entire countries, leaving in their wake families and communities torn apart and cut off from any notion of sustainable development. In these situations, humanitarian assistance is the necessary first aid before major surgery and rehabilitation. The problem is that all too often it is the first aiders, the humanitarian agencies, who are thrust into the front line of assisting communities in rebuilding after disaster. Disaster recovery, the key theme for the *World Disasters Report 2001* is attracting an increasing share of agencies resources. Whether it is working on post-conflict situations or trying to rebuild entire communities after hurricanes or drought, disaster recovery is the more complex, the less publicized but vital partner to disaster response.

To order the *World Disasters Report,* please contact:

International Federation of Red Cross and Red Crescent Societies
P.O. Box 372, CH-1211 Geneva 19, Switzerland.
Fax: (41) (22) 730 49 56 E-mail: wdrorder@ifrc.org

Index

A

B

C

D

E

F

J

K

L

M

N

O

P

R

S

T

U

V

W

Y

Z

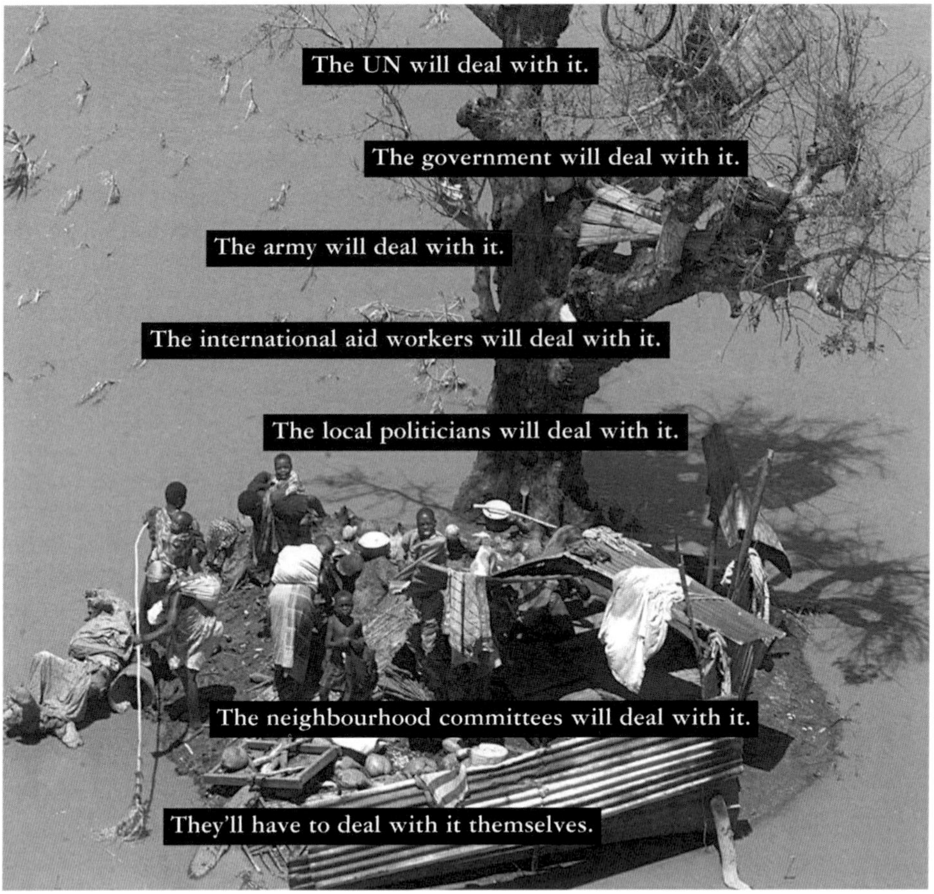

Beyond conflict

The International Federation of Red Cross and Red Crescent Societies, 1919-1994

Daphne A. Reid and **Patrick F. Gilbo**

352 pages, illustrated throughout
24 x 30.5 cm, cloth
ISBN 92-9139-041-0, 70 Swiss francs

Beyond conflict looks back on 75 years of service to humanity. The book chronicles the evolution of the International Federation from its founding to its maturity, using photographs, posters and original documentation. It follows the challenges, hopes and accomplishments of those who sought to build a dynamic organization with universal appeal. It focuses on the people whose work on behalf of national Red Cross and Red Crescent societies gave the organization its strength, while enabling the simple ideals of service and volunteerism to survive amid the tensions of an increasingly complex and difficult world.

To order this publication, please contact the International Federation:
P.O. Box 372, 1211 Geneva 19, Switzerland.
Telephone (41-22) 730 42 22, telefax (41-22) 733 03 95, e-mail secretariat@ifrc.org

Heritage

Dedication

This book is dedicated to Carolyn, Stephanie, and Richard; to my mother and to my father's memory; to my students of recent years, and those of my colleagues who have encouraged me in this task; and to all people everywhere working to preserve their own heritage, however they define it. I especially dedicate the book to the National Trust of Australia and similar organisations world-wide.